Machine Learning
in Production

The Pearson Addison-Wesley Data & Analytics Series

   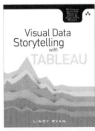 

Visit **informit.com/awdataseries** for a complete list of available publications.

The **Pearson Addison-Wesley Data & Analytics Series** provides readers with practical knowledge for solving problems and answering questions with data. Titles in this series primarily focus on three areas:

1. **Infrastructure:** how to store, move, and manage data

2. **Algorithms:** how to mine intelligence or make predictions based on data

3. **Visualizations:** how to represent data and insights in a meaningful and compelling way

The series aims to tie all three of these areas together to help the reader build end-to-end systems for fighting spam; making recommendations; building personalization; detecting trends, patterns, or problems; and gaining insight from the data exhaust of systems and user interactions.

Make sure to connect with us!
informit.com/socialconnect

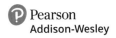 

Machine Learning in Production

Developing and Optimizing Data Science Workflows and Applications

Andrew Kelleher
Adam Kelleher

✦✦ Addison-Wesley

Boston • Columbus • New York • San Francisco • Amsterdam • Cape Town
Dubai • London • Madrid • Milan • Munich • Paris • Montreal • Toronto • Delhi • Mexico City
São Paulo • Sydney • Hong Kong • Seoul • Singapore • Taipei • Tokyo

For information about buying this title in bulk quantities, or for special sales opportunities (which may include electronic versions; custom cover designs; and content particular to your business, training goals, marketing focus, or branding interests), please contact our corporate sales department at corpsales@pearsoned.com or (800) 382-3419.

For government sales inquiries, please contact governmentsales@pearsoned.com.

For questions about sales outside the U.S., please contact intlcs@pearson.com.

Visit us on the Web: informit.com/aw

Library of Congress Control Number: 2018954331

ISBN-13: 978-0-13-411654-9
ISBN-10: 0-13-411654-2

1 19

❖

This book is dedicated to our lifelong mentor, William F. Walsh III.
We could never thank you enough for all the years of support and
encouragement.

❖

Contents

Foreword   xv

Preface   xvii

About the Authors   xxi

I: Principles of Framing   1

1   The Role of the Data Scientist   3
1.1   Introduction   3
1.2   The Role of the Data Scientist   3
     1.2.1   Company Size   3
     1.2.2   Team Context   4
     1.2.3   Ladders and Career Development   5
     1.2.4   Importance   5
     1.2.5   The Work Breakdown   6
1.3   Conclusion   6

2   Project Workflow   7
2.1   Introduction   7
2.2   The Data Team Context   7
     2.2.1   Embedding vs. Pooling Resources   8
     2.2.2   Research   8
     2.2.3   Prototyping   9
     2.2.4   A Combined Workflow   10
2.3   Agile Development and the Product Focus   10
     2.3.1   The 12 Principles   11
2.4   Conclusion   15

3   Quantifying Error   17
3.1   Introduction   17
3.2   Quantifying Error in Measured Values   17
3.3   Sampling Error   19
3.4   Error Propagation   21
3.5   Conclusion   23

4   Data Encoding and Preprocessing   25
4.1   Introduction   25
4.2   Simple Text Preprocessing   26
     4.2.1   Tokenization   26

4.2.2 N-grams   27

4.2.3 Sparsity   28

4.2.4 Feature Selection   28

4.2.5 Representation Learning   30

4.3 Information Loss   33

4.4 Conclusion   34

5 **Hypothesis Testing   37**

5.1 Introduction   37

5.2 What Is a Hypothesis?   37

5.3 Types of Errors   39

5.4 P-values and Confidence Intervals   40

5.5 Multiple Testing and "P-hacking"   41

5.6 An Example   42

5.7 Planning and Context   43

5.8 Conclusion   44

6 **Data Visualization   45**

6.1 Introduction   45

6.2 Distributions and Summary Statistics   45

6.2.1 Distributions and Histograms   46

6.2.2 Scatter Plots and Heat Maps   51

6.2.3 Box Plots and Error Bars   55

6.3 Time-Series Plots   58

6.3.1 Rolling Statistics   58

6.3.2 Auto-Correlation   60

6.4 Graph Visualization   61

6.4.1 Layout Algorithms   62

6.4.2 Time Complexity   64

6.5 Conclusion   64

II: **Algorithms and Architectures   67**

7 **Introduction to Algorithms and Architectures   69**

7.1 Introduction   69

7.2 Architectures   70

7.2.1   Services   71

7.2.2   Data Sources   72

7.2.3   Batch and Online Computing   72

7.2.4   Scaling   73

7.3   Models   74

7.3.1   Training   74

7.3.2   Prediction   75

7.3.3   Validation   76

7.4   Conclusion   77

8   Comparison   79

8.1   Introduction   79

8.2   Jaccard Distance   79

8.2.1   The Algorithm   80

8.2.2   Time Complexity   81

8.2.3   Memory Considerations   81

8.2.4   A Distributed Approach   81

8.3   MinHash   82

8.3.1   Assumptions   83

8.3.2   Time and Space Complexity   83

8.3.3   Tools   83

8.3.4   A Distributed Approach   83

8.4   Cosine Similarity   84

8.4.1   Complexity   85

8.4.2   Memory Considerations   85

8.4.3   A Distributed Approach   86

8.5   Mahalanobis Distance   86

8.5.1   Complexity   86

8.5.2   Memory Considerations   87

8.5.3   A Distributed Approach   87

8.6   Conclusion   88

9   Regression   89

9.1   Introduction   89

9.1.1   Choosing the Model   90

9.1.2   Choosing the Objective Function   90

9.1.3   Fitting   91

9.1.4   Validation   92

9.2   Linear Least Squares   96
    9.2.1   Assumptions   97
    9.2.2   Complexity   97
    9.2.3   Memory Considerations   97
    9.2.4   Tools   98
    9.2.5   A Distributed Approach   98
    9.2.6   A Worked Example   98
9.3   Nonlinear Regression with Linear Regression   105
    9.3.1   Uncertainty   107
9.4   Random Forest   109
    9.4.1   Decision Trees   109
    9.4.2   Random Forests   112
9.5   Conclusion   115

10 Classification and Clustering   117
10.1 Introduction   117
10.2 Logistic Regression   118
    10.2.1 Assumptions   121
    10.2.2 Time Complexity   121
    10.2.3 Memory Considerations   122
    10.2.4 Tools   122
10.3 Bayesian Inference, Naive Bayes   122
    10.3.1 Assumptions   124
    10.3.2 Complexity   124
    10.3.3 Memory Considerations   124
    10.3.4 Tools   124
10.4 K-Means   125
    10.4.1 Assumptions   127
    10.4.2 Complexity   128
    10.4.3 Memory Considerations   128
    10.4.4 Tools   128
10.5 Leading Eigenvalue   128
    10.5.1 Complexity   129
    10.5.2 Memory Considerations   130
    10.5.3 Tools   130
10.6 Greedy Louvain   130
    10.6.1 Assumptions   130
    10.6.2 Complexity   130

10.6.3 Memory Considerations   131

10.6.4 Tools   131

10.7 Nearest Neighbors   131

10.7.1 Assumptions   132

10.7.2 Complexity   132

10.7.3 Memory Considerations   133

10.7.4 Tools   133

10.8 Conclusion   133

11 Bayesian Networks   135

11.1 Introduction   135

11.2 Causal Graphs, Conditional Independence, and Markovity   136

11.2.1 Causal Graphs and Conditional Independence   136

11.2.2 Stability and Dependence   137

11.3 D-separation and the Markov Property   138

11.3.1 Markovity and Factorization   138

11.3.2 D-separation   139

11.4 Causal Graphs as Bayesian Networks   142

11.4.1 Linear Regression   142

11.5 Fitting Models   143

11.6 Conclusion   147

12 Dimensional Reduction and Latent Variable Models   149

12.1 Introduction   149

12.2 Priors   149

12.3 Factor Analysis   151

12.4 Principal Components Analysis   152

12.4.1 Complexity   154

12.4.2 Memory Considerations   154

12.4.3 Tools   154

12.5 Independent Component Analysis   154

12.5.1 Assumptions   158

12.5.2 Complexity   158

12.5.3 Memory Considerations   159

12.5.4 Tools   159

12.6 Latent Dirichlet Allocation   159

12.7 Conclusion   165

13 Causal Inference   167

13.1 Introduction   167

13.2 Experiments   168

13.3 Observation: An Example   171

13.4 Controlling to Block Non-causal Paths   177

13.4.1 The G-formula   179

13.5 Machine-Learning Estimators   182

13.5.1 The G-formula Revisited   182

13.5.2 An Example   183

13.6 Conclusion   187

14 Advanced Machine Learning   189

14.1 Introduction   189

14.2 Optimization   189

14.3 Neural Networks   191

14.3.1 Layers   192

14.3.2 Capacity   193

14.3.3 Overfitting   196

14.3.4 Batch Fitting   199

14.3.5 Loss Functions   200

14.4 Conclusion   201

III: Bottlenecks and Optimizations   203

15 Hardware Fundamentals   205

15.1 Introduction   205

15.2 Random Access Memory   205

15.2.1 Access   205

15.2.2 Volatility   206

15.3 Nonvolatile/Persistent Storage   206

15.3.1 Hard Disk Drives or "Spinning Disks"   207

15.3.2 SSDs   207

15.3.3 Latency   207

15.3.4 Paging   207

15.3.5 Thrashing   208

15.4 Throughput   208

15.4.1 Locality   208

15.4.2 Execution-Level Locality   208

15.4.3 Network Locality   209

15.5 Processors   209

    15.5.1 Clock Rate   209

    15.5.2 Cores   210

    15.5.3 Threading   210

    15.5.4 Branch Prediction   210

15.6 Conclusion   212

16 Software Fundamentals   213

16.1 Introduction   213

16.2 Paging   213

16.3 Indexing   214

16.4 Granularity   214

16.5 Robustness   216

16.6 Extract, Transfer/Transform, Load   216

16.7 Conclusion   216

17 Software Architecture   217

17.1 Introduction   217

17.2 Client-Server Architecture   217

17.3 N-tier/Service-Oriented Architecture   218

17.4 Microservices   220

17.5 Monolith   220

17.6 Practical Cases (Mix-and-Match Architectures)   221

17.7 Conclusion   221

18 The CAP Theorem   223

18.1 Introduction   223

18.2 Consistency/Concurrency   223

    18.2.1 Conflict-Free Replicated Data Types   224

18.3 Availability   225

    18.3.1 Redundancy   225

    18.3.2 Front Ends and Load Balancers   225

    18.3.3 Client-Side Load Balancing   228

    18.3.4 Data Layer   228

    18.3.5 Jobs and Taskworkers   230

    18.3.6 Failover   230

18.4 Partition Tolerance   231

   18.4.1 Split Brains   231

18.5 Conclusion   232

19 Logical Network Topological Nodes   233

19.1 Introduction   233

19.2 Network Diagrams   233

19.3 Load Balancing   234

19.4 Caches   235

   19.4.1 Application-Level Caching   236

   19.4.2 Cache Services   237

   19.4.3 Write-Through Caches   238

19.5 Databases   238

   19.5.1 Primary and Replica   238

   19.5.2 Multimaster   239

   19.5.3 A/B Replication   240

19.6 Queues   241

   19.6.1 Task Scheduling and Parallelization   241

   19.6.2 Asynchronous Process Execution   242

   19.6.3 API Buffering   243

19.7 Conclusion   243

Bibliography   245

Index   247

Foreword

This pragmatic book introduces both machine learning and data science, bridging gaps between data scientist and engineer, and helping you bring these techniques into production. It helps ensure that your efforts actually solve your problem, and offers unique coverage of real-world optimization in production settings. This book is filled with code examples in Python and visualizations to illustrate concepts in algorithms. Validation, hypothesis testing, and visualization are introduced early on as these are all key to ensuring that your efforts in data science are actually solving your problem. Part III of the book is unique among data science and machine learning books because of its focus on real-world concerns in optimization. Thinking about hardware, infrastructure, and distributed systems are all steps to bringing machine learning and data science techniques into a production setting.

Andrew and Adam Kelleher bring their experience in engineering and data science, respectively, from their work at BuzzFeed. The topics covered and where to provide breadth versus depth are informed by their real-world experience solving problems in a large production environment. Algorithms for comparison, classification, clustering, and dimensionality reduction are all presented with examples of specific problems that can be solved with each. Explorations into more advanced topics like Bayesian networks or deep learning are provided after the framework for basic machine learning tasks is laid.

This book is a great addition to the Data & Analytics Series. It provides a well-grounded introduction to data science and machine learning with a focus on problem-solving. It should serve as a great resource to any engineer or "accidental programmer" with a more traditional math or science background looking to apply machine learning to their production applications and environment.

—*Paul Dix, series editor*

Preface

Most of this book was written while Andrew and Adam were working together at BuzzFeed. Adam was a data scientist, Andrew was an engineer, and they spent a good deal of time working together on the same team! Given that they're identical twins of triplets, it was confusing and amusing for everyone involved.

The idea for this book came after PyGotham in New York City in August 2014. There were several talks relating to the relatively broadly defined field of "data science." What we noticed was that many data scientists start their careers driven by the curiosity and excitement of learning new things. They discover new tools and often have a favorite technique or algorithm. They'll apply that tool to the problem they're working on. When you have a hammer, every problem looks like a nail. Often, as with neural networks (discussed in Chapter 14), it's more like a pile driver. We wanted to push past the hype of data science by giving data scientists, especially at the time they're starting their careers, a whole tool box. One could argue the context and error analysis tools of Part I are actually more important than the advanced techniques discussed in Part III. In fact, they're a major motivator in writing this book. It's very unlikely a choice of algorithm will be successful if its signal is trumped by its noise, or if there is a high amount of systematic error. We hope this book provides the right tools to take on the projects our readers encounter, and to be successful in their careers.

There's no lack of texts in machine learning or computer science. There are even some decent texts in the field of data science. What we hope to offer with this book is a comprehensive and rigorous entry point to the field of data science. This tool box is slim and driven by our own experience of what is useful in practice. We try to avoid opening up paths that lead to research-level problems. If you're solving research-level problems as a junior data scientist, you've probably gone out of scope.

There's a critical side of data science that is separate from machine learning: engineering. In Part III of this text we get into the engineering side. We discuss the problems you're likely to encounter and give you the fundamentals you'll need to overcome them. Part III is essentially a Computer Science 201-202 crash course. Once you know what you're building, you still have to address many considerations on the path to production. This means understanding your toolbox from the perspective of the tools.

Who This Book Is For

For the last several years there has been a serious demand for good engineers. During the Interactive session of SXSW in 2008 we heard the phrase "accidental developer" coined for the first time. It was used to describe people playing the role of engineer without having had formal training. They simply happened into that position and began filling it out of necessity. More than a decade later we still see this demand for developers, but it's also begun to extend to data scientists. Who fills the role of the "accidental data scientist"? Well, it's usually developers. Or physics undergraduates. Or math majors. People who haven't had much if any formal training in all the disciplines required of a data scientist. People who don't lack for technical training, and have all the prerequisite curiosity and ambition to succeed. People in need of a tool box.

This book is intended to be a crash course for those people. We run through a basic procedure for taking on most data science tasks, encouraging data scientists to use their data set, rather than the tools of the day, as the starting point. Data-driven data science is key to success. The big open secret of data science is that while modeling is important, the bread and butter of data science is simple queries, aggregations, and visualizations. Many industries are in a place where they're accumulating and seeing data for the very first time. There is value to be delivered quickly and with minimal complexity.

Modeling is important, but hard. We believe in applying the principles of agile development to data science. We talk about this a lot in Chapter 2. Start with a minimal solution: a simple heuristic based on a data aggregation, for example. Improve the heuristic with a simple model when your data pipeline is mature and stable. Improve the model when you don't have anything more important to do with your time. We'll provide realistic case studies where this approach is applied.

What This Book Covers

We start this text by providing you with some background on the field of data science. Part I, "Principles of Framing," includes Chapter 1, "The Role of the Data Scientist," which serves as a starting point for your understanding of the data industry.

Chapter 2, "Project Workflow," sets the context for data science by describing agile development. It's a philosophy that helps keep scope small, and development efficient. It can be hard to keep yourself from trying out the latest machine learning framework or tools offered by cloud platforms, but it pays off in the long run.

Next, in Chapter 3, "Quantifying Error," we provide you with a basic introduction to error analysis. Much of data science is reporting simple statistics. Without understanding the error in those statistics, you're likely to come to invalid conclusions. Error analysis is a foundational skill and important enough to be the first item in your tool kit.

We continue in Chapter 4, "Data Encoding and Preprocessing," by discovering a few of the many ways of encoding the real world in the form of data. Naturally this leads us to ask data-driven questions about the real world. The framework for answering these questions is hypothesis testing, which we provide a foundation for in Chapter 5, "Hypothesis Testing."

At this point, we haven't seen many graphs, and our tool kit is lacking in communicating our results to the outside (nontechnical) world. We aim to resolve this in Chapter 6, "Data Visualization," where we learn many approaches to it. We keep the scope small and aim to mostly either make plots of quantities we know how to calculate errors for, or plots that resolve some of the tricky nuances of data visualization. While these tools aren't as flashy as interactive visualizations in d3 (which are worth learning!), they serve as a solid foundational skill set for communicating results to nontechnical audiences.

Having provided the basic tools for working with data, we move on to more advanced concepts in Part II, "Algorithms and Architecture." We start with a brief introduction to data architectures in Chapter 7, "Data Architectures," and an introduction to basic concepts in machine learning in Chapter 8, "Comparison." You now have some very handy methods for measuring the similarities of objects.

From there, we have some tools to do basic machine learning. In Chapter 9, "Regression," we introduce regression and start with one of the most important tools: linear regression. It's odd to start with such a simple tool in the age of neural networks and nonlinear machine learning, but linear regression is outstanding for several reasons. As we'll detail later, it's interpretable, stable, and often provides an excellent baseline. It can describe nonlinearities with some simple tricks, and recent results have shown that polynomial regression (a simple modification of linear regression) can outperform deep feedforward networks on typical applications!

From there, we describe one more basic workhorse of regression: the random forest. These are nonlinear algorithms that rely on a statistical trick, called "bagging," to provide excellent baseline performance for a wide range of tasks. If you want a simple model to start a task with and linear regression doesn't quite work for you, random forest is a nice candidate.

Having introduced regression and provided some basic examples of the machine learning workflow, we move on to Chapter 10, "Classification and Clustering." We see a variety of methods that work on both vector and graph data. We use this section to provide some basic background on graphs and an abbreviated introduction to Bayesian inference. We dive into Bayesian inference and causality in the next chapter.

Our Chapter 11, "Bayesian Networks," is both unconventional and difficult. We take the view that Bayesian networks are most intuitive (though not necessarily easiest) from the viewpoint of causal graphs. We lay this intuition as the foundation for our introduction of Bayesian networks and come back to it in later sections as the foundation for understanding causal inference. In the Chapter 12, "Dimensional Reduction and Latent Variable Models," we build off of the foundation of Bayesian networks to understand PCA and other variants of latent factor models. Topic modeling is an important example of a latent variable model, and we provide a detailed example on the newgroups data set.

As the next to last data-focused chapter, we focus on the problem of causal inference in Chapter 13, "Causal Inference." It's hard to understate the importance of this skill. Data science typically aims to inform how businesses act. The assumption is that the data tells you something about the outcomes of your actions. That can only be true if your analysis has captured causal relationships and not just correlative ones. In that sense, understanding causation underlies much of what we do as data scientists. Unfortunately, with a view toward minimizing scope, it's also too often the first thing to cut. It's important to balance stakeholder expectations when you scope a project, and good causal inference can take time. We hope to empower data scientists to make informed decisions and not to accept purely correlative results lightly.

Finally, in the last data-focused chapter we provide a section to introduce some of the nuances of more advanced machine learning techniques in Chapter 14, "Advanced Machine Learning." We use neural networks as a tool to discuss overfitting and model capacity. The focus should be on using as simple a solution as is available. Resist the urge to start with neural networks as a first model. Simple regression techniques almost always provide a good enough baseline for a first solution.

Up to this point, the platform on which all of the data science happens has been in the background. It's where you do the data science and is not the primary focus. Not anymore. In the last part of this book, Part III, "Bottlenecks and Optimizations," we go in depth on hardware, software, and the systems they make up.

We start with a comprehensive look at hardware in Chapter 15, "Hardware Fundamentals." This provides a tool box of basic resources we have to work with and also provides a framework to discuss the constraints under which we must operate. These constraints are physical limitations on what is possible, and those limitations are realized in the hardware.

Chapter 16, "Software Fundamentals," provides the fundamentals of software and a basic description of data logistics with a section on extract-transfer/transform-load, commonly known as ETL.

Next, we give an overview of design considerations for architecture in Chapter 17, "Architecture Fundamentals." Architecture is the design for how your whole system fits together. It includes the components for data storage, data transfer, and computation, as well as how they all communicate with one another. Some architectures are more efficient than others and objectively do their jobs better than others. Still, a less efficient solution might be more practical, given constraints on time and resources. We hope to provide enough context so you can make informed decisions. Even if you're a data scientist and not an engineer, we hope to provide enough knowledge so you can at least understand what's happening with your data platform.

We then move on to some more advanced topics in engineering. Chapter 18, "The CAP Theorem," covers some fundamental bounds on database performance. Finally, we discuss how it all fits together in the last chapter, which is on network topology: Chapter 19, "Logical Network Topological Nodes."

Going Forward

We hope that not only can you do the machine learning side of data science, but you can also understand what's possible in your own data platform. From there, you can understand what you might need to build and find an efficient path for building out your infrastructure as you need to. We hope that with a complete toolbox, you're free to realize that the tools are only a part of the solution. They're a means to solve real problems, and real problems always have resource constraints.

If there's one lesson to take away from this book, it's that you should always direct your resources toward solving the problems with the highest return on investment. Solving your problem is a real constraint. Occasionally, it might be true that nothing but the best machine learning models can solve it. The question to ask, then, is whether that's the best problem to solve or if there's a simpler one that presents a lower-risk value proposition.

Finally, while we would have liked to have addressed all aspects of production machine learning in this book, it currently exists more as a production data science text. In subsequent editions, we intend to cover omissions, especially in the area of machine learning infrastructure. This new material will include methods to parallelize model training and prediction; the basics of Tensorflow, Apache Airflow, Spark, and other frameworks and tools; the details of several real machine learning platforms, including Uber's Michelangelo, Google's TFX, and our own work on similar systems; and avoiding and managing coupling in machine learning systems. We encourage the reader to seek out the many books, papers, and blog posts covering these topics in the meantime, and to check for updates on the book's website at adamkelleher.com/ml_book.

We hope you'll enjoy learning these tools as much as we did, and we hope this book will save you time and effort in the long run.

About the Authors

Andrew Kelleher is a staff software engineer and distributed systems architect at Venmo. He was previously a staff software engineer at BuzzFeed and has worked on data pipelines and algorithm implementations for modern optimization. He graduated with a BS in physics from Clemson University. He runs a meetup in New York City that studies the fundamentals behind distributed systems in the context of production applications, and was ranked one of FastCompany's most creative people two years in a row.

Adam Kelleher wrote this book while working as principal data scientist at BuzzFeed and adjunct professor at Columbia University in the City of New York. As of May 2018, he is chief data scientist for research at Barclays and teaches causal inference and machine learning products at Columbia. He graduated from Clemson University with a BS in physics, and has a PhD in cosmology from University of North Carolina at Chapel Hill.

Principles of Framing

Chapter 1, "The Role of the Data Scientist," provides background information about the field of data science. This should serve as a starting point to gain context for the role of data science in industry.

Chapter 2, "Project Workflow," describes project workflow and how it relates to the principles of agile software development.

Chapter 3, "Quantifying Error," introduces the concept of measurement error and describes how to quantify it. It then shows how to propagate error approximately through calculations.

Chapter 4, "Data Encoding and Preprocessing," describes how to encode complex, real-world data into something a machine learning algorithm can understand. Using text processing as the example case, the chapter explores the information that is lost due to this encoding.

Chapter 5, "Hypothesis Testing," covers this core skill for a data scientist. You'll encounter statistical tests and p-values throughout your work, and in the application of algorithms like least-squares regression. This chapter provides a brief introduction to statistical hypothesis testing.

Chapter 6, "Data Visualization," is the last subject before the unit on machine learning. Data visualization and exploratory data analysis are critical steps in machine learning, where you evaluate the quality of your data and develop intuition for what you'll model.

The Role of the Data Scientist

1.1 Introduction

We want to set the context for this book by exposing you to the focus on products, rather than methods, early on. Data scientists often make shortcuts, use rules of thumb, and forgo rigor. They do this in favor of speed and with reasonable levels of uncertainty with which to make decisions. The world moves fast, and businesses don't have time for you to write a dissertation on error bars when they need answers to hard questions.

We'll begin by describing how the sizes of companies put different demands on a data scientist. Then, we'll describe agile development: the framework for building products that keeps them responsive to the world outside of the office. We'll discuss ladders and career development. These are useful for both data scientists and the companies they work for. They lay out expectations that companies have for their scientists and help scientists see which traits the company has found useful. Finally, we'll describe what data scientists actually "do" with their time.

1.2 The Role of the Data Scientist

The role of the data scientist is different depending on the context. It's worth having an in-depth understanding of some of the factors that influence your role so you can adapt as your role changes. A lot of this chapter is informed by working within a company that grew from about 150 people to almost 1,500 in a few short years. As the size changed, the roles, supporting structure, management, interdepartmental communications, infrastructure, and expectations of the role changed with it. Adam came in as a data scientist at 300 people, and Andrew came in as an engineer at 150 people. We both stayed on as the company grew over the years. Here is some of what we learned.

1.2.1 Company Size

When the company was smaller, we tended to be generalists. We didn't have the head count to have people work on very specific tasks, even though that might have led to deeper analyses, depth of perspective, and specialized knowledge about the products. As a data scientist at the then-small company, Adam did analyses across several products and departments. As the company grew, the team roles tended to get more specialized, and data scientists tended to start working more on one product or a small number of related products. There's an obvious benefit: they can have deep knowledge of a sophisticated product, so they have fuller context and nuanced understanding that they might not be capable of if they were working on several different products.

A popular team structure is for a product to be built and maintained by a small, mostly autonomous team. We'll go into detail on that in the next section. When our company was smaller, team members often performed a much more general role, acting as the machine learning engineer, the data analyst, the quantitative researcher, and even the product manager and project manager. As the company grew, the company hired more people to take on these roles, so team members' roles became more specialized.

1.2.2 Team Context

Most of the context of this book will be for data scientists working in small, autonomous teams, roughly following the Agile Manifesto. This was largely developed in the context of software engineering, so the focus is on producing code. It extends well to executing data science projects. The manifesto is as follows:

- **Individuals and interactions** over processes and tools
- **Working software** over comprehensive documentation
- **Customer collaboration** over contract negotiation
- **Responding to change** over following a plan

The bold in this list indicates where the priorities lie. The items on the right of each line are still important, but the items on the left are the priorities. This means that team structure is flat, with more experienced people working alongside (rather than above) more junior people. They share skills with interactions like pair-coding and peer-reviewing each other's code. A great benefit to this is that everyone learns quickly from direct interactions with more senior teammates as peers. A drawback is that there can be a little friction when senior developers have their code reviewed by junior team members.

The team's overall goal is to produce working software quickly, so it's okay to procrastinate on documentation. There is generally less focus on process and more on getting things done. As long as the team knows what's going on and they're capable of onboarding new members efficiently enough, they can focus on the work of shipping products.

On the other side of this, the focus on moving fast causes teams to take shortcuts. This can lead to systems being more fragile. It can also create an ever-growing list of things to do more perfectly later. These tasks make up what is called *technical debt*. Much like debt in finance, it's a natural part of the process. Many argue, especially in smaller companies, that it's a necessary part of the process. The argument is that a team should do enough "paying the debt" by writing documentation, making cleaner abstractions, and adding test coverage to keep a sustainable pace of development and keep from introducing bugs.

Teams generally work directly with stakeholders, and data scientists often have a front-facing role in these interactions. There is constant feedback between teams and their stakeholders to make sure the project is still aligned with stakeholder priorities. This is opposed to contract negotiation, where the requirements are laid out and the team decouples from the stakeholders, delivering the product at a later date. In business, things move fast. Priorities change, and the team and product must adapt to those changes. Frequent feedback from stakeholders lets teams learn about changes quickly and adapt to them before investing too much in the wrong product and features.

It's hard to predict the future. If you come up with a long- or moderate-term plan, priorities can shift, team structure can change, and the plan can fall apart. Planning is important, and trying to stick to a plan is important. You'll do all you can to make a plan for building an amazing product, but you'll often have to respond quickly and agilely to change. It can be hard to throw out your favorite plans as priorities shift, but it's a necessary part of the job.

Data scientists are integral members of these teams. They help their teams develop products and help the product managers evaluate a product's performance. Throughout product development, there are critical decisions to make about its features. To that end, a data scientist works with product managers and engineers to formulate questions to answer. They can be as simple as "What unit on this page generates the most clicks?" and as complex as "How would the site perform if the recommender system didn't exist?" Data lets us answer these questions, and data scientists are the people who analyze and help interpret the data for making these decisions. They do this in the context of a dynamic team environment and have to work quickly and effectively in response to change.

1.2.3   Ladders and Career Development

Sometimes data scientists are contrasted against the data analyst. The data analyst has an overlapping skill set, which includes querying databases, making plots, doing statistics, and interpreting data. In addition to these skills, according to this view, a data scientist is someone who can build production machine-learning systems. If that were an apt view, then there might not be such a thing as a junior data scientist. It's not typical to start your career designing production machine-learning systems. Most companies have well-defined "ladders" for career advancement, with specific skills expected at each level.

The team's goal is to build and ship products. There are many skills that are critically important for this that have nothing to do with data. Ladders go beyond technical skills to include communication skills, the ability to understand project scope, and the ability to balance long- and short-term goals.

Generally, companies will define an "individual contributor" track and a "management" track. Junior scientists will start in the same place and shift onto a specific track as their skills develop. They generally start out being able to execute tasks on projects with guidance from more senior team members. They advance to being able to execute tasks more autonomously. Finally, they're the ones helping people execute tasks and usually take more of a role in project planning. The shift often happens at this point, when they hit the "senior" level of their role.

1.2.4   Importance

The data scientist, like everyone on their teams, has an important role. Analysis can lie on the "critical path" of a project's development. This means the analysis might need to be finished before a project can proceed and be delivered. If a data scientist isn't skillful with their analysis and delivers too slowly or incompletely, they might block progress. You don't want to be responsible for delaying the release of a product or feature!

Without data, decision-makers might move more toward experience and intuition. While these might not be wrong, they're not the best way to make decisions. Adding data to the decision-making process moves business more toward science. The data scientist, then, has a critical role in making business decisions more rational.

1.2.5 The Work Breakdown

Anecdotally, probably 80 to 90 percent of the work a data scientist does outside of interpersonal and managerial tasks is basic analysis and reporting on experimental and observational data. Much of the data the scientist has to work with is observational since experimental data takes time and resources to collect, while observational data is essentially "free" once you've implemented data collection. This makes observational data analysis methods important to be familiar with. You'll examine correlation and causation later in this book. You'll develop an understanding of observational data analysis methods by contrasting them with experimental data and an understanding of why observational results are often biased.

Many data scientists work primarily with experimental data. We'll cover experiment design and analysis in some detail as well. Good experiment design is hard. Web-scale experiments, while often providing large samples, don't guarantee you'll actually be able to measure the experimental effects you're looking for, even when they're large! Randomized assignment doesn't even guarantee you'll have correct experimental results (due to selection bias). We'll cover all of this and more later in the book.

The other 10 or so percent of the work is the stuff you usually read about when you hear about data science in the news. It's the cool machine learning, artificial intelligence, and Internet of Things applications that are so exciting and drive so many people toward the field of data science. In a very real sense, these applications are the future, but they're also the minority of the work data scientists do, unless they're the hybrid data scientist/machine learning engineer type. Those roles are relatively rare and are generally for very senior data scientists. This book is aimed at entry- to mid-level data scientists. We want to give you the skills to start developing your career in whichever direction you'd like so you can find the data science role that is perfect for you.

1.3 Conclusion

Getting things right can be hard. Often, the need to move fast supercedes the need to get it right. Consider the case when you need to decide between two policies, A and B, that cost the same amount to implement. You must implement one, and time is a factor. If you can show that the effect of policy A, $Y(A)$, is more positive than $Y(B)$, it doesn't matter how much more positive it is. As long as $Y(A) - Y(B) > 0$, policy A is the right choice. As long as your measurement is good enough to be within 100 percent of the correct difference, you know enough to make the policy choice!

At this point, you should have a better idea of what it means to be a data scientist. Now that you understand a little about the context, you can start exploring the product development process.

2

Project Workflow

2.1 Introduction

This chapter focuses on the workflow of executing data science tasks as one-offs versus tasks that will eventually make up components in production systems. We'll present a few diagrams of common workflows and propose combining two as a general approach. At the end of this chapter you should understand where they fit in an organization that uses data-driven analyses to fuel innovation. We'll start by giving a little more context about team structure. Then, we'll break down the workflow into several steps: planning, design/preprocessing, analysis, and action. These steps often blend together and are usually not formalized. At the end, you'll have gone from the concept of a product, like a recommender system or a deep-dive analysis, to a working prototype or result.

At that stage, you're ready to start working with engineers to have the system implemented in production. That might mean bringing an algorithm into a production setting automating a report, or something else.

We should say that as you get closer to feature development, your workflow can evolve to look more like an engineer's workflow. Instead of prototyping in a Jupyter Notebook on your computer, you might prototype a model as a component of a microservice. This chapter is really aimed at getting a data scientist oriented with the steps that start them toward building prototypes for models.

When you're prototyping data products, it's important to keep in mind the broader context of the organization. The focus should be more on testing value propositions than on perfect architecture, clean code, and crisp software abstractions. Those things take time, and the world changes quickly. With that in mind, we spend the remainder of this chapter talking about the agile methodology and how data products should follow that methodology like any other piece of software.

2.2 The Data Team Context

When you're faced with a problem that you might solve with machine learning, usually many options are available. You could make a fast, heuristic solution involving very little math that you could produce in a day and move on to the next project. You could take a smarter approach and probably achieve better performance. The cost is your time and the loss of opportunity to spend that time working on a different product. Finally, you could implement the state of the art.

That usually means you'd have to research the best approach before even beginning coding, implement algorithms from scratch, and potentially solve unsolved problems with how to scale the implementation.

When you're working with limited resources, as you usually are in small organizations, the third option usually isn't the best choice. If you want a high-quality and competitive product, the first option might not be the best either. Where you fall along the spectrum between the get-it-done and state-of-the-art approaches depends on the problem, the context, and the resources available. If you're making a healthcare diagnosis system, the stakes are much higher than if you're building a content recommendation system.

To understand why you'll use machine learning at all, you need a little context for where and how it's used. In this section, we'll try to give you some understanding of how teams are structured, what some workflows might look like, and practical constraints on machine learning.

2.2.1   Embedding vs. Pooling Resources

In our experience, we've seen two models for data science teams. The first is a "pool of resources" where the team gets a request and someone on the team fulfills it. The second is for members of the team to "embed" with other teams in the organization to help them with their work.

In the first "pool of resources" approach, each request of the team gets assigned and triaged like with any project. Some member of the team executes it, and if they need help, they lean on someone else. A common feature of this approach is that tasks aren't necessarily related, and it's not formally decided that a single member of the team executes all the tasks in a certain domain or that a single member should handle all incoming requests from a particular person. It makes sense to have the same person answer the questions for the same stakeholders so they can develop more familiarity with the products and more rapport with the stakeholders. When teams are small, the same data scientist will tend to do this for many products, and there's little specialization.

In the "embedded" approach, a data scientist works with some team in the organization each day, understanding the team's needs and their particular goals. In this scenario, the understanding of problems and the approaches are clear as the data scientist is exposed to them day to day. This is probably the biggest contrast between the "embedded" and "pool of resources" approaches. Anecdotally, the former is more common than the latter in small organizations. Larger organizations tend to have more need and resources for the latter.

This chapter has a dual focus. First we'll discuss the data science project life cycle in particular, and then we'll cover the integration of the data science project cycle with a technical project life cycle.

2.2.2   Research

The steps to develop a project involving a machine learning component aren't really different from those of an engineering project. Planning, design, development, integration, deployment, and post-deployment are still the steps of the product life cycle (see Figure 2.1).

There are two major differences between a typical engineering product and one involving a data science component. The first is that with a data science component, there are commonly

Figure 2.1   The stages of a product's life cycle

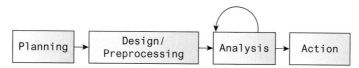

Figure 2.2   The independent life cycle of a data science task

unknowns, especially in smaller teams or teams with less experience. This creates the need for a recursive workflow, where analysis can be done and redone.

The second major difference is that many if not most data science tasks are executed without the eventual goal of deployment to production. This creates a more abridged product life cycle (see Figure 2.2).

The Field Guide to Data Science [1] explains that four steps comprise the procedure of data science tasks. Figure 2.2 shows our interpretation.

Here are the steps:

1. Build domain knowledge and collect data.

2. Preprocess the data. This involves cleaning out sources of error (e.g., removing outliers), as well as reformatting the data as needed.

3. Execute some analyses and draw conclusions. This is where models are applied and tested.

4. Do something with the result. Report it or refine the existing infrastructure.

2.2.3   Prototyping

The workflows we've outlined are useful for considering the process of data science tasks independently. These steps, while linear, seem in some ways to mirror the general steps to software prototyping as outlined in "Software Prototyping: Adoption, Practice and Management"[2]. Figure 2.3 shows our interpretation of these steps.

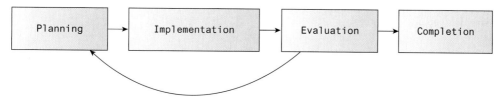

Figure 2.3   The life cycle of a software prototype

1. **Planning:** Assess project requirements.

2. **Implementation:** Build a prototype.

3. **Evaluation:** Determine whether the problem is solved.

4. **Completion:** If the needs are not satisfied, re-assess and incorporate new information.

2.2.4   A Combined Workflow

Sometimes these tasks are straightforward. When they take some time and investment, a more rigorous focus on process becomes crucial. We propose the typical data science track should be considered as being like a typical prototyping track for engineering projects. This is especially useful when the end goal is a component in a production system. In situations where data science influences engineering decisions or products that are brought to production, you can picture a combined product life cycle, as in Figure 2.4.

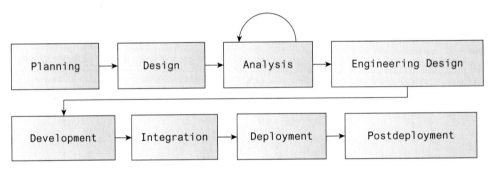

Figure 2.4   The combined product life cycle of an engineering project dependent on exploratory analysis

This approach allows data scientists to work with engineers in an initial planning and design phase, before the engineering team takes lessons learned to inform their own planning and design processes with technical/infrastructural considerations taken fully into account. It also allows data scientists to operate free of technical constraints and influences, which could otherwise slow progress and lead to premature optimization.

2.3   Agile Development and the Product Focus

Now that you understand how prototyping works and the product life cycle, we can build a richer context around product development. The end goal is to build a product that provides value to someone. That might be a product that performs a task, like translating languages for travelers or recommending articles to read on your morning commute. It might be a product that monitors heart rates for patients after surgery or tracks people's fitness as they work toward personal milestones. Common to each of these products is a *value proposition*.

When you're building a new product, you have a value proposition in mind. The issue is that it's likely untested. You might have good reason to believe that the proposition will be true: that users are willing to pay $1 for an app that will monitor their heart rate after surgery (or will tolerate some number of ads for a free app). You wouldn't be building it in the first place if you didn't believe in the value proposition. Unfortunately, things don't always turn out how you expect. The whole purpose of AB tests is to test product changes in the real world and make sure reality aligns with our expectations. It's the same with value propositions. You need to build the product to see whether the product is worth building.

To manage this paradox, we always start with a *minimum viable product*, or MVP. It's minimal in the sense that it's the simplest thing you can possibly build while still providing the value that you're proposing providing. For the heart rate monitor example, it might be a heart rate monitor that attaches to a hardware device, alerts you when you're outside of a target range, and then calls an ambulance if you don't respond. This is a version of an app that can provide value in the extra security. Any more features (e.g., providing a fancy dashboard, tracking goals, etc.), and you're going beyond just testing the basic value proposition. It takes time to develop features, and that is time you might invest in testing a different value proposition! You should do as little work as possible to test the value proposition and then decide whether to invest more resources in the product or shift focus to something different.

Some version of this will be true with every product you build. You can look at features of large products as their own products. Facebook's Messenger app was originally part of the Facebook platform and was split into its own mobile app. That's a case where a feature literally evolved into its own product. Everything you build should have this motivation behind it of being minimal. This can cause problems, and we have strategies to mitigate them. The cycle of software development is built around this philosophy, and you can see it in the concept of microservice architecture, as well as the "sprints" of the product development cycle. These leads us to the principles of the agile methodology.

2.3.1 The 12 Principles

The agile methodology is described with 12 principles [3].

1. Our highest priority is to satisfy the customer through early and continuous delivery of valuable software. The customer is the person you're providing value to. That can be a consumer, or it can be the organization you're working for. The reason you'd like to deliver software early is to test the value proposition by actually putting it in front of the user. The requirement that the software be "valuable" means you don't work so fast that you fail to test your value proposition.

2. Welcome changing requirements, even late in development. Agile processes harness change for the customer's competitive advantage. This principle sounds counterintuitive. When requirements for software change, you have to throw away some of your work, go back to the planning phase to re-specify the work to be done, and then do the new work. That's a lot of inefficiency! Consider the alternative: the customer needs have changed. The value proposition is no longer satisfied by the software requirements as they were originally planned. If you don't adapt your software to the (unknown!) new requirements, the value proposition, as executed by your software, will fail to meet the customer's needs. Clearly, it's better to throw away some work than to throw away the whole product without testing the value proposition! Even better, if the competition isn't keeping this "tight coupling" with their stakeholders (or customers), then your stakeholders are at a competitive advantage!

3. Deliver working software frequently, from a couple of weeks to a couple of months, with a preference to the shorter timescale. There are a few reasons for this. One of them is for consistency with the last principle. You should deliver software often, so you can get frequent feedback from stakeholders. That will let you adjust your project plans at each step of its development and make sure you're aligned with the stakeholders' needs as well as you can be. The time when you deliver value is a great time to hear more about the customer's needs and get ideas for new features. We don't think we've ever been in a meeting where we put a new product or feature in front of someone and didn't hear something along the lines of "You know, it would be amazing if it also did... ."

Another reason for this is that the world changes quickly. If you don't deliver value quickly, your opportunity for providing that value can pass. You might be building a recommender system for an app and take so long with the prototype that the app is already being deprecated! More realistically, you might take so long that the organization's priorities have shifted to other projects and you've lost support (from product managers, engineers, and others) for the system you were working on.

4. Businesspeople and developers must work together daily throughout the project. This principle is an extension of the previous two. Periodically meeting with the stakeholders isn't the only time to connect the software development process with the context of the business. Developers should at least also be meeting with product managers to keep context with the business goals of their products. These managers, ideally, would be in their team check-ins each day, or at the least a few times per week. This makes sure that not only does the team building the software keep the context of what they're working on, but the business knows where the software engineering and data resources (your and your team's time) are being spent.

5. Build projects around motivated individuals. Give them the environment and support they need, and trust them to get the job done. One sure way to restrict teams from developing things quickly is to have them all coordinate their work through a single manager. Not only does that person have to keep track of everything everyone is working on, but they need to have the time to physically meet with all of them! This kind of development doesn't scale. Typically, teams will be small enough to share a pizza and have one lead per team. The leads can communicate with each other in a decentralized way (although they do typically all communicate through management meetings), and you can scale the tech organization by just adding new similar teams.

Each person on a team has a role, and that lets the team function as a mostly autonomous unit. The product person keeps the business goals in perspective and helps coordinate with stakeholders. The engineering manager helps make sure the engineers are staying productive and does a lot of the project planning. The engineers write the code and participate in the project planning process. The data scientist answers questions for the product person and can have different roles (depending on seniority) with managing the product's data sources, building machine learning and statistical tools for products, and helping figure out the presentation of data and statistics to stakeholders. In short, the team has everything they need to work quickly and efficiently together to get the job done. When external managers get too involved in the details of team's operations, they can end up slowing them down just as easily as they can help.

6. The most efficient and effective method of conveying information to and within a development team is face-to-face conversation. A lot of communication is done over chat clients, through shared documents, and through email. These media can make it hard to judge someone's understanding of project requirements as well as their motivation, focus, and confidence for getting it done. Team morale can fluctuate throughout product development. People can tend to err on the side of agreeing to work that they aren't sure they can execute. When teams communicate face to face, it's much easier to notice these issues and handle them before they're a problem.

As a further practical issue, when you communicate over digital media, there can be a lot of other windows, and even other conversations, going on. It can be hard to have a deep conversation with someone when you aren't even sure if they're paying attention!

7. Working software is the primary measure of progress. Your goal is to prove value propositions. If you follow the steps we've already outlined, then the software you're building is satisfying stakeholders' needs. You can do that without implementing the best software abstractions, cleaning up your code, fully documenting your code, and adding complete test coverage. In short, you can take as many shortcuts as you like (respecting the next principle), as long as your software works!

When things break, it's important to take a retrospective. Always have a meeting to figure out why it happened but without placing blame on any individual. The whole team is responsible when things do or don't work. Make whatever changes are necessary to make sure things don't break in the future. That might mean setting a higher standard for test coverage, adding more documentation around certain types of code (like describing input data), or cleaning up your code just a little more.

8. Agile processes promote sustainable development. The sponsors, developers, and users should be able to maintain a constant pace indefinitely. When you're working fast, it's easy for your code to end up messy. It's easy to write big monolithic blocks of code instead of breaking it up into nice small functions with test coverage on each. It's easy to write big services instead of microservices with clearly defined responsibilities. All of these things get you to a value proposition quickly and can be great if they're done in the right context. All of them are also *technical debt*, which is something you need to fix later when you end up having to build new features onto the product.

When you have to change a monolithic block of code you've written, it can be really hard to read through all the logic. It's even worse if you change teams and someone else has to read through it! It's the type of problem that can slow progress to a halt if it isn't kept in check. You should always notice when you're taking shortcuts and consider at each week's sprint whether you might fix some small piece of technical debt so it doesn't build up too much. Remember that you'd like to keep up your pace of development indefinitely, and you want to keep delivering product features at the same rate. Your stakeholders will notice if they suddenly stop seeing you for a while! All of this brings us to the next point.

9. Continuous attention to technical excellence and good design enhances agility. When you have clear abstractions, code can be much more readable. When functions are short, clean, and well-documented, it's easy for anyone to read and modify the code. This is true for software development as well as for data science. Data scientists in particular can be guilty of poor coding standards: one character variable names, large blocks of data preprocessing code with no documentation, and other bad practices. If you make a habit of writing good code, it won't slow you down to do it! In fact, it'll speed up the team as a whole.

10. Simplicity—the art of maximizing the amount of work not done—is essential. Writing a good MVP can be an art. How do you know exactly the features to write to test your value proposition? How do you know what software development best practices you can skip to keep a sustainable pace of development? Which architectural shortcuts can you get away with now and in the long term?

These are all skills you learn with practice and that your manager and team will be good resources for advice. If you're not sure which product features really test the minimum value proposition, talk to your product manager and your stakeholders. If you're not sure how sloppy your code can be, talk to a more senior data scientist, or even to an engineer on your team.

11. The best architectures, requirements, and designs emerge from self-organizing teams. Some things are hard to understand unless you're working with them directly. The team writing the software is going to have the best idea what architectural changes are going to work the best. This is partly because they know the architecture well and partly because they know their strengths and weaknesses for executing it. Teams communicate with each other and can collaborate without the input of other managers. They can build bigger systems that work together than they could on their own, and when several teams coordinate, they can architect fairly large and complex systems without a centralized architect guiding them.

12. At regular intervals, the team reflects on how to become more effective and then tunes and adjusts its behavior accordingly. While the focus is on delivering value quickly and often and working closely with stakeholders to do that, teams also have to be introspective occasionally to make sure they're working as well as they can. This is often done once per week in a "retrospective" meeting, where the team will get together and talk about what went well during the past week, what didn't work well, and what they'll plan to change for the next week.

These are the 12 principles of agile development. They apply to data science as well as software. If someone ever proposes a big product loaded with features and says "Let's build this!" you should think about how to do it agilely. Think about what the main value proposition is (chances are that it contains several). Next, think of the minimal version of it that lets you test the proposition. Build it, and see whether it works!

Often in data science, there are extra shortcuts you can take. You can use a worse-performing model while you work on a better one just to fill the gap that the engineers are building around. You can write big monolithic functions that return a model just by copying and pasting a prototype from a Jupyter Notebook. You can use CSV files instead of running database queries when you need static data sets. Get creative, but always think about what you'd need to do to build something right. That might be creating good abstractions around your models, replacing CSV files with database queries to get live data, or just writing cleaner code.

To summarize, there are four points to the Agile Manifesto. Importantly, these are tendencies. Real life is not usually dichotomous. These points really reflect our priorities:

- Individuals and interactions over processes and tools

- Working software over comprehensive documentation

- Customer collaboration over contract negotiation

- Responding to change over following a plan

2.4   Conclusion

Ideally now you have a good idea of what the development process looks like and where you fit in. We hope you'll take the agile philosophy as a guide when building data products and will see the value in keeping a tight feedback loop with your stakeholders.

Now that you have the context for doing data science, let's learn the skills!

Quantifying Error

To kill an error is as good a service as, and sometimes even better than, the establishing of a new truth or fact.
—Charles Darwin

3.1 Introduction

Most measurements have some error associated with them. We often think of the numbers we report as exact values (e.g., "there were 9,126 views of this article"). Anyone who has implemented multiple tracking systems that are supposed to measure the same quantity knows there is rarely perfect agreement between measurements. The chances are that neither system measures the ground truth—there are always failure modes, and it's hard to know how often failures happen.

Aside from errors in data collections, some measured quantities are uncertain. Instead of running an experiment with all users of your website, you'll work with a sample. Metrics like retention and engagement you measure in the sample are noisy measurements of what you'd see in the whole population. You can quantify that noise and make sure you bound the error from sampling to something within reasonable limits.

In this chapter, we'll discuss the concept of error analysis. You'll learn how to think about error in a measurement, and you'll learn how to calculate error in simple quantities you derive from measurements. You'll develop some intuition for when error matters a lot and when you can safely ignore it.

3.2 Quantifying Error in Measured Values

Imagine you want to measure the length of a piece of string. You take out a ruler, stretch the string along the length of the ruler, and type the length you measure into a spreadsheet. You're a good scientist, so you know that you really shouldn't stop at one measurement. You measure it again and get a slightly different result. The string was stretched a little less; maybe it was a little misaligned on the ruler the first time. You repeat the process over and over again. You find the measurements plotted in Figure 3.1.

Figure 3.1   Several measurements of a string are given by the red dots along the number line. The true length of the string is shown with the vertical blue line. If you look at the average value of the measurements, it falls around the center of the group of red dots. It's higher than the true value, so you have a positive bias in your measurement process.

There is a true length to the string, but the string bends a little. To straighten it out to measure it, you have to stretch it a little, so the measurement tends to be a little longer than it should be. If you average your measurements together, the average will be a little higher than the true length of the string. This difference between the "expected" length from your measurements and the "true" length is called *systematic error*. It's also sometimes called *bias*.

If there is no bias, there is still some random spread your measurements take around the true value. On average you measure the true value, but each measurement is a little low or a little high. This type of error is called *random error*. It's what we commonly think of as *measurement noise*. We usually measure it with the standard deviations of the measurements around their average value.

If measurements have no systematic error, then you can take a large enough sample of them, average them together, and find the true value! This is a great situation to be in, if you're able to take several independent measurements. Unfortunately, it's not a common situation. Usually you can make only one measurement and expect that there is at least a little systematic error (e.g., data is only lost, so count measurements are systematically low).

Consider the case of tracking impressions on a web page. When a user clicks a link to the page on which you're tracking impressions, in some instances, they will not follow the link completely (but exit before arriving at the final page). Still closer to conversion, they may load the page but not allow the pixel tracking impressions on that page to be requested. Further, we may double-count impressions in the case a user refreshes the page for whatever reason (which happens quite a lot). These all contribute random and systematic errors, going in different directions. It's hard to say whether the measurement will be systematically low or high.

There are certainly ways to quantify errors in tracking. Server logs, for example, can tell the story of requests complete with response codes your tracking pixels may have missed. `tcpdump` or `wireshark` can be used for monitoring attempted connections that get dropped or disconnected before the requests are fulfilled. The main consideration is that both of these methods are difficult in real-time reporting applications. That doesn't mean, though, you can't do a sampled comparison of tracked impressions to impressions collected through these other less convenient more expensive means.

Once you've implemented your tracking system and checked it against some ground truth (e.g., another system, like Google Analytics), you'll usually assume the error in these raw numbers is small and that you can safely ignore it.

There is another context where you have to deal with systematic and random error, where you can't safely ignore the error. This comes up most often in AB testing, where you look at a performance metric within a subpopulation of your users (i.e., those participating in the experiment) and want to extrapolate that result to all of your users. The measurement you make with your experiment, you hope, is an "unbiased" measurement (one with no systematic error) of the "true" value of the metric (the one you would measure over the whole population).

To understand error from sampling, it'll be helpful to take a little side trip into sampling error. The end result is familiar: with each measurement, we should have random and systematic error in comparison to the "true" value.

3.3 Sampling Error

Sampling error is a very rich subject. There are entire books written about it. We can't hope to cover all of its intricacies here, but we can provide enough of an introduction to give you some working knowledge. We hope you'll continue reading more on your own!

Suppose you run a news website, and you want to know the average amount of time it takes you to read an article on your website. You could read every article on the site, record your reading time, and get your answer that way, but that's incredibly labor intensive. It would be great if you could read a much smaller number of the articles and be reasonably confident about the average reading time.

The trick you'll use is this: you can take a random *sample* of articles on the website, measure the reading time for those articles, and take the average. This will be a measurement of the average reading time for articles on the whole website. It probably won't match the actual average reading time exactly, the one you'd measure if you read all of the articles. This true number is called the *population* average since it's averaging over the whole population of articles instead of just a sample from it.

How close does the average read time in your sample compare with the average read time across the whole site? This is where the magic happens. The result comes from the central limit theorem. It says that the average of N independent measurements, μ_N, from a population is an unbiased estimate for the population average, μ, as long as you have a reasonably large number of samples. Even better, it says the random error for the sample average, σ_μ, is just the sample standard deviation, σ_N, divided by the square root of the sample size, $\sqrt{N}$:

$$\sigma_\mu = \frac{\sigma_N}{\sqrt{N}} \tag{3.1}$$

In practice, $N = 30$ is a pretty good rule of thumb for using this approximation. Let's draw a sample from a uniform distribution to try it.

First, let's make the population of reading times. Let's make it uniform over the range of 5 to 15 minutes and generate a population of 1,000 articles.

```
1  import numpy as np
2
3  population = np.random.uniform(5,15, size=1000)
```

and then sample 30 articles from it at random.

```
1  sample = np.random.choice(population, size=30, replace=False)
```

Note that in practice, you won't have access to a whole population to sample from. If these were the reading times of articles, none of the reading times is even measured when you start the process! Instead, you'd sample 30 articles from a database and then read those articles to generate your sample from the populations. We generate a population to sample from here, just so we can check how close our sample mean is to the population mean.

Note also that database queries don't sample randomly from the database. To get random sampling, you can use the rand() SQL function to generate random floats between 0 and 1. Then, you can sort by the random value, or limit to results with rand() < 0.05 for example, to keep 5 percent of results. An example query might look like this (NOTE: This should never be used on large tables):

```
SELECT article_id, rand() as r FROM articles WHERE r < 0.05;
```

Continuing, you can compute the population and sample means, as shown here:

```
1 population.mean()
2 sample.mean()
```

which for us returns 10.086 for the population and 9.701 for the sample. Note that your values will be different since we're dealing with random numbers. Our sample mean is only 3 percent below the population value!

Repeating this sampling process (keeping the population fixed) and plotting the resulting averages, the histogram of sample averages takes on a bell curve shape. If you look at the standard deviation of this bell curve, it's exactly the quantity that we measured earlier, σ_μ. This turns out to be extremely convenient since we know a lot about bell curves.

Another useful fact is that 95 percent of measurements that fall onto a bell curve happen within $\pm 1.96\sigma_\mu$ of the average. This range, $(\mu_N - 1.96\sigma_\mu, \mu_N + 1.96\sigma_\mu)$, is called the 95 percent confidence interval for the measurement: 95 percent of times you take a sample it will fall within this range of the true value. Another useful way to look at it is that if you take a sample, and estimate this range, you're 95 percent sure that the true value is within this range!

In the context of our example, that means you can expect roughly 95 percent of the time that our sample average will be within this range of the population average. You can compute the range as follows:

```
1 lower_range = sample.mean() - 1.96 * sample.std(ddof=1) /
2                         np.sqrt(len(sample))
3 upper_range = sample.mean() + 1.96 * sample.std(ddof=1) /
4                         np.sqrt(len(sample))
```

You use ddof=1 because here you're trying to estimate a population standard deviation from a sample. To estimate a sample standard deviation, you can leave it as the default of 0. The values we get here are 8.70 for the lower value and 10.70 for the upper. This means from this sample, the true population value will be between 8.70 and 10.70 95 percent of the time. We use an interval like this to estimate a population value.

Notice that the denominator is $\frac{1}{\sqrt{N}}$, where N is the size of the sample. The standard deviation and the mean don't change with the sample size (except to get rid of some measurement noise), so the sample size is the piece that controls the size of your confidence intervals. How much do they change? If you increase the sample size, $N_{new} = 100N_{old}$, increasing the sample 100 times, the factor is $\frac{1}{\sqrt{N_{new}}} = \frac{1}{\sqrt{100N_{old}}} = \frac{1}{10}\frac{1}{\sqrt{N_{old}}}$. You can see, then, that the error bars only shrink to one-tenth of their original size. The error bars decrease slowly with the sample size!

We should also note that if the number of samples is comparable to the size of the whole population, you need to use a finite-population correction. We won't go into that here since it's pretty rare that you actually need to use it.

Note that you can get creative with how you use this rule. A *click-through rate* (CTR) is a metric you're commonly interested in. If a user views a link to an article, that is called an *impression*. If they click the link, that is called a *click*. An impression is an opportunity to click. In that sense, each impression is a trial, and each click is a success. The CTR, then, is a *success rate* and can be thought of as a probability of success given a trial.

If you code a click as a 1 and an impression with no click as a 0, then each impression gives you either a 1 or a 0. You end up with a big list of 1s and 0s. If you average these, you take the sum of the outcomes, which is just the number of clicks divided by the number of trials. The average of these binary outcomes is just the click-through rate! You can apply the central limit theorem. You can take the standard deviation of these 1/0 measurements and divide by the square root of the number of measurements to get the standard error. You can use the standard error as before to get a confidence interval for your CTR measurement!

Now that you know how to calculate standard errors and confidence intervals, you'll want to be able to derive error measurements on calculated quantities. You don't often care about metrics alone but rather *differences* in metrics. That's how you know, for example, if one thing is performing better or worse than another thing.

3.4   Error Propagation

So, assume you've done all the work to take good random samples of data for two measurements, and you've calculated standard errors for the two measurements. Maybe these measurements are the click-through rates of two different articles. Suppose you'd like to know if one article is clicking better than the other. How can you find that out?

A simple way is to look at the difference in the click-through rates. Suppose article 1 has CTR p_1 with standard error σ_1 and article 2 has CTR p_2 with standard error σ_2. Then the difference, d, is $d = p_1 - p_2$. If the difference is positive, that means $p_1 > p_2$, and article 1 is the better clicking article. If it's negative, then article 2 clicks better.

The trouble is that the standard errors might be bigger than d! How can you interpret things in that case? You need to find the standard error for d. If you can say you're 95 percent sure that the difference is positive, then you can say you're 95 percent sure that article 1 is clicking better.

Let's take a look at how to estimate the standard error of an arbitrary function of many variables. If you know calculus, this will be a fun section to read! If you don't, feel free to skip ahead to the results.

Start with the Taylor Series, which is written as follows:

$$f(x) \approx \sum_{n \geq 0}^{N < \infty} \frac{(x - a)^n}{n!} \tag{3.2}$$

If you let f be a function of two variables, x and y, then you can compute up to the first order term.

$$f(x, y) \approx f(x_0, y_0) + \frac{\partial f}{\partial x}(x - x_0) + \frac{\partial f}{\partial y}(y - y_0) + \mathcal{O}(2) \tag{3.3}$$

Here, $\mathcal{O}(2)$ denotes terms that are of size $(x - x_0)^n$ or $(y - y_0)^n$ where n is greater than or equal to 2. Since these differences are relatively small, raising them to larger powers makes them very small and ignorable.

When x_0 and y_0 are the expectations of x and y, you can put this equation in terms of the definition of variance, $\sigma^2 = \langle (f(x, y) - f(x_0, y_0))^2 \rangle$, by subtracting $f(x_0, y_0)$ from both sides, squaring, and taking expectation values. You're dropping terms like $(x - x_0)(y - y_0)$, which amounts to assuming that the errors in x and y are uncorrelated.

$$\sigma_f^2 \approx \left(\frac{\partial f}{\partial x}(x - x_0) + \frac{\partial f}{\partial y}(y - y_0) \right)^2$$
$$= \left(\frac{\partial f}{\partial x} \right)^2 \sigma_x^2 + \left(\frac{\partial f}{\partial y} \right)^2 \sigma_y^2 \tag{3.4}$$

Just taking the square root gives you the standard error we were looking for!

This formula should work well whenever the measurement errors in x and y are relatively small and uncorrelated. Small here means that the relative error, e.g., σ_x / x_0, is less than 1.

You can use this formula to derive a lot of really useful formulae! If you let $f(x, y) = x - y$, then this will give you the standard error in the difference that you wanted before! If you let $f(x, y) = x/y$, then you get standard error in a ratio, like the standard error in a click rate due to a measurement error in clicks and impressions!

You'll give a few handy formulae here for reference. Here, c_1 and c_2 will be constants with no measurement error associated with them. x and y will be variables with measurement error. If you ever like to assume that x or y has no error, simply plug in $\sigma_x = 0$, for example, and the formulae will simplify.

$f(x, y)$	σ_f
$c_1 x - c_2 y$	$\sqrt{c_1^2 \sigma_x^2 + c_2^2 \sigma_y^2}$
$c_1 x + c_2 y$	$\sqrt{c_1^2 \sigma_x^2 + c_2^2 \sigma_y^2}$
x/y	$f \sqrt{\left(\left(\frac{\sigma_x}{x}\right)^2 + \left(\frac{\sigma_y}{y}\right)^2 \right)}$
xy	$f \sqrt{\left(\left(\frac{\sigma_x}{x}\right)^2 + \left(\frac{\sigma_y}{y}\right)^2 \right)}$

In the previous section, we talked about the case of tracking web page impressions. Let's take a look at how the error in impression data (call it 0.4 percent) and the error in click data (call it 3.2 percent) affects the calculation of CTR as defined here:

$$CTR = \frac{\text{clicks}}{\text{impressions}} \tag{3.5}$$

For shorthand, let's let *clicks* be c and *impressions* be i. Let's also choose the number of impressions to be 10,540 and the number of clicks to be 844.

Now, you can just plug all of this into the formula in the table for a quotient! You can use $f = c/i$. You just re-arrange it by dividing by f on both sides.

$$\frac{\sigma_f}{f} \approx \sqrt{\left(\left(\frac{\sigma_c}{c}\right)^2 + \left(\frac{\sigma_i}{i}\right)^2\right)} \tag{3.6}$$

$$= \sqrt{0.032^2 + 0.004^2} \tag{3.7}$$

$$= 0.0322 \tag{3.8}$$

We end up with about 3.2 percent error in the click-through rate. Small errors for the numbers going into quotients (or products, too) give comparable percent errors in the results. These percent errors, or *relative* errors, add in quadrature. This means the new percent error is the square root of the sum of squares of the percent errors of the inputs. You'll find a different result for differences: the errors magnify!

Suppose you have a CTR $p_1 = 0.03$, with a 10 percent error, or $\sigma_1 = 0.003$. Suppose you have a $p_2 = 0.035$, also with 10 percent error, $\sigma_2 = 0.0035$. You can compute the error using the previous formula for $f = p_2 - p_1 = 0.005$. You find $\sigma_f = 0.0046$. That gives a percent error of $\sigma_f/f = 0.0046/0.005 = 0.92$, or 92 percent error! You took two measurements that were reasonably precise, and the difference you calculated ended up with huge error! This is because the errors add in quadrature (not the relative errors!), and the quantities *subtract*, leaving the magnitude of the difference much smaller. The error then grows relative to the difference, and you get a large relative error. You need much more precision to say for sure that p_2 is a higher click rate than p_1!

3.5 Conclusion

This concludes the discussion of error and error propagation. You'll dive much deeper into confidence intervals, p-values, and hypothesis testing in Chapter 5.

Ideally, after reading this section, you have some intuition for error and how it changes with sample sizes. You should be able to calculate confidence intervals for experiment results and do some basic calculations with those calculated results. You should have some intuition that when you add or subtract noisy quantities, the noise can grow. This shows how hard it can be to estimate differences between quantities!

Data Encoding and Preprocessing

4.1 Introduction

Data preprocessing is an important step in machine learning. It's the first step and a place where there is a lot of room for subjective decision-making, which can reduce the information content of your data in ways you'll learn about in this chapter.

Generally, data preprocessing is the process of mapping raw data into a format that is ready to pass into a machine-learning algorithm. You can assume for now that there's no uncertainty in the data that you're encoding, and you'll revisit the problem of uncertainty in later chapters. For now, you'll learn how you can encode measurements in a way an algorithm can understand. You can also take steps to make sure your models perform as well as possible on your data. That can mean removing features to reduce the number of parameters your model has to learn, multiplying features together to capture interactions between them, or even combining features in more complicated ways to capture relationships your model won't be likely to find on its own.

For now, let's use logistic regression as an example. A logistic regression model takes a variable, x, and produces a probability, $P(Y = 1) = 1/e^{-\beta_1 x + \beta_0}$, that an outcome will happen. Here, you encode the outcome as a variable Y. Either Y happens or it doesn't. If it happens, you can say $Y = 1$, and if it doesn't, you can say $Y = 0$. Y is called a *binary* variable. The coefficients β_0 and β_1 are parameters that you have to choose to make the model fit the data as well as possible.

This way of encoding these types of outcomes has a nice property. Let Y_i be the ith measurement of Y, and let there be N total measurements in the data set. If you average all the outcomes, you get the following:

$$\bar{Y} = \sum_{i=1}^{N} Y_i/N$$

This is just the number of occurrences of $Y = 1$ divided by the number of data points. That's just the estimate for the probability that $Y = 1$! It's a handy trick.

You can use the logistic regression algorithm to find values of the βs that do the best job of estimating the true probability that $Y = 1$. You'll learn more about how this works later, but it's clear from how the model is written, as an algebraic formula with x in it, that x has to be a number.

Why do you need to change the format of your data? Suppose Y represents whether a user on a website clicks a hyperlink. Suppose you want to predict these clicks using the title of the article that is being linked to. If you'd like to use the logistic regression model (or a more suitable variant of it that takes the same inputs!), then you have to change the title into a number like x that you can put into the model.

You'll see a strategy for doing this in the next section, where you'll see some basic text processing techniques.

4.2   Simple Text Preprocessing

The first technique that will accomplish the task of putting a title into a logistic regression algorithm will be tokenization. This technique lets you break up a title into terms. Then, you can encode each term like you encode the outcome, which is as a binary variable if it's in the title or not. There are some strengths and weaknesses to this approach, which you'll see.

4.2.1   Tokenization

Tokenization is a pretty simple concept. The basic idea is that you think the individual terms in a title are important for predicting the outcome, so you'll encode each one based on how much it occurs in the title.

Let's look at the title "The President vetoed the bill." You think titles with *President* in them might get clicked more often. The reason is that the president is important, and people want to hear about what he's doing. You can encode the presence of the word *President* as $x = 1$, so any title with *President* in it has $x = 1$, and any title without it has $x = 0$. Then, you're free to put it into the algorithm and get predictions out. You could stop here, but you notice some problems.

First, most titles aren't about the president. You'd do a lousy job if you just used a single token. Second, not all titles about the president have the term *President* in them. Even if you were right that people are interested in reading about the president, maybe you should include titles that have *White House*, *POTUS*, and other related terms. Finally, we haven't really addressed how to deal with multiword terms like *White House*. *White* and *House* mean something very different by themselves. You'll learn how to deal with this in the next section when we talk about n-grams.

A next step you can take is to allow there to be many different xs, one for each token. You'll call them $x_1, x_2, ..., x_v$ for v different tokens. These v tokens will be your *vocabulary*. They represent all the words your algorithm knows about. How might you tokenize the sentence from earlier into v tokens? You can just split the sentence into a list of terms, like so:

```
1 | ['The', 'President', 'vetoed', 'the', 'bill']
```

You can achieve this by just splitting on spaces, as shown here:

```
1  sentence = "The President vetoed the bill"
2  tokenized_sentence = sentence.split(' ') # split on spaces
```

Now, you have all the tokens. Next, you should define your vocabulary by enumerating all the distinct terms, as shown here:

```
1  vocabulary = {token: i for i, token
2                         in enumerate(set(tokenized_sentence))}
```

These instances of i are the subscripts for each of the x_i variables. Here you get the following:

```
1  print vocabulary
2  {'The': 0, 'President': 1, 'vetoed': 2, 'the': 3, 'bill': 4}
```

For example, if $x_1 = 1$, then the title has the term *President* in it. Notice that *the* appears twice and is counted separately because of the different capitalization. In general, you may choose to lowercase words instead. You should try both ways and see what works better for your problem.

Now, you need a way to represent the whole list of terms in a title, instead of a single term. You do this with a *vector*. You can lay out all the terms in the title in a row, and each column corresponds to one term in the vocabulary. If the term is in the title, the column gets a 1; otherwise, it gets a zero. This sentence, with this vocabulary, would be represented as *sentence_vector* = [1, 1, 1, 1, 1] since each term in the vocabulary is present. Compare with a different sentence using the same vocabulary defined earlier, "The President went to the store." You'd represent this as [1, 1, 0, 1, 0]. The only terms in the vocabulary are *The, the, and President.*

A vector written like this is often known as a *bag of words* since the encoding has lost the order of the terms. You've jumbled them all together, like taking the sentence apart and just throwing the terms in a bag. You can do a little better than this by respecting the order of terms, as you'll see in the next section. For now, let's think more about how these words influence the model.

There's a careful balance to strike when you're preprocessing text. On the one hand, the more terms you have in your vocabulary, the more parameters your model needs to have. In the case of logistic regression to predict a class from a piece of text, you have one parameter for each term in your vocabulary. If there are infrequent terms or terms with small relationships to the output, you won't learn their parameters very precisely. If those parameters are used in prediction, they'll add more noise to the output, and your model can perform worse by including them than by ignoring them. In practice, you might want to eliminate some terms from the vocabulary by calculating their dependence with the output, like with the chi-squared test or Fisher's exact test. You can keep the number of terms that cross-validate the best on your validation set.

Now, we'll explain how you can allow some nonlinearity in linear models by using n-grams.

4.2.2   N-grams

A great way to respect the order of terms in a sentence is by using *n-grams*. The simplest version is a unigram, which is just a single-word token. The simplest nontrivial example is a bigram, which is a sequence of two words that appear consecutively in a sentence.

To see the strength in this, consider the sentence "The President lives in the White House." If you just use unigrams, you lose the ordering of *White House* and just consider them as the words *White* and *House*. They aren't as meaningful apart as they are together. The solution is to add a new *term* to the vocabulary, which is the pair of those terms together.

There is still a little ambiguity. You might have the bigram and both terms that comprise it in the vocabulary! Do you encode it as having all three? Typically, you would first tokenize the text into lists of terms. Then, you'd collapse all bigrams into unigrams, usually by merging them together with an underscore. For example, *White House* would become ['*White*', '*House*'] and then just [*White_House*]. Then, if either of *White* or *House* remains, they'll be picked up separately.

You don't normally have to implement all of this yourself. You can use packages like scikit learn's vectorizer, in *sklearn.feature_extraction.text.CountVectorizer*.

4.2.3   Sparsity

Once you've settled on a vocabulary that includes n-grams, you'll notice a new problem. Not every title will contain every word in the vocabulary, so the title vectors are almost all zeros! These are called *sparse* vectors, because there's very little (nontrivial) data in them. The problem is that they can take up a lot of computer memory. If you have 300,000 terms in your vocabulary and you have 1,000 titles, then you have 300,000,000 entries in your data matrix! That takes a lot of space for so little data!

Instead of encoding a vector as a long list of zeros with a few nonzero entries, it's much more efficient to encode them by saying which entries aren't zero. It makes handling math a little trickier, but fortunately most of this has been worked out for us! There's a great implementation of spark vector and matrix math in the *scipy.sparse* library.

The easiest form for constructing sparse matrices is the sparse coordinate format. Instead of a vector like [0, 1, 0, 0, 0], you would just write a list with entries like (*row, column, value*). In this case, we'd encode the vector as [(0, 1, 1)]. In general, you might be working with lots of vectors, so the first entry tells you which vector you're working with. Here, it's just zero. The next entry tells you which column has the nonzero entry. The last entry tells you what the value of the entry is.

The downside of this approach is that you need three values to encode a single nonzero entry in the matrix. It saves space only if less than one-third of the entries in the matrix is nonzero. This will usually be the case for reasonably large sets of documents, with reasonably large vocabularies.

There is another problem that comes up with such large numbers of columns: algorithm performance can suffer if there are too many columns of data. Sometimes it will be useful to limit to only the most important terms. You can do this by choosing a set of "features" to keep and discarding the rest.

4.2.4   Feature Selection

Feature selection is a general term that applies well outside the context of text analysis. Typically, you'll have a combination of text features, numerical features, and categorical features. You'll want to throw away any that aren't useful for solving the problem you're working on. You need a way to measure the usefulness of a feature so you can decide whether to include it.

Consider, for example, linear regression on a large number of variables. Consider including some binary features that are completely irrelevant, so their true coefficients should be 0. If you include these variables with a finite data set, you'll generally find a value different from zero because of measurement error. Assuming a Gaussian sampling distribution for these coefficients with standard deviation σ, and assuming k coefficents of irrelevant variables are active for a prediction, then you'd add noise to your prediction for y with a standard deviation of $\sqrt{k}\sigma$ (use the error propagation formulae for sums)! Clearly we'd be better off throwing away some of these features.

There are many ways to do this in practice. We'll talk about two: testing for dependence and using a prediction method called *lasso regression*.

With the first method, you want to find words that correlate highly with the outcome you're trying to predict. You can do this using an χ^2 test since you're working with categorical (two categories, in this case) data. A good implementation is in the scikit learn (also called sklearn) library, in *sklearn.feature_selection.SelectKBest*. You can use it with the score metric *sklearn.feature_selection.chi2*. This will find the features that are most informative of the outcome and select the top k of these, where you specify the value of k to use. Let's try a quick example. You'll start with a sequence of sentences. For a dumb prediction task, you'll see if a dog lover likes or dislikes the sentences. The sentences and outcomes will be as follows:

```
1  X = ["The dog is brown",
2        "The cat is grey",
3        "The dog runs fast",
4        "The house is blue"]
5  y = [1, 0, 1, 0]
```

where $y = 1$ indicates the person likes the sentences and $y = 0$ otherwise. You can tokenize this as follows:

```
1  from sklearn.feature_extraction.text import CountVectorizer
2
3  vectorizer = CountVectorizer()
4  X_vectorized = vectorizer.fit_transform(X)
5  X_vectorized.todense()
```

which produces the following output:

```
matrix([[0, 1, 0, 1, 0, 0, 0, 1, 0, 1],
        [0, 0, 1, 0, 0, 1, 0, 1, 0, 1],
        [0, 0, 0, 1, 1, 0, 0, 0, 1, 1],
        [1, 0, 0, 0, 0, 0, 1, 1, 0, 1]], dtype=int64)
```

Each column is a word in the vocabulary, and each row is a sentence. The entries show how many times each word occurs in the vocabulary. Notice that while you can recover the list of words used in the sentence, you can't recover the order of the words. You've lost that information with this encoding. This is the *bag of words* approach to preprocessing we discussed earlier.

You can select the most important features now. You'll choose the top feature, which you hope will be the word *dog*.

```
1 from sklearn.feature_selection import SelectKBest
2 from sklearn.feature_selection import chi2
3
4 feature_selector= SelectKBest(k=2)
5 feature_selector.fit_transform(X_vectorized, y).todense()
```

This That produces the new *X* matrix with fewer columns, as shown here:

```
matrix([[1],
        [0],
        [1],
        [0]], dtype=int64)
```

You probably want to know what words these columns correspond to, so you can check that by looking at the "support" of the feature selector, as shown here:

```
1 feature_selector.get_support()
```

This produces the following output:

```
array([False, False, False, True, False, False, False, False, False,
       False])
```

Here, you can see the fourth and ninth entries are kept. To check which words these correspond to, you'll reference this against the vectorizer's vocabulary, as shown here:

```
1 np.array(vectorizer.get_feature_names())[feature_selector.get_support()]
```

This gives the result you hoped for.

```
array(['dog'], dtype='<U5')
```

The second method you might use is randomized lasso, as implemented in the package *sklearn.linear_model.RandomizedLasso*. It ties the feature selection to the model you'd likely use, the lasso model, and works for binary and real-valued data. It's appropriate for the case when you have a mixture of text and other data types. This model will give you a set of scores for features, and you can select the *k* best of these for your prediction task. It also has a `fit_transform` method you can use to automatically reduce your data matrix.

4.2.5   Representation Learning

The ideal would be if you didn't have to make any of these subjective choices. It would be great if a computer could do that for you. These vectors you use to represent text are called *representations*. If a machine could learn how to map the text to a vector, that would be *representation learning*.

When you represent a sentence by a list of tokens, you lose the meaning of the sentence. A word like *bush* could mean "a shrub" or "the former president." The context is lost from the tokenization. You really want a system that can go beyond n-grams and understand the real meaning of words in context. You want a system that can understand grammar and represent a piece of text in a "space of meaning." This is a major aim of modern natural language processing. With it, you could understand the nuance of sarcastic text, the meaning of jokes, and the nuance of puns. Without it, you can usually take only rule-based approaches to understanding these nuances of language.

Representation learning is one of the more interesting and powerful avenues in neural network research. It has led to groundbreaking performance on a broad array of tasks, like image classification and text translation. It is beyond the scope of this book, but we encourage you to check out the recent text by Goodfellow et al. [4].

Just to see an example of how a neural network can capture more information than these simple encodings, we'll try something a little different. We can train a network to tell apart the ordering of words! You'll use a toy example with just two words, but the same process applies to much more complicated sequences.

You'll use a recurrent neural network (RNN) to do this job. First, let's make the data, as shown here:

```
1  x = []
2  y = []
3  for i in range(1000):
4      x.append([0, 1])  # ['a', 'b']
5      y.append(-1)
6      x.append([1, 0])  # ['b', 'a']
7      y.append(1)
```

So, the sequence ['a', 'b'] maps to −1, and the sequence ['b', 'a'] maps to 1. Now, let's create the neural network in Keras.

```
1  from keras.layers import Input, Embedding, Dense, SimpleRNN
2  from keras.models import Model
3
4  alphabet_size = 2
5  embedding_size = 4
6  sequence_length = 2
7
8  input_sequence = Input(shape=(sequence_length,))
9  embedding = Embedding(alphabet_size,
10                       embedding_size,
11                       input_length=sequence_length)(input_sequence)
12 h1 = SimpleRNN(10, return_sequences=False)(embedding)
13 y_out = Dense(1, activation='linear')(h1)
14
15 model = Model(inputs=[input_sequence], outputs=[y_out])
16 model.compile('RMSProp', loss='mean_squared_error')
```

The Input is where the input is transformed into a data type the network understands. The Embedding is the first representation, where each word is turned into a vector. In this case, you (arbitrarily) chose a vector of length 4, but you can experiment with different lengths if you like. At this point, the sequence of word tokens has been converted into a sequence of vectors. That's still not a good form to use for a regression task. At the next stage, the SimpleRNN converts the sequence of vectors into a single vector that represents the whole sequence. This is where the magic happens, and this is a representation you can now put into a regression problem! The next layer, Dense, is actually just a linear regression on the representation found for the text sequences. You put it all together into a Model object and specify a training algorithm and metric to optimize (minimize the mean-squared error).

You can call the fit method on this model and fit it to the data.

```
model.fit(x, y, epochs=10)
```

It will iterate over the data several times, training the model as it goes. The output looks like this:

```
Epoch 1/10
2000/2000 [==============================] - 0s - loss: 0.7239
Epoch 2/10
2000/2000 [==============================] - 0s - loss: 0.1111
Epoch 3/10
2000/2000 [==============================] - 0s - loss: 2.3685e-06
Epoch 4/10
2000/2000 [==============================] - 0s - loss: 0.0000e+00
Epoch 5/10
2000/2000 [==============================] - 0s - loss: 0.0000e+00
Epoch 6/10
2000/2000 [==============================] - 0s - loss: 0.0000e+00
Epoch 7/10
2000/2000 [==============================] - 0s - loss: 0.0000e+00
Epoch 8/10
2000/2000 [==============================] - 0s - loss: 0.0000e+00
Epoch 9/10
2000/2000 [==============================] - 0s - loss: 0.0000e+00
Epoch 10/10
2000/2000 [==============================] - 0s - loss: 0.0000e+00
```

You can see it has found the target. Calling the predict method, you can see that it has found the alternating −1 and 1 that you'd expect from the training data, where the following:

```
model.predict(x)
```

produces this:

```
array([[-1.],
       [ 1.],
       [-1.],
       ...,
       [ 1.],
       [-1.],
       [ 1.]], dtype=float32)
```

The interesting representation, the vectorized sequences, is deep inside the network. It's often hard to visualize these representations, and direct inspection can be unenlightening. It's also often possible to find nice visualizations for the layers, as in convolutional networks where you can see the pixel shapes as images that the network is looking for.

You'll learn a little more about neural networks in the advanced chapters of this book, but much detail on neural networks is beyond the scope of this book.

4.3 Information Loss

We've talked a lot about reducing your data in this chapter, but what we really mean is transforming your data in a way that probably loses some information.

Consider the original example, "The President vetoed the bill." You'd represent this as something the machine sees more as ['*the*' : 2, '*President*' : 1, '*vetoed*' : 1, '*bill*' : 1]. If you're smart, you could guess what the sentence is saying, but it's clear you lost a lot of information when you mapped the sentence to the bag of words.

It turns out that information content is critically important when you're doing a prediction problem. If you can't reverse a data transformation, then you've lost some information. A theorem from information theory says that as you gain more information in X (that relates to Y), your prediction for Y will get better and better. The more information you lose during preprocessing, the more you set yourself back from the start. A simple example to illustrate this point is the case of tokenization.

There's another theorem from information theory called the *data-processing inequality*. It says that when you process data (as in preprocessing), you can end up only with less than or equal to the amount of information you started with. There are no creative ways to slice the data that will add information, unless you incorporate more data from an outside source. To illustrate this, you can turn a continuous variable into a discrete variable using quantile discretization and test the transformed version on the same prediction problem.

First, let's generate some linear data and fit a linear model. You'll check R^2 to see how well your model works.

```
1  from sklearn.linear_model import LinearRegression
2  import pandas as pd
3
4  x = np.random.normal(size=1000)
5  y = x  + 0.1*np.random.normal(size=1000)
6  X = pd.DataFrame({'x': x, 'y': y})
7
8  model = LinearRegression()
9  model.fit(X[['x']], X['y'])
10 model.score(X[['x']], X['y'])
```

This returns an R^2 of 0.99. Now, you'll discretize using pandas.qcut and pandas.get_dummies and check the R^2 on the new model, as shown here:

```
1  x_discretized = pd.get_dummies(pd.qcut(x, [0., 0.25, 0.5, 0.75, 1.])).
2                  values[:, 1:]
3  model.fit(x_discretized, X['y'])
4  model.score(x_discretized, X['y'])
```

which returns a lower R^2 of 0.85. This is because you've lost information due to data processing!

Note that as usual with dummy encoding, you have to drop one column of the data. This is because it contains redundant information with the other columns: if all the entries are zero, then the 1 was in the missing column. Dropping the extra column is not a source of information loss.

This tells us that the more you do to the data, the more opportunity you have for information loss. This is a strong argument for relatively minimal preprocessing. Encode the data just enough to get it into the algorithm to start with, and try running your task. If it works, great. Try adjusting the preprocessing a little to see if you can improve things, but don't get carried away cutting away your data too early.

Another way to lose information is by aggregating data. An aggregation is when a collection of numbers go into a calculation and a single number (or smaller collection of numbers) is the result. Common examples are sums, averages, variances, and medians.

Suppose you have a sample of website users and a statistic for each user, like the number of articles on the website that the user has read. Often, the only data that is available is that which is reported by a third party. This data is often just aggregations of the data for the individual users. Instead of the number of articles each user has read, you might have the total number of reads of articles (the sum of the individual user statistics). You might instead have the average articles read per user (the average of the user statistics).

In each of these cases, you have a single number that is calculated from a collection of numbers. Since you don't have access to the original, more granular data, you can't calculate other statistics from it. There's no way, for example, to compute the standard deviation in article views per user, so there's no way you can derive error bounds on the mean that was reported. When you can work only with aggregations of data, your ability to do more in-depth analysis can be very limited. You can no longer slice the data different ways based on user attributes. You can't even calculate other aggregations. For this reason, it's best to record data with as much granularity as you are able.

4.4 Conclusion

In this chapter, you saw how to take raw data and transform it in a way that can be passed into a machine-learning model. We hope you've gathered that it's a complicated process and that it can be very specific to each case you work on. It's worth putting the time in to make sure everything is working as expected. It's much more often the data source or the preprocessing that is the problem when a model fails to work than it is the model itself.

There are many options for preprocessing and many parameters that control the process. Parameters can be caps on word frequencies, a number of features to select, the dimensions of embeddings, and so on. Without a principled approach, it's hard to make sure you choose the best parameters for your model. If you're working with many parameters, it can be worth looking into parameter search strategies. Scikit learn provides some search tools, and frameworks like Google's Cloud ML offer parameter search tools as well. That subject is beyond the scope of this book, but we hope you'll explore it on your own when you discover that you're spending too much time adjusting parameters, retraining your model, and repeating.

Hypothesis Testing

5.1 Introduction

Now that you know how to encode data, you can start making some use of it! A common task is to say statistics from different samples are different from one another. For example, you might have data from an AB test, and you'd like to say the average number of articles shared by users in the test group is higher than the number of pages shared by users in the control group. How can you be sure the difference isn't due to random error from sampling? How can you be sure there's really a difference? These questions fall in the domain of *hypothesis testing*.

In this chapter, we'll address a few related questions. We'll often frame questions in the context of AB testing because hypothesis testing is often used there. We'll build up some machinery for answering questions with hypothesis testing and then pick up the discussion later in the book, where we can answer even more interesting questions by running basic machine learning models on our AB test data.

Hypothesis testing is one of the most important tools in a data scientist's toolkit. When a company needs to decide whether to take a certain action (e.g., make a change to a product), the best way to see what it will do is to run an experiment. To make the right decision from the experimental data, you have to use statistical hypothesis testing to get the right results!

5.2 What Is a Hypothesis?

Say you want to test whether a hypothesis is true or false. By *hypothesis* we really just mean a statement about the world that may or may not be true. In a typical AB test, the hypothesis might be "Users who experience variant A come back to the website more often than users who experience variant B." You usually want to phrase hypotheses more precisely, using equalities or inequalities. In this example, say you have to measure a revisit rate for users in variant A, r_A, and the revisit rate for users in variant B, r_B. This hypothesis translates into $r_A > r_B$.

If you're interested in one rate being strictly greater than another, you want a one-sided hypothesis test. If you had a different hypothesis, where you were just testing that they're the same rate, $r_A = r_B$, then you want to know if the test group's rate is higher, $r_A > r_B$, or lower, $r_A < r_B$. For this, you want to use a two-tailed hypothesis test.

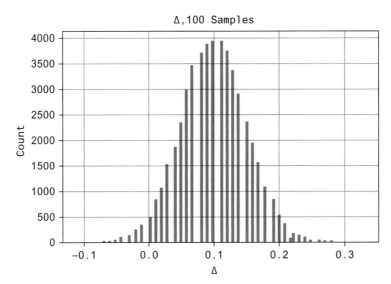

Figure 5.1 $r_B - r_A$ where each rate was measured after k successes for 100 trials. The true rates are $r_B = 0.2$ and $r_A = 0.1$, so the difference centers around 0.1. The test was run 50,000 times to estimate the sampling distribution for the difference. As you increase the number of trials upward from 100, the histogram fills in and becomes even more Gaussian.

You know from the central limit theorem that an average, like these rates, should have a Gaussian sampling distribution when you have a lot of data (usually, 30 success data points is a good rule of thumb). If you plot the distribution of differences in the rates you calculate from samples of size N, you'll get (approximately) the Gaussian in Figure 5.1. You look at the difference because it nicely centers at 0 when the rates are equal. If r_A is higher, then $r_A - r_B$ will tend to be positive, but you might find it to be negative just by chance.

You want to know, given the measured difference, how likely it is that you'll find $r_A > r_B$, or equivalently $r_A - r_B > 0$, by chance, when r_A is not actually higher. If you calculate the odds of getting a measurement at least as large as ours by chance, then you know the odds that you're wrong when you say "There's a positive effect."

If the two values are equal, then you have a distribution for the statistic. That will be the distribution you'll use when you're wondering how likely it is to get a measurement as large as this, given that there's no effect. If that's the case, then the sampling distribution of $r_A - r_B$ centers at 0, and the standard deviation is just the standard error from before, $\sigma = \sigma_N / \sqrt{N}$, where you have N data points, and the standard deviation calculated with this sample is σ_N. If you normalized the measurement by the standard error, then you get a nice normal distribution for the statistic $Z = (r_A - r_B)/(\sigma_N / \sqrt{N})$. This is called the Z statistic.

You can calculate the odds of getting a Z statistic as large as the one you've measured using this normal distribution. The shaded area is the region where the statistic is at least as large as ours. The odds of getting such a statistic under this distribution is just equal to that area.

Generally, you'd like to set a cutoff for the Z statistic called a *critical value*. Say you'd like to say "If greater than 5 percent chance that I would find an effect as large as the one I've found by chance, I don't want to say that I've found an effect." If you find the value for the Z statistic where there's a 5 percent chance of measuring a greater value, then any Z statistic lower than that has an even greater chance of being measured when there's no effect. That means you don't want to say you have found an effect any time the measurement is lower than this critical value. This probability of making a mistake, 5 percent, is your *p-value*.

Five percent ($p = 0.05$) is a common choice of p-value in the social sciences, where the amount of data is limited. The odds of making a mistake are about 1 in 20. In the worst case, you can expect 5 percent of experiments to come to a wrong conclusion! In a data science setting, you're often free to choose much lower chances of error. Particle physicists use a "five sigma" rule to say they've detected a new particle. This corresponds to a p-value of around $p = 0.0000003$, or about one in three million. There have been three sigma ($p = 0.0013$) detections that were later overturned when trying to meet the five sigma standard!

There are other tests than this z-test, where you use other test statistics, but this is a nice common example. If you have a smaller sample size, a t-test might be more appropriate. In practice, you usually just search around for a test that is appropriate for the problem you're working on.

5.3   Types of Errors

There are four outcomes in hypothesis testing, and two are errors. We don't need to discuss in detail the cases where you find an effect where there really is an effect or the case where you find no effect where there is no effect.

The two error cases are where there is no effect but you find one due to sampling error and where there is an effect but you fail to find it. These are called Type I and Type II errors, respectively. When you choose the probability of finding an effect when there is none, you're directly making a choice about the probability of making a Type I error. You're indirectly making a choice about Type II errors.

If you fix the p-value, then the sample size determines the probability of a Type II error. The way to control Type II errors is to decide on the size of an effect in which you are interested (say, a 3 percent increase in revisit rates). Then, knowing the variance of the revisit rate distribution beforehand and choosing a p-value, you can find a sample size that will give you a good chance of finding an effect that is equal to or larger than the minimum value you've chosen. This is called a *power calculation*.

A study that doesn't have a large enough sample size to detect an effect of a size the investigators care about is called *underpowered*. A typical choice for the power is around 80 percent. That is, you'd like an 80 percent chance of finding an effect if the true effect is larger than the minimum value you set. For 80 percent power and $p = 0.05$, a good rule of thumb for the sample size is as follows:

$$N = 16\sigma^2/\Delta^2$$

where σ is the standard deviation of the outcome you're measuring, and Δ is the minimum difference you'd like to measure. For example, suppose the revisit rate is typically $r_B = 0.05$, and the standard deviation in revisits is $\sigma = 0.05(1 - 0.05)$ (since it's binomial). You can assume the test group standard deviation is similar. If you'd like to measure a 3 percent effect, you want $\Delta = 0.03 * 0.05 = 0.0015$. Then the sample size you'd need for 80 percent power at $p = 0.05$ is in the ballpark of $N = 16{,}000$.

5.4   P-values and Confidence Intervals

Often people report the statistic they've measured along with the odds of getting a value at least that extreme by chance (the p-value). This isn't a great way to report results. There is still uncertainty in the true value of what you're trying to measure, so reporting a result without error bars is misleading. Even worse, nontechnical people will tend to read your p-value as how sure you are that you're reporting the "right" answer, which is nonsense.

While it may be useful to sacrifice some truth for clarity in a business setting, you'll likely want to report results more carefully for your technical team. For that reason, you should report confidence intervals (that is, the error bars!) instead of an expected value with a p-value.

To drive the point in a little further, consider an example. We've made a measurement as shown by the confidence intervals in Figure 5.2. The p-value in this figure is extremely small—well beyond the typical $p = 0.05$. We've established that we're very sure that the effect is not zero. But how big is it?

From the p-value and the expected value alone, you don't really get a good idea for the possibilities. You've only bounded the true value between a few percent of the expected value and about twice the expected value. All this measurement is telling you is that there is a positive effect. The size of

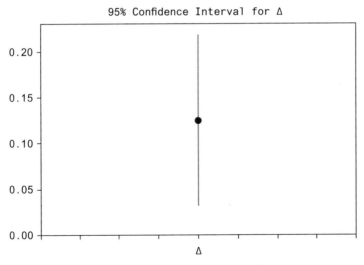

Figure 5.2   This shows a 95 percent confidence level for Δ, the difference between r_B and r_A. This is for 200 trials. The p-value for a t-test is 0.0090, which is well below the $p = 0.05$ significance level, but the confidence interval is $(0.03, 0.21)$. The upper bound is more than five times the lower bound! Even though you can be sure the difference is positive, you really have no idea what the true difference is without more data.

the effect, even the order of magnitude, is not determined well because you have too little data. The takeaway is that statistical significance does not imply precise measurement!

You can get a confidence interval for the difference in rates, as in this example, by using the error propagation formulae for a difference. If $\Delta = r_A - r_B$ and they have standard errors like σ_Δ, σ_a, and σ_b, then you can calculate the error like this:

$$\frac{\sigma_\Delta}{\Delta} = \sqrt{\left(\frac{\sigma_a}{r_A}\right)^2 + \left(\frac{\sigma_b}{r_B}\right)^2} \tag{5.1}$$

In other words, the errors add in quadrature. This is bad since the difference tends to get smaller while the errors tend to get bigger. This makes the relative error in differences in measurements get larger than the relative error in the input measurements. If each input has 10 percent error, then the output should have $\sqrt{2}10\%$, or about 14.4 percent error.

You can use this with the $z = 1.96$ value for the 95 percent confidence interval, so you find a confidence interval for the difference of $(\Delta - 1.96\sigma_\Delta, \Delta + 1.96\sigma_\Delta)$.

5.5 Multiple Testing and "P-hacking"

There is a lot of subtlety to p-values and hypothesis testing. One of the trickier aspects is multiple testing. Suppose you do ten AB tests and estimate a p-value of $p = 0.05$ for each result. What are the odds that you made a Type I error on at least one test?

For each individual test, the odds are given by the p-value, $p = 0.05$. The subtlety comes when you consider the tests as a group. The odds of discovering an effect when there isn't one is $p = 0.05$. The odds of not making this mistake on a test is $1 - p = 0.95$. The odds of not making a mistake on two tests is $(0.95)(0.95) = 0.90$, so the odds of making a mistake on two tests is $1 - 0.90$, or 10 percent! If you apply this to ten tests, you calculate $1 - 0.95^{10} = .40$. There's a 40 percent chance you'll have made a mistake on a test! In general, for a p-value of p, this formula is $p_{mistake} = 1 - (1 - p)^n$ for n tests. This is the problem with multiple testing. If p is small, this is approximately $p_{mistake} = np$.

The problem is even more subtle. If you do an AB test and then split the data different ways or measure different metrics with their own p-values, then each split or each measurement is another test. The practice of starting with a calculation that isn't statistically signficant and splitting the data until you find a p-value less than the original cutoff (usually 0.05) is called *p-hacking*. The analyst doesn't take into account multiple testing, so the true p-value is no longer $p = 0.05$.

A common way to account for multiple testing is to use the Bonferroni correction for the p-value. Using the formula $p_{mistake} = np$, you can say that if you're doing n tests, your new significance level should be $p_{new} = p/n$. That way, when you calculate the probability of making a mistake, $p_{mistake} = np_{new} = p$, so it's just the original p-value!

It's good practice to decide on what you'll measure before you even start collecting the experimental data. You can do power calculations with observational data, and you can do this with an eye toward using the Bonferroni correction to make sure you have a large enough sample size for all of the analyses you're planning.

If you find no effect after the experiment and want to continue slicing the data, you should think of that process as a search for new hypotheses rather than a search for a real result. You will no longer have statistically significant effects if you slice the data too many ways. The new hypothesis should be tested with a future experiment.

5.6   An Example

Let's work an example for fun. Imagine you're doing some exploratory work to design a study. You have 100 data points on each of 100 variables, $X_1, ..., X_{100}$. You're interested in predicting another variable, Y. In this case, you're working in an organization that can collect more data, but it's expensive. You really want to narrow down the set of variables you're collecting data for, so you want to be sure there's a good, strong correlation between the X variables you choose and Y.

Let's generate some toy data to illustrate how you'd solve this problem. In this example, only one of the Xs, say X_1, will actually correlate with Y. The rest will have no correlation but might have nonzero sample correlation! That means if you were to measure that variable for many more data points, you'd find the correlation goes to zero—you just happened to get unlucky with the small sample.

Let's generate this data now.

```
1  import pandas as pd
2  import numpy as np
3
4  X = pd.DataFrame(np.random.normal(size=(100,100)),
5                   columns=['X_{}'.format(i + 1) for i in range(100)])
6  X['Y'] = X['X_1'] + np.random.normal(size=100)
```

You can compute the Pearson correlation without p-values just using the data frame's `corr` method, and you can see many entries much larger than 0 (try it!).

Let's start running some hypothesis tests. You have 100 to run in total, where you measure the correlation with each X with Y. You'll use the Pearson correlation implemented in SciPy since it gives a p-value with the correlation against the null hypothesis that the correlation is zero. To do this correctly, you'll use a Bonferroni correction to adjust the p-value for multiple testing. You're testing so many hypotheses that you're certain to get some $p < 0.05$ just by chance. To adjust it for how many tests you're running, you'll use the new confidence threshold $\alpha = 0.05/n$, where n is the number of tests you're running. Here, that gives $\alpha = 0.0005$. That means you'll need a strong correlation to be able to detect it! This is a general problem with multiple testing: the more tests you run, the stronger the effects (or the more data), so you need to be sure you've found true effects.

Run the following code:

```
1  from scipy.stats import pearsonr
2  alpha = 0.05
3  n = len(X.columns) - 1
4  bonferroni_alpha = alpha / n
5  for xi in X.columns:
6      r, p_value = pearsonr(X[xi], X['Y'])
7      if p_value < bonferroni_alpha:
8          print(xi, r, p_value, '***')
```

```
9       elif p_value < alpha:
10          print(xi, r, p_value)
```

That produces the following output (for us—your results will differ):

```
X_1 0.735771451720503 2.799057346922578e-18 ***
X_25 -0.20322243350571845 0.04257172321036264
X_32 0.2097009042175228 0.036261143690351785
X_38 0.20496594851035607 0.040789547879409846
X_67 -0.26918780734103714 0.006764583272751602
X_70 -0.33455121155458417 0.0006688593439594529
X_76 0.20437622718079831 0.04138524622687304
X_91 -0.21485767438274925 0.03181701367805414
X_92 0.23895175142700853 0.016653536509189357
Y 1.0 0.0 ***
```

You can see the first entry, where you check the correlation with X_1 and Y, has a p-value around 10^{-18}. It's certainly not by chance and is well below our threshold of $p < \alpha = 0.0005$. The rest of the Xs here are not significant at our new confidence level, but they are without doing our multiple testing correction! This illustrates the danger of not being careful about multiple testing. Some of these correlations are fairly strong, at around $r = -0.33$!

You see then that it's important to be careful about how many hypotheses you're testing. In this example, our recommendation would be to definitely record the variable X_1, but the rest show correlations that are probably just due to chance. You'd save a lot of money over measuring everything at the $p < 0.05$ level!

5.7   Planning and Context

We've covered the technical details of hypothesis testing but haven't said much about the product side of it. Generally, there are many criteria you care about. Suppose your experiment boosts clicks and shares, but visit time decreases significantly. Should you implement the change? You'll work with the members of your team to identify your primary objectives (e.g., "increase engagement") and a set of secondary health metrics to make sure the change you're making doesn't do substantial damage (e.g., "doesn't hurt ad revenue").

After identifying your main objective and secondary criteria that you'll need to consider, you can create a list metrics that measure your main objective and the other criteria. You might choose "time on the site," "pages per session," and "visits per user" as your engagement metrics, "net ad clicks" and "total ad impressions" as secondary metrics to measure ad health, and "total page views," "shares per user," and "clicks per user" as some other secondary health metrics to measure site health.

After deciding all of your metrics, you should get an idea of what some healthy levels might be for them to change. Can you stand to have "net ad clicks" decrease by half a percent if "ad impressions" increase by 1 percent? Could the number of page views users have in a session decrease slightly if the number of sessions goes up slightly? It's a good idea (though not a requirement) to have some idea about the answer to these questions, at least for your primary criteria, before starting the test.

You need to take extra care when you care about small changes in metrics. The sample size you need grows quickly as the size of the effect you care about decreases. A good rule of thumb [5] is that to detect a difference Δ in the outcome between the test and control group, $\Delta = Y(1) - Y(0)$, when the variance in the outcome is $Var(Y) = \sigma^2$, you need a sample size N given by roughly the following to get statistically significant results at the 95 percent confidence level 80 percent of the time you run the experiment. The noisier the outcome, the larger the samples you'll need as well.

$$N = \frac{16\sigma^2}{\Delta^2}, \tag{5.2}$$

Realistically, you'll be performing experiments over a long period of time for the same product. You'll probably go through some very abridged version of this process the first experiment you run (especially at smaller companies) and continue refining it as the product becomes more mature. Most people won't worry about sample sizes or the effect size (Δ) the first time they run the experiment and will start worrying about it later after noticing they ended up with large error bars. The previous formula is arguably most useful when you're looking after the fact and asking "How much bigger would my sample size have had to be to get significance at the level I care about?"

5.8   Conclusion

In this chapter, we covered one of the most common and important tools a data scientist uses: hypothesis testing. There is a lot more you can do from here, such as developing more robust tests, looking at conditional test results (e.g., what is the result for the most frequent users?), and examining other test statistics and contexts. We haven't even begun to scratch the surface of AB test architectures, checks of randomized assignment, and a host of other subjects that are beyond the scope of this book. We recommend [5], [6], and [7] for more information about web experiments, and [8] for general information on experiment design.

Ideally, you at least have a good idea about the process of running and analyzing an AB test. You should be comfortable pulling data and running significance tests to see which metrics have moved and bringing those results to your team to have a discussion about what the next steps are after the experiment.

6

Data Visualization

6.1 Introduction

When you need to present data to your team or when you just need a better look at what's going on in the data, plotting is a great way to see the relationships in your data in ways that aren't as clear from just looking at summary statistics. Here, we'll focus mostly on the basic concepts of plotting different types of data to reveal something about the distributions that underlie the data.

We won't cover the entire area of thought around the qualitative design of data visualizations that make representations of data both clear and appealing to laypeople. We'll focus instead on the more objective aspects of data visualization: how can you visualize sample from a distribution in a way that reflects where the probability mass lies? How can you visualize data in higher and higher dimensions? How can you visualize far more data points than you can fit in a single image? These are problems that, in many cases, have simple solutions.

As you gain proficiency with the basics, you can start to explore other packages that make visually appealing plots easier to make. Seaborn for Python is a great example. Pandas and matplotlib have some nice, more obscure features that can make visually appealing plots as well.

6.2 Distributions and Summary Statistics

Imagine the case where some relatively static process generates data points. These data points can consist of one or more variables. For example, if you're working in a news organization, authors will be writing articles, and each article will have some number of measured attributes. These might include the section of the site the article was written for, who wrote it, the time it was written, and a set of tags for the article. Once the article is published, you will have measured some traffic statistics for the article: the number of clicks it received on the website, the number of referrals from social media platforms, the click-through rate, the share rate, and many others.

You want to get an idea of what this data looks like, so you'll want to make some plots to understand all of these variables and their relationships to each other. A good place to start is just to plot 1-D distributions of each of the measured variables.

6.2.1   Distributions and Histograms

Here, we'll give two examples that correspond to two common cases: when the variable is discrete and when the variable is continuous. Some examples of discrete variables are authors of articles, the section the article was written for, and the number of clicks the article receives. Some examples of continuous variables are the click-through rate for an article (which is bounded between zero and one) and the time an article was published.

Often, it makes sense to treat a discrete variable as a continuous one. When there is a clear ordering to the variable and the intervals and ratios make sense, then you can treat the discrete variable as continuous. This is true for the total referrals an article receives (which must be integers), the clicks an article receives, and many other variables. With this in mind, let's look at some plots and talk about what they mean.

First, let's look at how many times we show content from each section of the site. This will give us an idea of the experience users have on the site. Figure 6.1 shows a plot of articles from each section of the site.

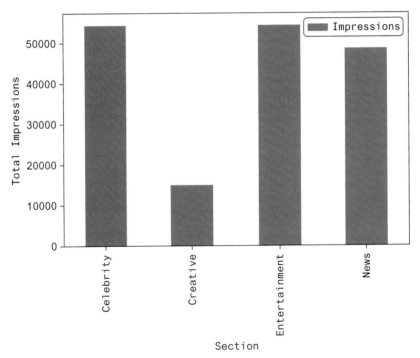

Figure 6.1   A bar chart showing the number of times an article from each section of a website was shown

You can see from the graph that celebrity content and entertainment content show roughly the same amount, followed by news content and then creative (advertising) content. This gives you a good picture of the total quantity of impressions each item accounts for, but it doesn't give as clear a picture of how they relate proportionately to one another. A better way to do this might be to rescale the y-axis so the values are what *fraction* of total impressions go into each category. You can see this plot in Figure 6.2.

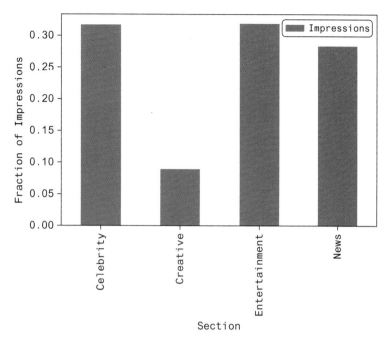

Figure 6.2   A bar chart showing the fraction of times an article from each section of a website was shown

This graph is called a discrete *distribution* since it says how impressions are distributed over each of the items. If you chose an impression at random from this data set, the y-axis tells you the probability that impression was of a piece of content in each of these sections.

There is another nice way to show a distribution. Since all of the values add up to 1, you can imagine each section is accounting for its "piece of the pie." A pie chart can do a good job of showing how important each piece is, as in Figure 6.3.

These plots work well because the x-axis is a discrete variable. They don't work as well when the x-axis has a continuous variable. One common approach that lets you make some similar plots is to turn the continuous x-axis into a discrete one. Let's take the click-through rates, for example. These are real numbers between zero and one and can take on any value within that interval. If we want to see what click rates articles typically have, we could divide the interval into segments and count the number of articles in each segment. This is the continuous version of a bar chart, called a *histogram*, like in Figure 6.4.

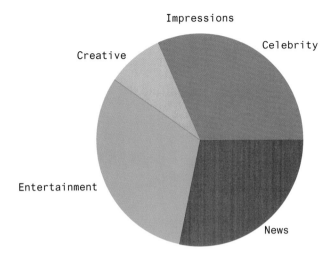

Figure 6.3 A pie chart showing the fraction of times an article from each section of a website was shown

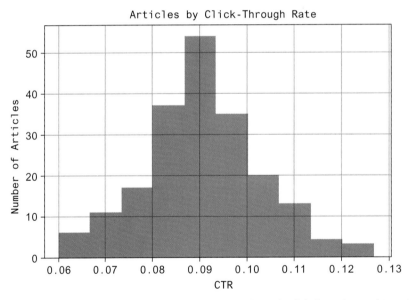

Figure 6.4 A histogram showing the count of articles within each click-through rate interval. We've set ten intervals in this example.

This can be a clunky way to show how data is distributed. A much nicer way can be to smooth out the graph using a method called *kernel density estimation*, pictured in Figure 6.5. The y-axis then tells you how many articles are within a small range of each point. These can be normalized (divided by a constant) to get a continuous probability distribution for the CTR of the articles.

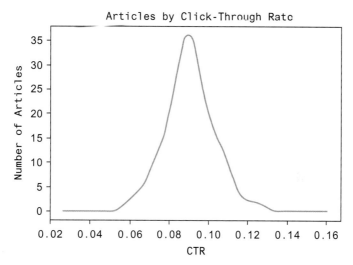

Figure 6.5   A graph showing a kernel density estimate of the CTR distribution

Often, you'll make a plot of a distribution and find something very uninformative, like Figure 6.6.

This picture has a "long-tailed" distribution, where the bottom 80 percent of the articles account for only around 20 percent of the views and the top 20 percent account for 80 percent of the views. When you have a long-tailed distribution, it's hard to make much sense of the data from a regular histogram. This is because the extreme data points are so far out to the right, so the data all gets squished into the first bin. You end up with one bin containing almost all of the data.

A simple trick to make the extreme values closer to everything else is to take a logarithm of the data. Many plotting packages, like pandas in Python, will have built-in arguments for plotting log axes. Here is the same plot, in Figure 6.7, but taking the log of the y-axis. Note that 10^0 is just 1, 10^1 is 10, 10^2 is 100, and so on.

Note that now the logged y-axis makes all of the bins much more comparable in height, even though some are thousands of times higher than the others. Histograms are best to use for communication within quantitative teams or to very quantitatively literate stakeholders.

Finally, there's a plot that does a nice job of showing the features of the long tail of the distribution called complementary cumulative distribution function (CCDF). It's plotted with logs on both

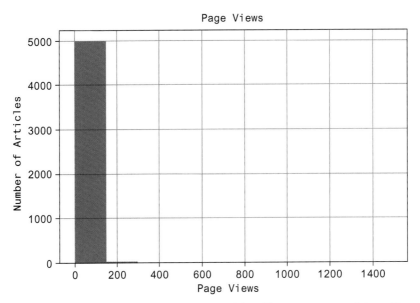

Figure 6.6   A typical distribution for page views to articles. There are many articles with very little traffic and a relatively small number accounting for most of the traffic.

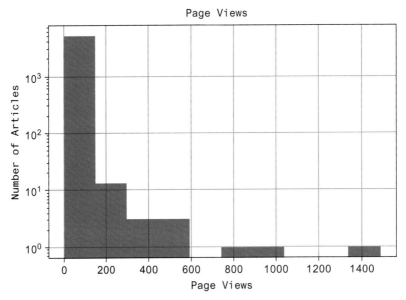

Figure 6.7   Now, the extremely tall bins are squished down, and you can see the bins with only a single data point.

axes, like in Figure 6.8. It says "For each data point, how many data points have values larger than or equal to this one?" It starts at one on the far left (where 100 percent of the data has larger values) and goes down and to the right, where finally only a single data point is at the end.

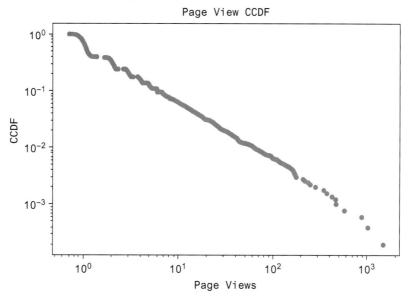

Figure 6.8 A typical distribution for page views to articles. There are many articles with very little traffic and a relatively small number accounting for most of the traffic. The y-axis is the fraction of articles with page views greater than or equal to the x-axis value.

These CCDFs are also called *survival plots*. If instead of "page views" the data was "time a component failed," then the plot shows the fraction of components surviving past time t.

All of these plots do a good job of showing how our 1-D metrics are distributed, but they're not useful for seeing how the different variables relate to one another. To see this, you need higher dimension plots.

6.2.2 Scatter Plots and Heat Maps

There is a lot more power when you're working with higher-dimensional data. Suppose you're looking at the distribution of referrals from other websites to articles on a website and you see the data in Figure 6.9.

If this were all the data we had, we couldn't do a whole lot more analysis. It looks like there might be more referrals in the lower range than we'd expect, but we really can't say without extra data to build a stronger argument.

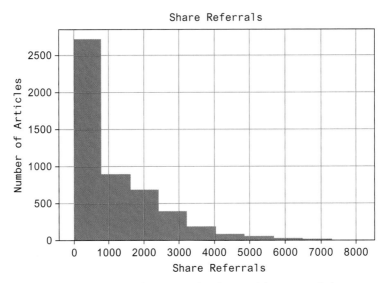

Figure 6.9   A hypothetical distribution for share referrals to articles on a website

Suppose we also have the number of clicks each article receives on our website. If we want to see how the two relate to each other, we can make a *scatter plot*, as in Figure 6.10. This is a simple way to visualize a lot of raw data.

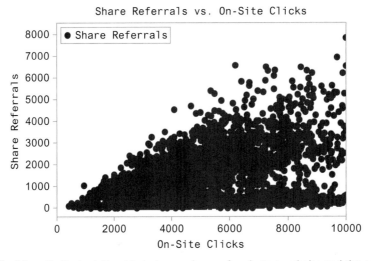

Figure 6.10   A hypothetical relationship between share referrals to a website and the on-site clicks for each of those articles

From this graph, it looks like there's a noisy linear relationship between on-site clicks and share referrals for a lot of the data, but there seems to be something funny going on. It looks like there are two distinct groups of data points with a gap between them. Let's see if we can draw this out better with a different type of plot: a heat map. You can think of the color as a third dimension. In this case, we'll use it to indicate the number of data points at an x-y location.

You'll end up with the same problem as before when there are some histogram bars that are much higher than the others. In this case, there will be one very dark bar in the histogram, and the whole thing will look washed out as in Figure 6.11.

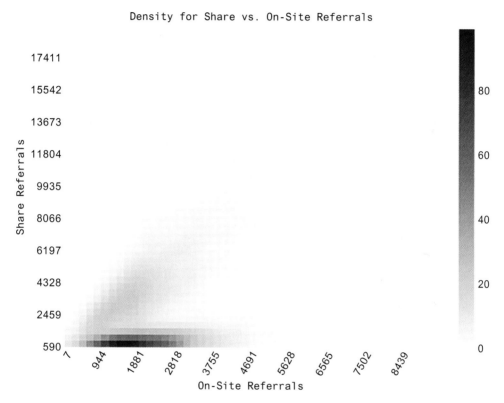

Figure 6.11 A hypothetical relationship between share referrals to a website and the on-site clicks for each of those articles. This is a washed-out heatmap since some x-y values have much higher densities of points than the others.

You can get much nicer results if you take logs of all the entries. In both of these graphs we've also smoothed out the data with a Gaussian filter (a typical thing to do when showing heatmaps). You can see what the final result looks like in Figure 6.12, where we've taken logs of all of the entries. Since the log of zero is negative infinity, we've added 1 to each value before taking the log.

Now it's pretty clear that there are two distinct groups of points with their own linear trends. If we could bring in more data, we could figure out what's going on here.

Suppose we've asked around, and people have said, "When I publish an article for news, it tends to get many more views than when I publish one for entertainment." That would give us an idea that

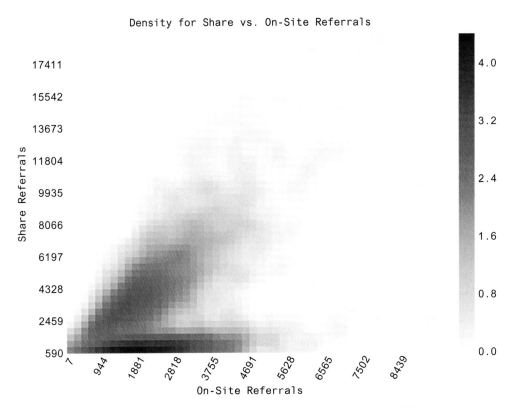

Figure 6.12   A better display of the relationship between share referrals and clicks using the loga-rithmic function to "flatten" the range.

the section of the site we're publishing to might play a role here. Since we're looking at two distinct groups of points, we also have reason to believe that there might be some discrete-valued piece of data that accounts for the two distinct groups.

Let's bring in some more data and see if we've found what accounts for the difference here. We'll make the same plots, in Figures 6.13 and 6.14, but for each section separately.

You can see in these plots that there is only one trend in each graph, so we've found the variable that separates the two groups of data points! Is there a good way now to represent the differences between these groups?

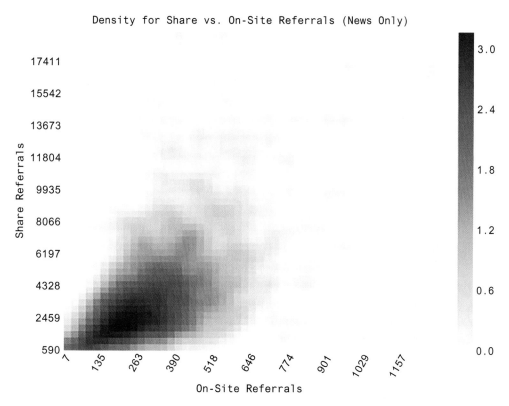

Figure 6.13 A hypothetical relationship between share referrals to a website and the on-site clicks for each of those articles. This plot is for the hypothetical "news" articles only.

6.2.3 Box Plots and Error Bars

We'd like to look into these groups and get a better understanding of how they're similar and how they're different. One way to do this is with the methods of the previous section, where we compute statistics, like means, and look at the p-values associated with them. You can take the average number of share referrals in each section and test whether they're statistically significantly different from each other.

We might want to visually explore the data to form hypotheses to test (ideally, with an independent data set). We can convey much more information than just the means. A box and whiskers plot (e.g., Figure 6.15) is a common way to show several statistics from a distribution, in a way that gives you a sense of what the underlying distribution looks like. It's much cleaner to read

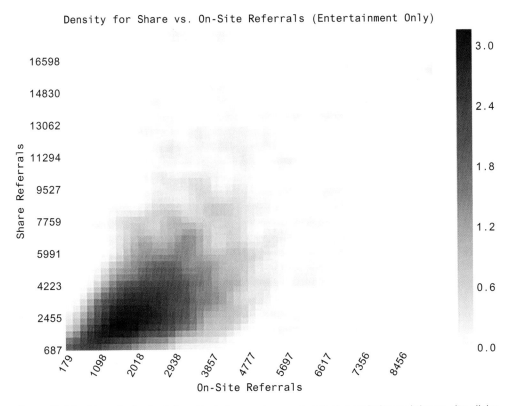

Figure 6.14   A hypothetical relationship between share referrals to a website and the on-site clicks for each of those articles. This plot is for the hypothetical "entertainment" articles only.

and to compare against other distributions. In pandas, the box plot shows the median in the middle of the box as a red line. It shows the 25th and 75th percentiles of the data as the bottom and top of the box and shows the maximum and minimum values of the distribution as the whiskers. Other software packages might show something different, so be sure to read the documentation on yours so you're sure of what you're looking at.

You see that the click distributions are similar to each other. What you're more interested in is the shares, which you saw are distinctly different. If you plot the box and whisker plots for the shares, you find the graphs shown in Figure 6.16.

You can see from this procedure that data visualizations are useful for developing hypotheses. Trends that are suggested by numerical data can become obvious from graphs. Fluency with data distributions and their visualizations are a key piece of data analysis and a required step when you're designing a machine-learning algorithm. Without understanding the distributions you're working with, you'll see that it's hard to build a good model.

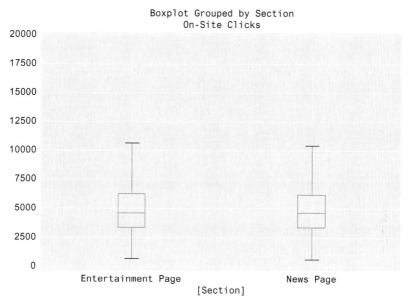

Figure 6.15   This box plot shows some statistics of the click distribution to articles on the website. We can see the distributions are basically the same, so we don't care to test whether there's any significant difference between these two sections with respect to the clicks that they get.

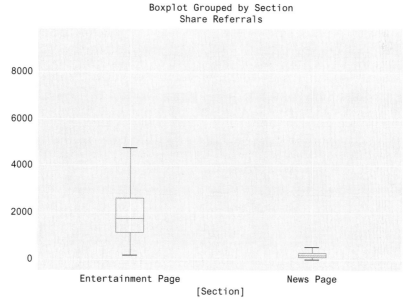

Figure 6.16   This box plot shows some statistics of the share referral distribution to articles on the website. You can see the distributions are very different. You might like to do a hypothesis test here to see that the difference is significant. You might have enough practice to know that given these means, interquartile distances, and data set sizes, the means are clearly statistically significantly different.

6.3   Time-Series Plots

Up to this point, you've worked only with samples from a distribution where each sample is independent from the others. What if the samples are drawn over time? In this case, the number of referrals, for example, to one article might be correlated with those to the next article simply because there were the same number of people on the website from one time step to the next.

If you plot the total clicks to each article over time, this property of the clicks being correlated from one time step to the next is called *auto-correlation*.

Generally, time-series data can be noisy. It's useful to calculate statistics of the time series that are themselves time series. These can cut through the noise and let you see the underlying trends.

6.3.1   Rolling Statistics

Here, we publish one article per day, so conveniently the article indexes correspond to the time indexes. In general, you'd want to look up a time each article was published and use the actual publish time to do this analysis.

First, you can plot the raw data in time series (Figure 6.17). Let's look at the total clicks each article receives plotted against the day it was published.

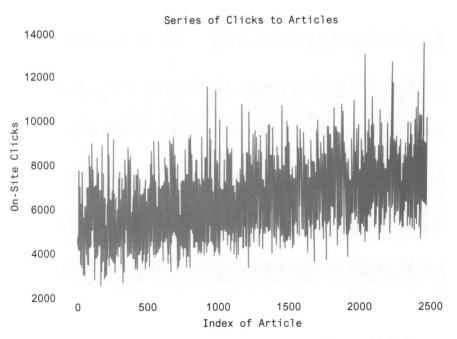

Figure 6.17   The raw data of clicks to articles versus the day the article was published

You can immediately see that articles tend to get more and more views over time. We'd guess that this is because the website grows in popularity over time, but it's hard to say without looking for other data to support this hypothesis.

This data is noisy. If you want to get a cleaner picture of how the data varies over time, you can take a *rolling mean.* This means that at each data point, you take the average of some number, w, of points around it. Different implementations will average data points before the point of focus, after it, or both before and after. You should be familiar with the choices your package makes.

While moving averages are useful for seeing trends in the data, they can introduce artifacts. For example, if the point of interest is a trough (or low point) in the raw data and there is a spike in the window ahead of the point, you can end up with a peak in the moving average at the same point! We've plotted some moving averages of this time-series from Figure 6.17 in Figures 6.18 and 6.19. You can see that while you'd hope the randomness around the trend averages out into a nice straight line, it doesn't in practice! If there's enough noise, it can take a large amount of data to get a good average. The 10-point average is still very noisy, while the 100-point average has many spurious trends around the true (linear) trend.

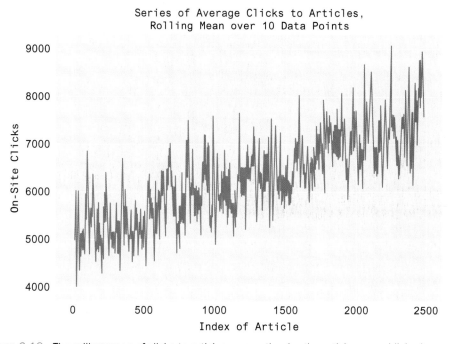

Figure 6.18   The rolling mean of clicks to articles versus the day the article was published

The solution to get a nice trend is to use more data points in the moving average. That will cause the noise to decrease like $\sigma/\sqrt{n}$ for n points, and σ the standard deviation of the noise around the trend. That might mean you have to think about averages over much longer times than you'd like or that you need higher time resolution data (more samples per unit time). You might also plot the standard error in the mean to make it clearer what apparent trends might just be noise.

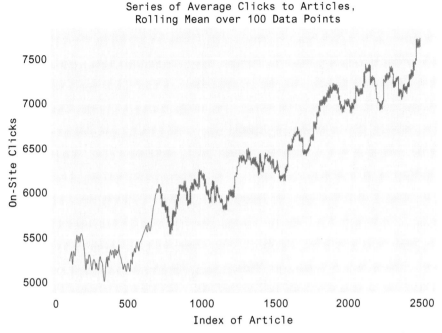

Figure 6.19   The rolling mean of clicks to articles versus the day the article was published

There are other packages, like the forecast package in R, that decompose a time series into a trend, periodic, and noise component.

6.3.2   Auto-Correlation

You might care to know how correlated the data is from one time step to the next. Let's look at this plot in Figure 6.20 for the time-series clicks data.

The x-axis is the *lag*. If you pick a data point, say at the index *i*, then the data point at lag 10 is the one at $i - 10$. If you want to know the lag 1 auto-correlation, you take each data point and compute the correlation with all data points at lag 1 from those. You can repeat this procedure at all lags, and that will tell you how strong the time dependence is in the data.

You can see that the auto-correlation is pretty strong at small lags: there does seem to be some substantial time dependence in the data, in the sense that if a data point is high, the next one tends to be high as well (roughly a 0.25 correlation). This correlation continues through time, and you can see the correlation is still pretty strong as far as 500 steps forward.

Here, the horizontal lines are the 95 percent and 99 percent confidence intervals on the "no auto-correlation" null hypothesis. If each data point were drawn independently, this plot would show no auto-correlation: only about 5 percent of the measurements would be outside of the 95 percent confidence bound.

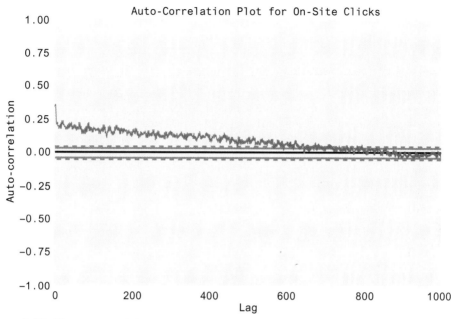

Figure 6.20   The auto-correlation plot of on-site clicks

Checking the auto-correlation will tell you whether a time-series model is important or whether you can get away ignoring time and predicting outcomes based on other features in the data.

6.4   Graph Visualization

An interesting and difficult area of data visualization is how to visualize the complex relationships between many items. A special case of this is the case of *graph* visualization.

A graph is a set of objects and a set of connections between those objects. These are very general objects and can be anything from the set of chemicals in your body and the reactions that produce them to the set of people on a social network and their "friend" connections.

To draw a graph, people usually draw points or circles for the objects and lines connecting the points to represent the connections between them.

The connections in a graph can have direction to them, as in the case where chemicals X and Y produce chemical Z. In this case, X and Y's connections to Z would have arrows pointing toward Z. They can be undirected, as in the case where two individuals are friends with each other, so their connection is symmetric.

You can imagine that when the number of connections gets large, pictures of graphs can get very messy and complicated. If a graph has N objects, then it can have as many as $N(N-1)/2$ connections (assuming objects don't connect to themselves). For a graph with only 100 objects, there can be as many as 4,950 connections!

6.4.1   Layout Algorithms

It's a tricky problem to decide how to lay out a graph in a way that tells you something about the structure of it. People often hope to learn about the structure of the graph from visualizing it. In particular, they're often interested in whether there are obvious "clusters" in the graph.

By clusters, we mean a collection of objects in the graph that are far more connected to each other than they are to the rest of the graph. This is a tricky thing to measure in general, and straightforward measures of clustering can have nuanced and interesting problems. We'll dive more into this later when we talk more about graph algorithms. A useful sanity check is to visualize the graph and make sure the clusters you've detected align with the clusters that are apparent in the graph visualization (if there are any!).

How can you visualize the graph? Figure 6.21 shows what you get if you just randomly place the objects and their connections in an area.

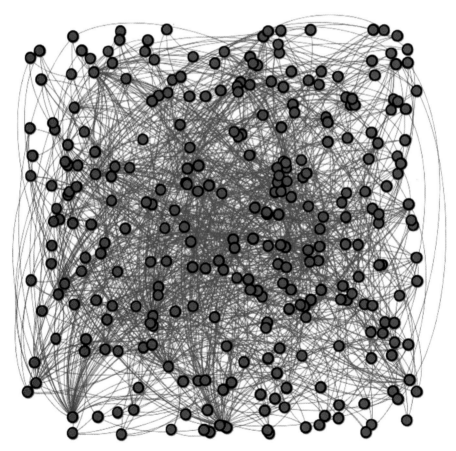

Figure 6.21   Graph visualizations that don't use the structure of the graph are unenlightening. You can do better than this!

You can see that there's nothing enlightening here. It looks like a random assortment of objects and connections. You can do a lot better!

You can imagine that each connection between objects is like a spring, pulling the objects together. Then, you can imagine each object repels every other object, so they're held closely together only by the springs. The result is that if a set of nodes are well interconnected, they'll form dense clusters or knots, while everything else tends to stretch out and fly apart. If you apply that to the graph (using ForceAtlas2 in Gephi), you can get the visualization in Figure 6.22.

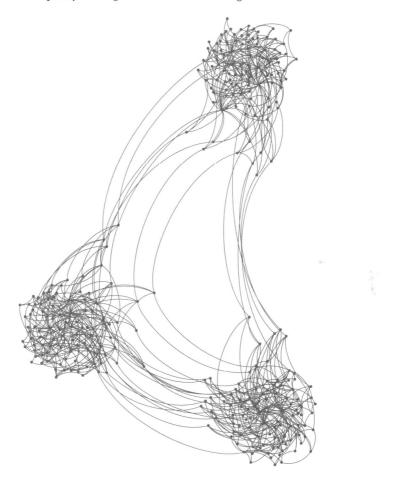

Figure 6.22   This visualization relies on the edges to attract nodes to each other, and the nodes themselves repel each other. This results in interconnected nodes getting grouped together, and the groups tend to push one another apart. You can get a nice picture of the structure from this layout, but it can be computationally expensive. It's intractable for large graphs.

You can see clearly here that there are three clusters in the graph that are loosely connected by a few extra connections. This graph was built using three random, disconnected components that were attached together by adding a few more connections at random. This is clear just from the visualization.

These are great algorithms for small graphs, but you'll see that they can be intractable for moderately sized or large graphs. Generally, they're good for graphs up to around a few hundred thousand nodes. After that, you need to use a different technique, like h3-layout.

6.4.2 Time Complexity

Most small-scale layout algorithms run with something like the following procedure:

```
1  # main loop
2  for step in num_steps:
3      for node in graph:
4          force = calculate_force(node)
5          new_position = update_position(force)
6
7  # force calculation
8  def calculate_force(node):
9      force = zero_vector
10     for other_node in graph:
11         force += update_force(node, other_node)
12     return force
```

You can see from this algorithm, each time calculate_force is called, you have to iterate over every object (node) in the graph. Within each step, you have to call this function once for each node in the graph! This results in N^2 calls to update_force. Even if this function has a fast runtime, these N^2 calls to it cause the algorithm to slow down tremendously for even moderately sized graphs. Even if the call takes just a microsecond, a graph with 100,000 nodes would make 10^{10} calls, resulting in about 10,000 seconds runtime. A graph with 500,000 nodes would take around 70 hours!

This problem, where the runtime grows with the square of the input, is our first look at the *time complexity* of an algorithm. Generally, when the runtime grows like the square of the input, the algorithm is not considered scalable. Even if you parallelize it, you only reduce the runtime by a constant factor. You might make it scale to slightly larger inputs, but the scaling problem still exists. The runtime will still be long for just slightly larger inputs. This can be okay in some applications, but it doesn't solve the problem of quadratic time complexity.

6.5   Conclusion

In this chapter, we covered some of the basics of data visualization. These can be useful when you're presenting results to your team, writing reports or automated emails to send to stakeholders, or sharing information with the rest of your team.

When you're making data visualizations, always consider your audience. A fellow data scientist might be interested in error bars, detailed labels and captions, and much more information contained in the plots. Stakeholders might be interested in only one quantity being bigger than another or the graph going "up and to the right." Don't include more detail than necessary. A plot can easily become overwhelming and push attention away from itself rather than ease the presentation of the data. Always consider removing tick marks and lines, moving labels and numbers down into captions, and simplifying labels however you can. Less is more.

II

Algorithms and Architectures

In this part, we cover algorithms and architectures. Specifically, we cover some of the basics to give you a feel for some of the elements of data infrastructure. And then we describe a basic process happening in this environment: model training.

Chapter 8, "Comparison," covers a useful collection of metrics and ways to compute them: similarity metrics. These can be especially useful for simple content recommendations systems but are useful to have in your toolbox whatever your domain.

Chapter 9, "Regression," describes supervised machine learning from the point of view of regression. The focus is less on the estimation error and more on the prediction and training problems. The chapter starts with linear regression and then moves to polynomial regression. It wraps up with random forest regression.

Chapter 10, "Classification and Clustering," includes the basics of discrete supervised models (e.g., classification) and unsupervised machine learning. It covers several clustering algorithms, some of which are very scalable.

Chapter 11, "Bayesian Networks," provides some preliminaries for understanding Bayesian networks and uses causal Bayesian networks to derive some intuition about them.

Chapter 12, "Dimensional Reduction and Latent Variable Models," describes a few useful Bayesian models and provides examples of how to use them.

Chapter 13, "Causal Inference," is a primer on understanding causal relationships and a good starting point for a deep and interesting field. Correlation does not imply causation. Machine learning is all about understanding correlative relationships.

Chapter 14, "Advanced Machine Learning," is an overview of the trade-off between model capacity and overfitting. Neural network models in Keras demonstrate these concepts.

7

Introduction to Algorithms and Architectures

7.1 Introduction

You have most of the background in place now and can finally start machine learning! There are two main settings in which you'll run machine-learning applications. The first setting is on a local computer, or *workstation*. This is usually for the purposes of a small, one-off analysis. The second context is in a *production environment* where a task is automated with relatively long-term support.

An example of a small, one-off analysis would be to find terms in article titles that correlate with higher click rates. You might do this analysis to report to a team of writers so they can experiment with the terms in their titles to increase click rates. An example of something that might run in a production environment is a recommendation system that runs on a website. The system has to run fully automated and should raise alarms if it's ever not working properly.

The requirements of each of these settings are different. Most elementary machine-learning books will make you proficient at machine learning in the first setting while almost entirely ignoring the second. Our focus will mainly be on the second setting.

Generally, you will prototype an application on a local machine, so the work to develop an application for production is strictly greater than the work for a one-off analysis. Often, you'll have a useful one-off analysis, and you'll be asked to automate it. In this way, you'll need to turn a machine-learning job that runs on your computer into one that runs automatically on a server. We generally call this *productionizing* a machine-learning job. You take a job running on your personal development machine and have it run on a production machine. An example would be turning a script that ranks the importance of terms in an ad with respect to click-through rates on that ad into a service that powers a real-time dashboard that writers can consult at their leisure.

When we're developing a prototype that might run in production, we like to use Jupyter Notebooks. Jupyter Notebooks allow you to write notes along with your code and include plots with those notes. The key advantages over using a development tool or the old-fashioned text editor and terminal are the tools for data visualization. Jupyter Notebooks can show plots inline and have nice formatting for printed data frames, as shown in Figure 7.1. This makes it easy to check intermediate results while you're writing your script in a way that's more insightful than printing lines of output to a terminal or checking variables at a breakpoint.

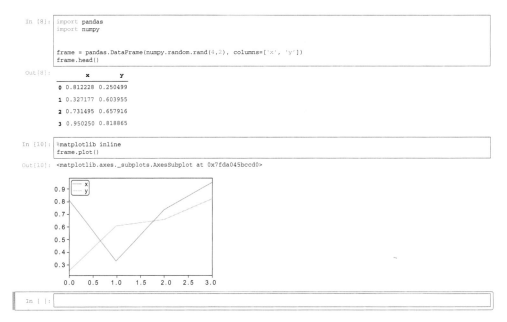

```
In [8]:   import pandas
          import numpy

          frame = pandas.DataFrame(numpy.random.rand(4,2), columns=['x', 'y'])
          frame.head()
```

```
Out[8]:          x         y

          0  0.812228  0.250499

          1  0.327177  0.603955

          2  0.731495  0.657916

          3  0.950250  0.818865
```

```
In [10]:  %matplotlib inline
          frame.plot()
```

```
Out[10]:  <matplotlib.axes._subplots.AxesSubplot at 0x7fda045bccd0>
```

```
In [ ]:
```

Figure 7.1   A Jupyter Notebook with a basic visualization of a data frame

Once you've developed a script and it runs in a Jupyter Notebook, you've finished the prototype, or one-off analysis. If you then need to productionize the job, there is a lot of work to do. Where does the data live in production? How will the model results be used in the real world? Does the job run quickly enough, or do you need to speed it up? Does the model serve results quickly enough, or will you need to scale it up by deploying to many machines with many workers? How will you update the model? How will you know if the model is broken? What do you do about edge cases, where there is missing data? The second part of the book seeks to answer all of these questions. The remainder of this chapter will cover the basics of the parts of a machine-learning model and the basics of computing architectures. The chapters that follow will cover the details of some common applications.

7.2   Architectures

This isn't much of a book on computer architecture, so we'll choose a functional definition. By *architecture*, we mean the design of the computer systems (including servers, databases, caches, etc.) and how they communicate to get a job done.

A *separation of concerns* refers to the partitioning of applications, code blocks, and other systems of objects in computer science. The degree to which "concerns" are "separated" varies from one system to another. Systems with many interdependencies are said to have a *weak* separation of concerns; a totally independent system responsible for its own job, is said to have a *strong* separation of concerns.

One example is the training and prediction steps of a machine-learning algorithm. A weak separation might have training and prediction both running on the same server, as part of the same block of code. You might call a function called `train` on your input data, which returns a model, and then a function called `predict` that takes your model and the data to predict with.

In contrast, a strong separation of concerns might have the training step and the prediction step running on two different servers or processes. Now, training and prediction happen independently of each other. You might still have a `train` and `predict` function on each server, and they might still run the same code, but they're not tied together in the same script. Changes to the training infrastructure, especially for scaling, are now independent from changes to the prediction infrastructure. Services and microservices, small and independent processes that run on servers, are a nice way to achieve this separation.

Generally, we'll be working with service-oriented architectures (SOAs). These have strong *separations of concerns*, and we think you'll find it natural to implement machine-learning systems in this context.

7.2.1 Services

A *service* is a stand-alone unit of a larger system that provides some particular function. Services can be thought of as the black boxes that comprise a system. One example might be a service that provides the article-viewing history for a user of a media site. Another service might provide a set of statistics about an article. Another service might spin up computing clusters to do large machine-learning jobs. Another might postprocess the results of a machine-learning job to make them accessible via yet another service.

These jobs are colloquially referred to as *concerns* of the service. To the extent they are disjoint, we have established a strong separation of concerns as defined earlier.

The standards for services vary from organization to organization, but these are some common requirements:

- Services are black boxes, in that their logic is hidden from their users.

- Services are autonomous, in that they are responsible for the function they serve.

- Services are stateless and return either their value or an error. You should be able to restart a service without it affecting the system.

- Services should be reusable. This is especially useful with machine-learning systems, where you might have a linear regression fitting service that can serve many needs.

The "12-factor rules" offer a broad overview of a good, opinionated set of requirements for services. They can be found at https://12factor.net/.

Your organization may have its own standard for what services are, and you should consult your engineering teams for what the organization's standards are.

For a great reference on microservices, we recommend [9].

7.2.2   Data Sources

You'll generally work with many types of data sources, as none is appropriate for every application.

Databases are great for storing large amounts of data but can be relatively slow at returning results. They read data from a disk, and the read time or disk IO is usually the limiting factor for web applications. For read-heavy applications, one way around this bottleneck is with *caching*. This technique stashes commonly used data so it is readily available in memory rather than being "paged" from disk.

A *cache* is an application that holds data in memory, often in a key: value format, making it available to other applications over a well-defined protocol. Redis is a one example. Caches can return results quickly, often 1,000 times faster than reading from disk. Again, they do this by storing data in memory rather than exclusively on disk. The reason we don't always just use a cache over a database is that memory is expensive and caches are ephemeral. For this reason, you'll often be limited by the size of your cache. There are strategies for keeping the size down, like having a finite lifetime for items in the cache called a *time to live* (TTL). Cache entries are deleted after that lifetime passes. Another approach to *cache eviction* is known as *least recently used* (LRU). This approach ejects the least recently used items to make way for newer, more popular cache entries.

Sometimes you'll need to work with large amounts of data. These will often be in cloud storage, like Amazon's S3 storage or Google's cloud storage. These can store large amounts of data cheaply, but they can present a locality problem: to process the data, you must download it first. Working with large data sets, this download time can be significant.

One strategy for operating on large data sets in batches is to use Hadoop file system (HDFS) storage on a cluster. This makes the data local to the cluster, so you need a large data set ready to be analyzed. Maintaining clusters, though, can be expensive.

Another strategy for working with large data sets is to sidestep the issue of locality by accessing the data *before* it is written to disk. You can do this by reading the data as it is produced and performing operations on one or a few data points at a time. As events occur that are relevant to training your model, for example, a message is sent from the user to a message handler that incorporates the data into your model. These streams of messages are often called *data streams*. There are many pieces of software that can do this. Kafka, RabbitMQ, and NSQd are a few examples.

7.2.3   Batch and Online Computing

Many algorithms can be categorized by whether they operate on all data points at once or on one or a few at a time in mini-batches. Algorithms that operate on data points one or a few at a time can operate in real time. These are called *online algorithms*.

You can have a service read a data stream and transform each data point by turning an article title into a word vector. That service can produce a new data stream that will be consumed by another service that trains a regression model to see which terms in the title best predict click rates. That service can save its model periodically to a database. A final service can read the database on request and power a dashboard that will show the best clicking terms! This is a real-time or almost real-time architecture for term importances.

A different way to perform this task is with batch computing. Instead of processing data one data point at a time, it can be easier to process it all in a big batch (say, the last hour's data) on a schedule and update the database all at once. In this case, you could just have one big service that does the updating. In this way, you can trade reusability and separation of concerns for simplicity and speed of development.

Of course, you could also have the batch system operate with several services that operate like the real-time system, where each saves the result of its batch processing and sends an event along the data stream to tell the next service there is data to be processed. There are many types of jobs that need to know about several data points at a time, so you'd have to write a batch processing job instead of an online one.

7.2.4 Scaling

Many services have to do a lot of work. If you're training a model on a large event stream, the data processing might be more than a single thread can handle. In that case, you can use many *threads of execution* to do work independently *in parallel* to handle the whole load. Another place this is common is when an API needs to handle a large request load. If you have a prediction service, for example, that gives article recommendations, you might have one request per page view on your site. For a large site, this can amount to hundreds or even tens of thousands of requests per second!

There are many ways to scale a production system. Typically the first approach is *vertical* scaling. This refers to the process of increasing the capacity of a single host in a network. If your service is running on multiple hosts already, this would refer to increasing the capacity of a portion of or the whole network. The main problem with vertical scaling is that as capacity of an individual node increases, it becomes disproportionately more expensive compared to adding a second node with similar specifications. Vertical scaling is often the preferred first approach because of the simplicity of "throwing hardware at the problem." Typically no code changes are required with this approach.

Often the second approach to scaling an application is *horizontal* scaling. More hosts are added to the network to divide capacity between them. This typically also requires the introduction of a *load balancer*, which directs a given request to a host that (probably) isn't already busy. Again, this usually doesn't require application changes, so it is pretty simple compared to the next type of scaling. It has more complexity compared to vertical scaling, however, because of the introduction of a load balancer and the increased size of the network.

The next approach to scaling a system is to change the machinery running the application. This approach can take many forms. It means using a cache if one isn't already being used or changing the database engine. It could mean choosing a different app server, or running more instances of the app server on a given host. It's more complex than vertical or horizontal scaling alone because it requires some knowledge of the application and product to get a sense of the best approach to scaling.

The last approach to scaling a production system is to make application-level changes. The last approach to scaling a production system is to make actual changes to the application's code. Imagine the case where a service's runtime grows quadratically with the size of the input data. It could already take hours to run. Doubling the cluster size would halve that time. It could still take an hour! If you can't increase your cluster size faster than the rate at which runtime increases, you need to improve your code.

This can take many forms. Most commonly people look for ways to make fragments of code faster first. Database calls are batched. Unnecessary loops and nestings are avoided. Network calls are made asynchronous. After these steps, the core algorithm being run is adapted to be faster. Sometimes this means finding a trade-off between speed and accuracy.

One example of this is locally sensitive hashing (LHS), which is the mechanism behind many collaborative filtering implementations (which we will discuss in another chapter). An initial approach to collaborative filtering might take the more precise metric of a Jaccard similarity between groups, calculating unions and intersections between sets. This union typically runs in $O(|M| + |N|)$ for sets M and N. The intersection runs in at least $O(argmin(|M|, |N|))$ and at worst $O(|M| * |N|)$. If M and N are the same size, you've got exactly the case where your time complexity grows quadratically with the size of your inputs. This is an excellent use case where you should change your algorithm from using Jaccard similarity to the less precise, but faster, locally sensitive hashing. Locally sensitive hashing has a time complexity that is bounded by the number of hash functions the user chooses to use. That number also limits the *accuracy* of the result.

7.3   Models

Machine-learning models need to learn about the world before they're useful. They learn by examining data and remembering something about the data. This is often done by having the model store a set of numbers called *parameters*.

Suppose you're interested in estimating the monthly expenses of households, y. You can try to predict expenses using some knowledge about the households. You know heating and cooling costs increase with the square footage of a house, x_1, and that these are significant household expenses. You also know that food costs are a major expense and increase with the number of members of the household, x_2.

You can write a linear model like this as an estimate of household expenses:

$$y = \beta_1 x_1 + \beta_2 x_2 \tag{7.1}$$

You don't know the values of your parameters, β_1 and β_2, but you can estimate them using a linear regression model. This step is called *training* the model.

7.3.1   Training

There are many algorithms used to train machine learning models, and a useful division again is between *batched* and *online* training algorithms.

Many models, like linear regression, will give algebraic formulae for calculating the parameters. Then, all you have to do is take your data matrix of observations and calculate the resulting parameters. This is feasible whenever the data matrix is small enough to fit in memory or small enough that the algorithm's runtime is acceptably fast. This is a *batched* calculation for the model parameters.

When the input data is too large or you need a more efficient algorithm, you might change over to doing online calculation of the coefficients. Instead of having an algebraic formula for the coefficients in the linear model, you might instead take an online approach, where you adjust the coefficients with every data point (or mini-batch of data points) that you pass into the training algorithm. A common approach for this is called *stochastic gradient descent*, and there are many other approaches. You'll learn more about stochastic gradient descent when we cover neural networks in Chapter 14.

Let's think about the household expense model again. It is common to partition your data set into two (usually) uneven portions. You might reserve 80 percent of your training data as the "training set" and the remaining 20 percent as the "test set". This assures you can get a relatively accurate measure of the quality of our model by first training on 80 percent of a data set and then using the known values for the remaining 20 percent to estimate important metrics like precision and recall.

After this testing step, you use all your past household data to train the model. You've estimated the model parameters β_1 and β_2. Now, you have data about a new household, so you know x_1 and x_2. You'd like to make your best guess about what their expenses are. When you plug the data into your linear regression model to get an estimate for y, you have completed the *prediction* step.

7.3.2   Prediction

The prediction step uses the parameters you've learned during the training step. Generally, these will be separate processes, and you'll want a way the training process can communicate model parameters to the prediction process. The basic idea is that after training a model, you'll save the model parameters (or the model object itself) to an external data store. You can then have the training service notify the prediction service with an event, and it will load the model from the data store. We'll get into those details later in the book when we discuss machine-learning architecture in Chapter 14.

In the linear regression example, a prediction service would have the parameters you've learned from some training data and take requests that pass in values for x_1 and x_2 from a different data set (usually, from some time after training your model). The service would use the parameters you've learned to do the multiplication to calculate $y = \beta_1 x_1 + \beta_2 x_2$, and it would return a response containing the calculated value of y for the parameters β_1 and β_2 you've estimated.

In general, your data distributions might change over time. That can mean that the correlations between x_1 or x_2 and y might change over time. If those correlations change, then your regression coefficients are no longer the same as you'd measure on the new data. Your predictions will have some error because of the difference in the correlations between the training data and the data you're trying to predict with. We'll address this problem a little more in the next section on validation. First, we'll discuss a little about scaling.

If the request rates for predictions are relatively low, as they might be if this household income data is used by employees within a company to estimate client's household income, you'll be able to handle the load with even a single server that returns income data. The request rates will probably be low enough that even a single thread on a relatively small machine could handle it if you weren't worried about availability or redundancy.

If the model is user-facing, as it might be on a financial planning website, you will probably have a much higher request load. You'll probably need several processes doing the work. If the request rate is high enough, you may need several machines spread out over a wide network and a mechanism to balance the requests across all of them.

Finally, now that you have a predictive model, you want to make sure it works on data the model has never seen before. When you did your training, you held out some data that wasn't used to learn the model parameters. Testing the model on this data will give you a measurement of the prediction error. If the data comes from the same distributions that real examples will come from when the model is applied, you can expect similar prediction error.

7.3.3   Validation

Generally, model validation is an attempt to see how well your model will perform when it's being used for its intended prediction task. There can be a couple of ways the model might fail to perform well for its prediction task. First, the model may have failed to train for technical reasons that are specific to the model, like accidentally dividing by zero (or close to zero) or parameters getting very large because of numerical problems. Second, the data distribution might change between training time and prediction time. Third, your model may be learning the training data too well, in the sense that it memorizes exact training examples instead of learning the pattern in the data. This is called *overfitting*, and we'll discuss it in more detail when we cover more advanced machine learning topics in Chapter 14.

To combat these failures, you'll want to do *model validation* before sending the parameters to be used for prediction (e.g., before sending them to the prediction service). If something about the training failed, you wouldn't want to run the new model parameters in production! You'd probably want to retry the algorithm with different settings (the parameters defining the settings are called *hyperparameters*) or raise an alert so the model can be fixed.

In the simplest case, you'll split your training data into two sets: a training set and a validation set. You'll use the training set to learn the model parameters, and you'll use the validation set to test the model. To test the model, you'll predict the outcomes for the y variable, usually denoted as $\hat{y}$, and compare these with the actual y values. This is a test to see that your model can predict outcomes that it hasn't seen before on data that is from the same distribution as your training data. This is great for checking that the model hasn't failed because of numerical reasons and that your model hasn't overfit the data. This procedure isn't good for making sure your model performs well on new data, in a context where the data distributions might be changing over time.

In addition to the validation at training time, as described in the previous paragraph, you'll also want to validate a live model to make sure it continues to perform well as the data distribution changes. To do this, you can save real predictions that your system makes and wait for the outcome event, y, to actually happen. You can pair these two pieces of data together and accumulate data points as prediction happens over time. You can then calculate your validation metric on a moving window of the past several predictions to see whether the validation metric is drifting over time.

To compare the predicted and actual values, you'll usually compute a number that measures your model's performance. In this case, the mean squared error is an appropriate number.

$$MSE = \sqrt{\Sigma_{i=1}^{N}(y_i - \hat{y}_i)^2} \qquad (7.2)$$

We'll go into some detail in Chapter 14 on the different metrics available and where each is appropriate. You can compare the metric with a reference value to see whether the model is performing well enough before saving the parameters.

7.4   Conclusion

In this chapter, we gave you the high-level view of how to build a production machine-learning system. We used this view to explain the different parts of a machine-learning model and how in building an external-facing service there can be a training step distinctly different from the external prediction/query interface. Ideally, we've convinced you these models divide naturally into separate training and prediction services and shown you a rough picture of how to scale these services from small data sets all the way up to very large ones!

8

Comparison

8.1 Introduction

We'll start with a useful collection of algorithms that are also used as elements of other algorithms. Comparison algorithms take a pair of objects and say how similar they are to each other.

Some example use cases might be finding articles about similar subjects or audiences for news recommendations, finding songs or movies with similar descriptors, or finding documents that are similar to a search query. We'll only scratch the surface of this class of algorithms, but we'll present some nice pedagogical development for simple implementations.

Which is the best comparison algorithm to use depends on the context. From the ones you'll see here, many of them are simple heuristics or just natural, easy solutions to implement. Whenever you're implementing a comparison, you generally have some goal in mind. Your choice of which algorithm to use should be guided by the input types for the algorithm (e.g., sets, fixed-length vectors, matrices, ranked lists, strings, etc.) and its performance for the context.

As an example, consider the task of recommending similar items on an ecommerce site. You might be interested in selling more recommended items, so the outcome you're interested in is "total sales per day." You might implement several comparison algorithms and AB test them against one another. The algorithms you implement depend on the input data you have available (e.g., metadata descriptions, sets of users interacting with each item, etc.), and the algorithm you end up choosing depends on the performance of each in context.

In this book, we'll have a lot of algorithm zoology. We'd like it to be useful as a desk reference, so we'll include summaries of algorithms and useful notes about them. You'll find the first here, for some comparison algorithms. To make the rest of this chapter self-contained, we'll include math preliminaries ahead of each algorithm where necessary.

8.2 Jaccard Distance

One concept that comes up many times in the theorems and definitions of the following algorithms is the concept of a *set*. Similarly, a *sequence* is used in many cases to define the domains over which certain operations take place. It's important to have a basic foundation for these ideas.

A set is a unique list of items with a size or *cardinality* of zero or more. A sequence is an ordered list of items allowed to repeat themselves. Let's look at a few concepts with respect to sets.

Jaccard Similarity Summary	
The Algorithm	Jaccard distance is a measure of how *similar* two sets are. A set compared with itself has a Jaccard similarity of one. Completely disjoint sets have a Jaccard similarity of zero.
Time Complexity	In Python, $O(|A| + |B|)$ on average. $O(|A||B|)$ worst case.
Memory Considerations	You'll want to store both sets in memory.

> **Definition 8.1. Union**
>
> The *union* of two sets, A and B, is denoted $A \cup B$ and is the set containing a unique combination of the elements of both sets A and B.
>
> For example, if $A = 1, 2, 3$ and $B = 2, 3, 4$, then
>
> $$A \cup B = \{1, 2, 3\} \cup \{2, 3, 4\} \tag{8.1}$$
> $$= \{1, 2, 3, 4\} \tag{8.2}$$

You can visualize this with a Venn diagram, as shown in Figure 8.1.

The Union of A and B   The Intersection of A and B

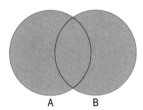   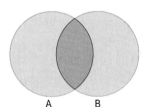

A   B   A   B

Figure 8.1   Elementary concepts in set theory

> **Definition 8.2. Intersection**
>
> The *intersection* of two sets, A and B, is denoted $A \cap B$ and is the set containing the elements *common* to both sets A and B.
>
> For example, if $A = 1, 2, 3$ and $B = 2, 3, 4$, then
>
> $$A \cap B = \{1, 2, 3\} \cap \{2, 3, 4\} \tag{8.3}$$
> $$= \{2, 3\} \tag{8.4}$$

8.2.1   The Algorithm

Jaccard distance is a measure of how *similar* two sets are. Exactly the same set has a Jaccard distance of 1. Completely disjoint sets have a Jaccard distance of 0.

> **Definition 8.3. Jaccard Distance**
>
> The *Jaccard distance* between two sets, *A* and *B*, is the cardinality of the *intersection* of the sets divided by the cardinality of the *union* of the sets.
>
> $$J(A, B) = \frac{|A \cap B|}{|A \cup B|} \tag{8.5}$$

8.2.2 Time Complexity

In the Python programming language, sets are implemented as hash tables. This makes maintaining their uniqueness simple. Lookups are $O(1)$ on average and $O(n)$ in the worst case [10].

Given two sets, A and B, computing the intersection then is $O(min(|A|, |B|))$. Computing the union of the sets is $O(|A| + |B|)$. These values are on average.

Combining them, we end up with a total complexity of $O(min(|A|, |B|) + |A| + |B|)$ on average, for Jaccard distance.

8.2.3 Memory Considerations

When calculating the Jaccard distance, it should be the case that both sets are stored in memory to ensure speedy computation.

8.2.4 A Distributed Approach

Consider the case when two sets, A and B, are very large, such that they can't fit on a single node. How can you take the Jaccard distance then? Or similarly, what happens when you have many parallel sets that you're interested in finding the Jaccard distance between? This is where you can turn to distributed systems.

In the distributed approach, we're interested in the problem of finding intersections and unions of sets with a parallelized approach. The formula for Jaccard distance requres the cardinality of the intersection and union of the sets. You don't actually need to keep the full sets in memory to represent them. You can compute them as statistics. This will save memory. We'll describe the architecture shown in Figure 8.2. For a fast and easy parallelized implementation, we suggest using PySpark with the native Python union and intersection methods!

Another approach to this problem would be to store the full sets, A and B, in a database that supports parallel reads (such as PostgreSQL or MySQL) and hash indexes (for roughly $O(1)$ lookups). We've already said you can't store all the data on a single node, so let's assume the database is horizontally sharded.

You can look up quickly whether a single element is in A or B or both by hashing the primary key for that element, addressing it to the correct database node, and doing a primary key lookup. You can't easily do a `JOIN` query to compute this all on the database because parts of the sets are on other nodes.

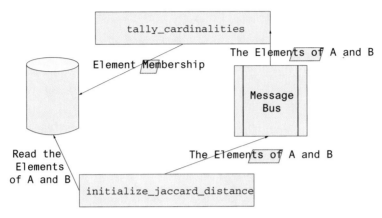

Figure 8.2   One of many possible architectures for computing Jaccard similarity in a distributed way

You know these sets are stored in the database. To kick off the Jaccard distance calculation for A and B, you should have a process, call it `initialize_jaccard_distance`, that reads the elements of the sets out of the database and sends a message to some other process, call it `tally_cardinalities`, that does the lookup and keeps a tally of what elements are in what sets.

You can store the results in `tally_cardinalities` (see Figure 8.2), but keeping state here is error prone. An unexpected error in reading from the database or tallying up some statistics could cause a loss of state. It's a better separation of concerns to send that information off to another process like back to the PostgreSQL or MySQL database.

The algorithm from here is simple. Realizing the elements of the intersection will be counted twice while the outer union will be counted once, you can use a little trick to fix the double-counting. Since the Jaccard distance is the intersection divided by the union, you can divide the intersection by 2 and subtract that number of elements from the union.

8.3   MinHash

It's not always tractable to store both sets in RAM to compute the union and intersection. Similarly, it can be substantial compute overhead to compare a large number of large sets (which is usually $O(n^2)$ in the number of sets as a factor to the previously noted complexity for Jaccard distance). When sets are very large, there are approximations to Jaccard distance available. *MinHash*, a version of *locality sensitive hashing*, is just such an approximation.

Locality sensitive hashing hashes elements of a space down to a smaller space. It's useful for approximate nearest neighbor algorithms. Here, we'll choose k random hash functions. For each function, we'll show how to hash each item in each set and find the set element that maps to the minimum of the hash function over each set. For each hash function, you'll keep track of how often the minimum set elements match.

It turns out the probability of matching is equal to the Jaccard similarity of the sets! The more hash functions you use, the more precise your estimate will be. Unfortunately, that also means you have to hash each set k times, so you'll want to keep k relatively small.

MinHash Summary	
The Algorithm	Compute approximate set similarity when both sets don't fit in memory using a hashing trick to reduce the dimension of the space of objects. A set of k MinHashes represents each set. N is the number of sets, and n is the number of elements in each set.
Time Complexity	$O(nk + N^2k)$
Memory Considerations	You'll want to store MinHash signatures for each set, so $O(kN)$ memory.

8.3.1 Assumptions

MinHash is an approximation. It's assumed you don't need an exact answer for similarity to effectively do a task.

8.3.2 Time and Space Complexity

You need to hash each set k times. If the sets are size n, then the time complexity is $O(nk)$. If you're comparing N sets, then there are $O(N^2)$ comparisons to make. Each comparison checks whether the MinHashes match, so run in $O(k)$ time. That makes the total $O(nk + N^2k)$. Much faster than computing the Jaccard similarity directly with set intersections!

8.3.3 Tools

You can find some nice code examples in Chris McCormick's blog post (http://mccormickml.com/2015/06/12/minhash-tutorial-with-python-code/), or get some pseudocode from Mining Massive Data Sets (https://www.amazon.com/Mining-Massive-Datasets-Anand-Rajaraman/dp/1107015359). It's fun and relatively easy to implement minhash using *hashlib* in Python.

Tools we can recommend for implementing LSH are the lshhdc package at https://github.com/go2starr/lshhdc for Python or lshkit, http://lshkit.sourceforge.net/, for C++. It's a little tricky to find a dedicated implementation of locally sensitive hashing for some reason. The algorithm is simple enough, though, to implement yourself if you want a version that needs to be maintained after deployment.

8.3.4 A Distributed Approach

MinHash gives an approximation of Jaccard similarity more efficiently than computing it exactly. The more precise the estimate, the more computationally expensive it gets.

Since MinHash is so much less computationally intense and you can specify the accuracy of the calculation, it is a pretty popular solution for taking the Jaccard distance of very large sets.

In MinHash you compute k hash functions where k is chosen to yield the desired accuracy in the Jaccard estimation. Since A and B are very large, their union and intersection don't change that much over time. This makes the first part of this algorithm a great candidate for a batched job to be run by cron.

You can create a cron task, `generate_signatures`, that reads all of A and asynchronously sends HTTP requests to hash all the elements to a load balancer, which relays those requests to one of many `hash_api` processes. These processes take the desired hash function, hash the element, and return the result. The architecture is illustrated in Figure 8.3.

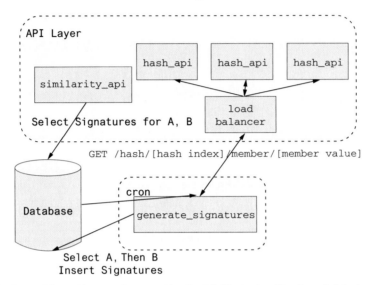

Figure 8.3   A possible architecture for executing the MinHash algorithm in a distributed way

In `generate_signatures`, all you have to keep in is the current minimum under each of k hash functions, not the hash of each element. The set of minimum elements under each hash function form the signature for the set.

Counting the number of elements for two sets that are the same under each hash function and then dividing by k gives the estimate for Jaccard similarity. Since the signatures are only k elements, you can create a `similarity_api` that sits around all day waiting to compare signatures and divide by k. This effectively separates the model-building and query portion of the algorithm.

8.4   Cosine Similarity

Cosine similarity measures the cosine of the angle between two vectors. When the angle is 0, the vectors are aligned, and the cosine is 1. When they are orthogonal, the angle is 90 degrees, and the cosine is 0. The cosine similarity is calculated easily by using the dot product, $\mathbf{v} \cdot \mathbf{w} = |\mathbf{v}||\mathbf{w}|\cos\theta$, and re-arranging, like so:

$$\cos\theta = \frac{\mathbf{v} \cdot \mathbf{w}}{|\mathbf{v}||\mathbf{w}|} \tag{8.6}$$

We can get a nice comparison between Jaccard distance and cosine similarity. You'll consider binary vectors that indicate the presence (1) or absence (0) of an object in a set. For example, you can consider vectors describing animals in images, where the universe of animals you'd like to consider contains only dogs and cats. An image with a dog in it has a 1 in the first entry but has a

0 if there is no dog. An image with a cat has a 1 in the second entry, or 0 if no cat. Now you have a way of representing the set of animals in an image as a binary vector, where, for example, $(1, 0)$ describes an image with only a dog, $(0, 1)$ an image with only a cat, and $(1, 1)$ an image with both a dog and a cat. $(0, 0)$ contains neither a dog nor a cat.

You can do some nice set operations with these vectors. First, consider an image with a dog and a cat, so the vector is $\mathbf{v} = (1, 1)$. Let's look at the product of $\mathbf{v}$ with itself. The product of two vectors is written $\mathbf{v} \cdot \mathbf{v} = \sum_{i=1}^{N} v_i v_i$, where v_i is the ith entry of $\mathbf{v}$. In this case, it's $1^2 + 1^2 = 2$. In general, it turns out to be the number of distinct elements in the set! If the set A is encoded as $\mathbf{V}$, then $|A| = \mathbf{v} \cdot \mathbf{v}$.

Suppose you have a second image with just a dog, with vector w encoding the set of animals B in that image. Let's see what happens when you multiply these vectors together. You get $1 \cdot 1 + 1 \cdot 0 = 1$. Since both had a dog, the 1s multiply and contribute to the sum. Since one of them had no cat, the 0 doesn't allow the one with a cat to contribute. It turns out the result is just the total objects that are in both images! In other words, the result is the size of the intersection of the two sets.

Since you have the sizes of each set and the intersection, you can also calculate the size of the union easily. It's simply the total number of objects in each set, minus the ones they have in common. It can be written as $|A \cup B| = \mathbf{v} \cdot \mathbf{v} + \mathbf{w} \cdot \mathbf{w} - \mathbf{w} \cdot \mathbf{v}$. Now, you can write the cosine similarity between binarized sets as follows:

$$cos\,\theta = \frac{|A \cap B|}{\sqrt{|A||B|}}. \tag{8.7}$$

You can see the difference is in the denominator, where the Jaccard distance uses the size of the union of A and B, while the cosine similarity uses the geometric mean of the sizes of the sets. The geometric mean is bounded above by the size of the larger of the two sets. The size of the union is bounded below by the size of the larger of the two sets. The denominator will thus tend to be smaller for the cosine similarity, so the cosine similarity will tend to be the larger quantity.

Cosine Similarity Summary	
The Algorithm	Measures the similarity between vectors. It works for sets as well as more general vector spaces (e.g., real numbers).
Time Complexity	$O(n)$, for n-dimensional vectors. N^2 where N is the number of sets to compare.
Memory Considerations	You'll want to store the vectors in memory. If there are dummy-encoded categorical variables, you'll probably want a sparse representation to save memory.

8.4.1 Complexity

The dot product for non-sparse n vectors involves n multiplications and $n - 1$ additions. That makes the complexity $\mathcal{O}(n)$.

If you use sparse vectors and a sparse representation, it depends on precisely how the vectors are represented. If the smaller vector has m nonzero entries, it should be $\mathcal{O}(m)$.

8.4.2 Memory Considerations

If you're using large vectors, you should consider a sparse representation.

8.4.3   A Distributed Approach

Cosine similarity has the same requirement for finding the union of a set that Jaccard distance does. We can repurpose our architecture for Jaccard distance here, with the same approach. The second part of this algorithm is just to find the cardinality of A and B. That is a simple divide-and-conquer style of query to each of our database shards. We count the cardinality on each shard and just add them.

8.5   Mahalanobis Distance

A more familiar special case of Mahalanobis distance is Euclidean distance. The Euclidean distance between two n-vectors, $\mathbf{v}$ and $\mathbf{w}$, is as follows:

$$d_E(\mathbf{w}, \mathbf{v}) = |\mathbf{v} - \mathbf{w}|^2 = \sum_{i=1}^{n}(v_i - w_i)^2. \tag{8.8}$$

Sometimes, you might have different units in different entries of your vectors. Suppose, for example, that your vectors were actually rows of real-valued data describing people, such as age, income, and IQ. If you wanted to evaluate how similar the two people were, it wouldn't make sense for income (maybe spread between \$0 and \$200000) and age (maybe between 18 and 68). A difference of a few percent in income would overwhelm a large difference in age. You need to change units to make everything more comparable.

If the data is (approximately) normally distributed, it makes sense to make the standard deviation your unit of variation in the data. If you scale the ith field by the inverse of its standard deviation, $1/\sigma_i$ over the data set, then the typical variation in each field becomes standardized to one unit. Now, it makes more sense to compare differences in each field. This is what happens naturally when you measure the Mahalanobis distance, defined as follows:

$$d_M(\mathbf{w}, \mathbf{v}) = \sum_{i=1}^{n} \frac{(w_i - v_i)^2}{\sigma_i^2}. \tag{8.9}$$

The units have been standardized, so now everything is measured in units of standard deviations.

Mahalanobis Distance Summary	
The Algorithm	Measures distance between vectors, scaling the units along each axis by that dimension's standard deviation.
Time Complexity	$O(Nn)$, for a set of N n-dimensional vectors.
Memory Considerations	You'll want to store the vectors in memory. If there are dummy-encoded categorical variables, you'll probably want a sparse representation to save memory.

8.5.1   Complexity

The calculation involves calculating each standard deviation over the whole data set. For N samples, the complexity is $\mathcal{O}(Nn)$.

8.5.2   Memory Considerations

If your dataset is large, it makes sense to sample to calculate the standard deviation.

8.5.3   A Distributed Approach

The Mahalanobis distance requires taking a difference between each feature of a vector, squaring it, and weighting it by the square of the variance of that feature across the data set.

Let's break this down into two problems. First let's find the variance of each feature in our data set. Again, if we have lots of vectors to compare, we'll find the variance doesn't change dramatically from one moment to the next. You can create a cron task called `compute_feature_variances` that computes the variance of each feature online. It will examine each feature of the data set, compute the variance, and store it in the database of your choice.

By storing each of our vector entries with its feature ID and by sharding on feature ID, you can compute the squared differences on each shard of the database before you read the data out. Similarly, by storing the variance with its feature ID and sharding on feature ID you can, indeed, run a portion of the whole sum on a single database shard. A schema for this is shown in Figure 8.4. Querying from an API allows you to reduce this to a single aggregation query on each node of the database cluster. The API would then add the portions of the sum to make the whole.

The architecture for this process could look like Figure 8.5.

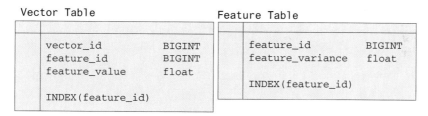

Figure 8.4   A schema for computing Mahalanobis distance on a SQL-like database

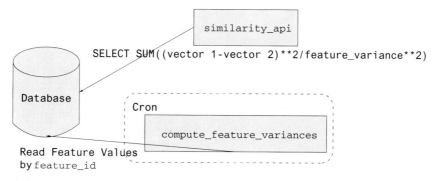

Figure 8.5   A possible architecture for computing Mahalanobis distance

8.6   Conclusion

In this chapter, you saw several useful algorithms for comparing items. While these methods are relatively simple, they're also powerful. You can compare article audiences with Jaccard similarity to find similar articles and could then power a recommender system. You can find similar users along some set of covariates and use that for matching in a web experiment or quasi-experiment.

These comparison methods are essential tools for your toolbox, and we hope you'll experiment on your own data.

You have the basic tools in place to begin machine learning. You can visualize and explore data sets to understand statistical dependence. You've developed an understanding of noise in data. You saw some useful tools to handling these data at a basic level, to discover similarities. It's time to be doing more advanced machine learning, and we'll start with regression.

9

Regression

9.1 Introduction

Model fitting is the process of estimating a model's parameters. In other chapters, we described linear regression as a specific example. Now, you'll develop that example with a little more detail. You'll find this same basic pattern throughout the book. It works well for linear regression, and you'll see the same structure for more advanced models like deep neural networks.

Generally, the first step is to start plotting the data with scatter plots and histograms to see how it is distributed. When you're plotting, you might see something like Figure 9.1. The constant slope to the data, even when there is a lot of noise around the trend, suggests that y is related linearly to x.

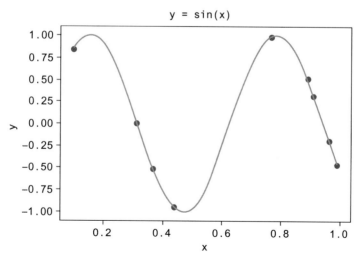

Figure 9.1 Random data from $y = sin(10x)$, along with the line for $y = sin(10x)$

In Figure 9.1, you can see that there's still a lot of spread to the y values at fixed values of x. While y increases with x on average, the predicted value of y will generally be a poor estimate of the true y

value. This is okay. You need to take more predictors of y into account to explain the rest of the variation of y.

9.1.1   Choosing the Model

Once you've explored the data distributions, you can write down your model for y as a function of x and some parameters. Our model will be as follows:

$$y = \beta x + \epsilon \tag{9.1}$$

Here, y is the output, β is a parameter of the model, and ϵ captures the noise in the y value from what you would expect just from the value of x. This noise can take on many different distributions. In the case of linear regression, you can assume that it's Gaussian with constant variance. As part of the model checking process, you should plot the difference between your model's output and the true value, or the *residual* to see the distribution of ϵ. If it's much different from what you expected, you should consider using a different model (e.g., a general linear model).

You could write this model for each y value explicitly, y_i (where i ranges from 1 to N when you have N data points), by writing it as follows:

$$y_i = \beta x_i + \epsilon_i \tag{9.2}$$

You could instead write these as column vectors, where

$$\mathbf{y} = \beta \mathbf{x} \tag{9.3}$$

and it will have the same meaning.

Often, you'll have many different x variables, so you'll want to write the following:

$$y_i = \beta_1 x_i 1 + \beta_2 x_i 2 + ... + \beta_j x_i j + \epsilon_i \tag{9.4}$$

Or you can write this more succinctly as the following:

$$\mathbf{y} = \mathbf{X}\beta + \epsilon \tag{9.5}$$

9.1.2   Choosing the Objective Function

Once you've chosen the model, you need a way of saying that one choice of parameter values is better or worse than another choice. The parameters determine the model's output for a given input. The objective function is usually decided based on the model's output by comparing it to known values.

A common objective function is the mean squared error. The error is just the difference between what the model thinks the y value should be, which you'll call $\hat{y}$, and the actual output, y. You could look at the average error but there's a problem. $\hat{y}$ could be arbitrarily far from y as long as for every positive error there is a negative error that cancels it out. This is true because when you take the average error (ME), you have to sum all the errors together, like so:

$$ME = \Sigma_{i=1}^{N}(y_i - \hat{y}_i) \tag{9.6}$$

Instead, you'd like only positive values to go into the average, so you don't get cancellation. An easy way to do this is to just square the errors before taking the average, giving you the mean squared error (MSE).

$$MSE = \Sigma_{i=1}^{N}(y_i - \hat{y}_i)^2 \tag{9.7}$$

Now, the smaller the mean squared error, the smaller the distance (on average) between the true y values and the model's estimates of the y values. If you have two sets of parameters, you can use one set to calculate the $\hat{y}$ and compute the MSE. You can do the same with the other set. The parameters that give you the smaller MSE are the better parameters!

You can automate the search for good parameters with an algorithm that iterates over choice of parameters and stops when it finds the ones that give the minimum MSE. This process is called *fitting* the model.

This isn't the only choice of objective function you could make. You could have taken absolute values, for example, instead of squaring the errors. What is the difference?

It turns out that when you use MSE and you have data whose mean follows a linear trend, the model that you fit will return the average value of y at x. If you use the absolute value instead (calculating the mean absolute deviation, or MAD), the model reports the median value of y at x. Either might be useful, depending on the application. MSE is the more common choice.

9.1.3 Fitting

When we say *fitting*, we generally mean systematically varying the model parameters to find the values that give the smallest value of the objective function. Generally, some objective functions should be maximized (likelihood is one example, which you'll see later), but here you're interested in minimizing functions. If an algorithm is designed to minimize an objective function, then you can maximize one by running that algorithm on the negative of the objective function.

We'll give a more thorough treatment later in the book, but a simple algorithm for minimizing a function is Newton's method, or gradient descent. The basic idea is that at a maximum or minimum, the derivative of a function is zero. At a minimum, the derivative (slope) will be negative to the left of the minimum and positive to the right.

Consider the one-dimensional case. We start at a random value of β and try to figure out if you should use a larger or smaller beta. If the slope of the objective function points downward at the value of β you've chosen, then you should follow it, since it points you toward the minimum. You should then adjust β to larger values. If it's a positive slope, then the objective function decreases toward the left, and you should use a smaller value of β. You can derive this very rigorously using more calculus, but the basic result is a rule for updating your value of β to find a better value. If you write your objective function as $f(\beta)$, then you can write the update rule as follows:

$$\beta_{new} = \beta_{old} - \lambda \frac{df}{d\beta} \tag{9.8}$$

You can see that if the derivative is positive, you decrease the value of beta. If it is negative, you increase the value of beta. Here, λ is a parameter to control how big the algorithm's steps are. You want it to be small enough that you don't jump from one side of a minimum clear across to the other. The best size will depend on the context.

Now, given a model and objective function, you have a procedure for choosing the best model parameters. You just write the objective function as a function of the model parameters and minimize it using this gradient descent method.

There are many ways you could do this minimization work. Instead of this iterative algorithm, you can write the objective function as a function of the parameters explicitly and use calculus to minimize it. There are also many variants of iterative algorithms like this one. Which is best for your job depends on the application.

9.1.4   Validation

After fitting your model, you need to test how well it works! You'll typically do this by giving it some data points and comparing its output with the actual output. You can calculate a score, often the same loss function you used to fit the model, and summarize the model performance. The problem with this procedure is when you validate the model on the same data you used to train it. Let's imagine an extreme case as an example.

Suppose your model had as much freedom as it liked to fit your data. Suppose also that you had only a few data points, like in Figure 9.1. If you try to fit a model to this data, you run the risk that the model overfits the data. To give you a parameter to adjust, you'll try to make a polynomial regression fit to this data. You can do this by making columns of data with higher and higher powers of x.

You'll plot a few different lines fit to the data with different powers of x, where you'll label the power by k, in Figure 9.2. In this figure, you can see the fit improving as k gets higher, until around $k = 5$. After $k = 5$, there's too much freedom in the model, and the function fine-tunes itself to the data set. Since this data is drawn from $y = sin(10x)$, you can see that you'll generalize much better to new data points with the $k = 5$ model, even though the $k = 8$ model fits the training data better. You say the $k = 8$ model is "overfit" to the data.

How, then, can you see when you're overfitting a model? The typical way to check is to reserve some of the data at training time and use it later to see how well a model generalizes.

You can do this, for example, using the `train_test_split` function from the sklearn package. Let's generate some new data and now compute the R^2 not only on the training data but also on a reserved set of test data.

First, we generate $N = 20$ data points.

```
1  import numpy as np
2
3  N = 20
4  x = np.random.uniform(size=N)
5  y = np.sin(x*10) + 0.05 * np.random.normal(size=N)
```

Next, let's split this into a train and test split. You'll train on the training data but hold the test data until the end to compute the validation scores. Typically you want your model to perform well, so you use as much training data as you can afford to train the model and validate with enough data to be sure the precision of your validation metric is reasonable. Here, since you're generating only 20 data points, you'll make a split into halves.

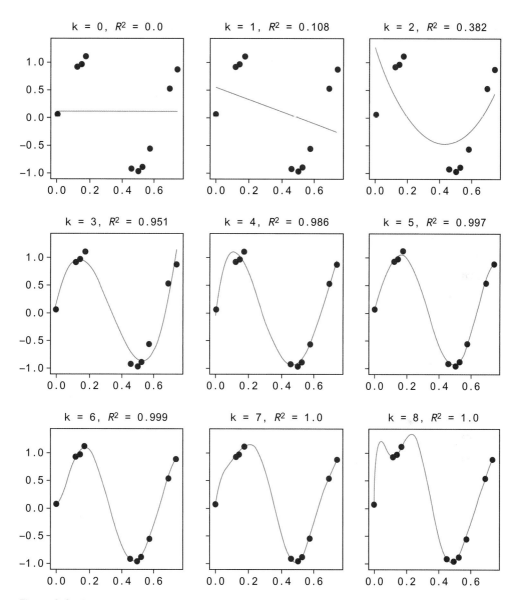

Figure 9.2   Random data from $y = sin(10x)$, along with the line for $y = sin(10x)$

```
1 from sklearn.model_selection import train_test_split
2
3 x_train, x_test, y_train, y_test = train_test_split(x, y,
4 train_size=10)
```

Now, you'll build up lots of columns of higher and higher powers of the *x* variable to run the polynomial regression. You'll use sklearn's linear regression to do the actual regression fit.

```
 1 k = 10
 2
 3 X = pd.DataFrame({'x^{}'.format(i): x_train**i for i in range(k)})
 4 X['y'] = y_train
 5
 6 X_test = pd.DataFrame({'x^{}'.format(i): x_test**i for i in range(k)})
 7 X_test['y'] = y_test
 8
 9 x_pred = np.arange(xmin, xmax, 0.001)
10 X_pred = pd.DataFrame({'x^{}'.format(i): x_pred**i for i in range(k)})
```

Now that you have train and test data preprocessed, let's actually run the regressions and plot the results.

```
 1 f, axes = pp.subplots(1, k-1, sharey=True, figsize=(30,3))
 2
 3 for i in range(k-1):
 4     model = LinearRegression()
 5     model = model.fit(X[['x^{}'.format(l) for l in range(i+1)]],
 6                       X['y'])
 7     model_y_pred = model.predict(
 8                       X_pred[['x^{}'.format(l) for l in range(i+1)]])
 9     score = model.score(X[['x^{}'.format(l) for l in range(i+1)]],
10                       X['y'])
11     test_score = model.score(
12                       X_test[['x^{}'.format(l) for l in range(i+1)]],
13                       X_test['y'])
14     axes[i].plot(x_pred, model_y_pred)
15     axes[i].plot(x, y, 'bo')
16     axes[i].set_title('k = {}, $R^2={}$, $R^2_t={}$'
17                       .format(i, round(score,3), round(test_score, 3)))
18 pp.ylim(-1.5,1.5)
```

This produces the data in Figure 9.3. You can see the R^2 gets better and better as *k* increases, but the validation R^2 doesn't necessarily keep increasing. Past $k = 4$ it seems to get noisy and sometimes increase while sometimes decreasing. Here, the validation and the training data are plotted on the same graph. When the trendline fails to match the validation data, the R^2 gets worse, even though the model does a good job of fitting the training data.

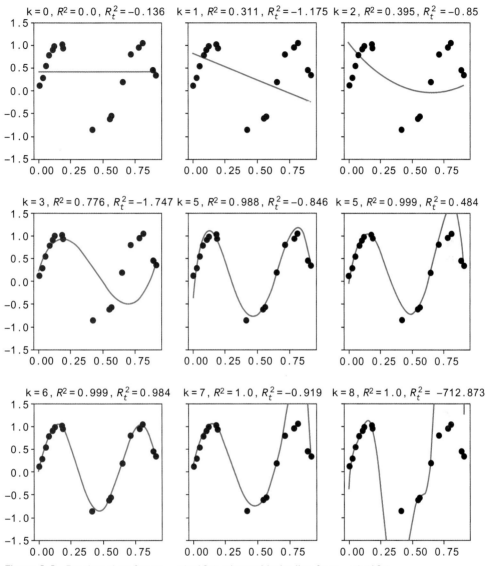

Figure 9.3   Random data from $y = sin(10x)$, along with the line for $y = sin(10x)$

These same basic principles can be applied in different ways. Another validation approach involves splitting the data into several slices and holding out one slice while training on the rest. This is called *k-fold cross-validation*. You can also train on all of the data but leave out a single data point at a time for validation. You can repeat this for each data point. This is called *leave-one-out cross-validation*.

Choosing a good model is a careful balance between giving your model enough freedom to describe the data but not so much that it overfits. You'll see these themes come up throughout the book, but especially when you look at neural networks in Chapter 14.

9.2   Linear Least Squares

Least squares refers to minimizing the square of the difference between the value at a point according to our data set and the value at that point according to the objective function. These values are known as *residuals*.

Least squares estimations can model equations with multiple independent variables, but for simplicity it's easier to consider simple linear equations.

In general you want to build a model of *m linear* equations with *k* coefficients weighting them.

To get the behavior of the model as close as possible to the function you're fitting, you minimize the function $||y - X\beta||^2$.

Here, X_{ij} is the jth feature of the ith data point. We show some data generated from such a model in Figure 9.4 (blue data points), along with the model that fits it (green line). Here, the coefficients have been fit to make sure the model has the correct slope ($\frac{1}{4}$) and y-intercept (2).

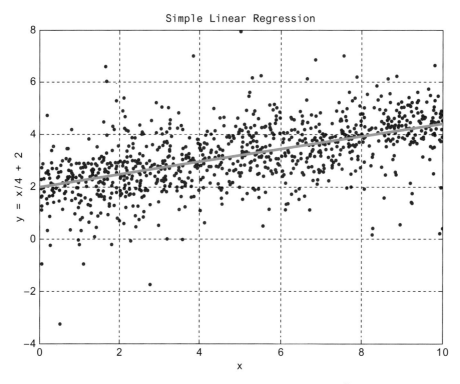

Figure 9.4   A curve fit to a randomly generated data set about the line $y = \frac{x}{4} + 2$ with linear regression

Linear Regression Summary	
The Algorithm	Linear regression is for predicting outcomes based on linear combinations of features. It's great when you want interpretable feature weights, want possible causal interpretations, and don't think there are interaction effects.
Time Complexity	$O(C^2 N)$, with C features and N data points. It's dominated by a matrix multiplication.
Memory Considerations	The feature matrix can get large when you have sparse features! Use sparse encodings when possible.

9.2.1 Assumptions

Ordinary least squares assumes errors have zero mean and equal variance. This will be true if the errors are Gaussian around the average y value at each x. If they are not Gaussian but the data is linear, consider using a general linear model.

9.2.2 Complexity

This complexity will be based on the algebraic approach to linear least squares model fitting.

You have to do the matrix multiplications given in the following formula:

$$\beta = (\mathbf{X}^T \mathbf{X})^{-1} \mathbf{X}^T \mathbf{y} \tag{9.9}$$

If N is the number of sample points and k is the number of features you're fitting, then the complexity is (with $N > k$), $k^2 N$.

9.2.3 Memory Considerations

Large matrix multiplications are usually run in a divide-and-conquer algorithm. When it comes to matrix multiplications in particular, it's often the case that it takes as much processing to send the matrix data across the network as it takes to do the multiplication locally. This is why "communication avoiding algorithms" like Cannon's algorithm exists. They minimize the amount of communication required to parallelize the task. Cannon's algorithm is among the most common and popular.

Part of Cannon's algorithm requires matrices to be broken into blocks, Since you choose the size of the blocks, you can choose the amount of memory required for this algorithm.

Another common approach is to just sample down the data matrix. Many common packages will report standard errors on regression coefficients. Use these metrics to help guide your choice of sample size.

Most often, you'll train a large-scale linear regression with SGD. There's a nice implementation in pyspark in the mllib package for doing this.

9.2.4   Tools

scipy.optimize.leastsq is a nice implementation in Python. This is also the method working under the hood for many of the other optimizations in scipy. scipy's implementation is actually a loose set of bindings on top of MINPACK's lmdif and lmdir algorithms (which are written in Fortran). MINPACK is also available in C++, though. If you want to minimize the dependencies for your application, numpy also has an implementation that can be found at *numpy.linalg.lstsq*. You can find implementations for least-squares regression in scikit-learn, in *sklearn.linear_model.LinearRegression*, or in the statsmodels package in *statsmodels.regression.linear_model.OLS*.

9.2.5   A Distributed Approach

To improve communication across the network, one of the keys is minimizing bandwidth. Each node at the beginning of a mesh of nodes pulls what data it needs from a database or archival source. It shifts the rows and columns appropriately for the next node and passes that information along. Each node operates on its own data to compute some portion of the resulting multiplication. Figure 9.5 illustrates this architecture.

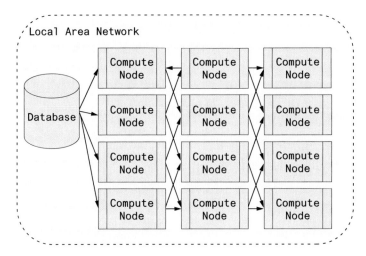

Figure 9.5   A possible architecture for computing distributed matrix multiplications

Alternatively, you can use the pyspark implementation!

9.2.6   A Worked Example

Now, let's actually run a linear regression. We'll use numpy and pandas to work with the data and statsmodels for the regression. First, let's generate some data.

```
1  from statsmodels.api import OLS
2  import numpy as np
3  import pandas as pd
4
5  N = 1000
6
7  x1 = np.random.uniform(90,100, size=N)
8  x2 = np.random.choice([1,2,3,4,5], p=[.5, .25, .1, .1, .05] size=N)
9  x3 = np.random.gamma(x2, 100)
10 x4 = np.random.uniform(-10,10, size=N)
11
12 beta1 = 10.
13 beta2 = 2.
14 beta3 = 1.
15
16 y = beta1 * x1 + beta3 * x3
17
18 X = pd.DataFrame({'$y$': y, '$x_1$': x1, '$x_2$': x2, '$x_3$': x3})
```

The independent variables are x_1, x_2, and x_3. The dependent variable, y, will be determined by these independent variables. Just for concreteness, let's use a specific example. Say the y variable is the monthly cost of living for a household and the x_1 variable is the temperature outside for the month, which you expect is a big factor and will significantly increase their housing costs. It will be summer, so the hotter it is, the more expensive the cooling bill. The x_2 variable will be the number of people living in the house, which directly leads to higher food costs, x_3. Finally, x_4 will be the amount spent on everything else. Families don't tend to keep track of this very well, and you're not able to measure it.

To get a feel for the data, you should make some plots and tables. You'll start by looking directly at a random sample of the data, shown in Figure 9.6.

This gives you some ideas for visualization. You can see the x_2 variable is small and discrete and that the y variable (total monthly expenses) tends to be a few thousand dollars.

To get a better picture of what variables are related to one another, you can make a correlation matrix (see Figure 9.7). The matrix is symmetric because the Pearson correlation between two variables doesn't care which variable is which: the formula gives the same result if they trade their places. You're curious which variables predict y, so you want to see which ones correlate well with it. From the matrix, you can just read the y column (or row) and see that x_1, x_2, and x_3 are all correlated with y. Notice that since household size (x_2) directly determines food cost (x_3), these two variables are correlated with each other.

Now that you've confirmed that all of these variables might be useful for predicting y, you should check their distributions and scatter plots. This will let you check what model you should use. Pandas' scatter matrix is great for this.

```
1  from pandas.tools.plotting import scatter_matrix
2  scatter_matrix(X, figsize=(10,10))
```

	x_1	x_2	x_3	y
178	96.593026	1	185.598228	4036.221255
605	92.363628	4	619.496338	4303.454053
885	91.407646	1	356.765700	4339.105906
162	94.560898	3	315.768688	2996.295793
311	98.333232	2	102.839859	2830.060009
449	93.401160	1	62.936118	4159.687843
923	97.722119	1	68.425069	3677.811971
411	95.013256	2	316.018205	3592.387199
651	95.034241	5	452.055364	3699.554499
749	93.654123	1	20.933010	2843.012500

Figure 9.6   A sample of data simulated for this housing data example. Here x_1 is the temperature outside. x_2 is the number of people living in the house. x_3 is the cost of food for the month.

	x_1	x_2	x_3	y
x_1	1.000000	0.024543	0.026800	0.090549
x_2	0.024543	1.000000	0.649954	0.340209
x_3	0.026800	0.649954	1.000000	0.504172
y	0.090549	0.340209	0.504172	1.000000

Figure 9.7   The correlation matrix for the housing data simulated earlier. You can see most variables are somewhat strongly correlated with each other, except for x_1.

It produced the plots in Figure 9.8.

When you're examining scatter plots, the standard convention is to place the dependent variable on the vertical axis and the independent variable on the horizontal axis. The bottom row of the scatter matrix has y on the vertical axis and the different x variables on the horizontal.

You can see there's a lot of noise in the data, but this is okay. The important thing is that the average y value at each x value follows the model. In this case, you want the average y value at each x value to be increasing linearly with x.

Looking at the bottom left plot in the matrix, you see the points don't seem to be getting higher or lower (on average) as you go from left to right in the graph. There seems to be a weak relationship between x_1 and y. Next, you see the data for x_2 is in bands at integer values of x_2. This is because x_2 is a discrete variable. Since there are many other factors that determine the value of y, there is some

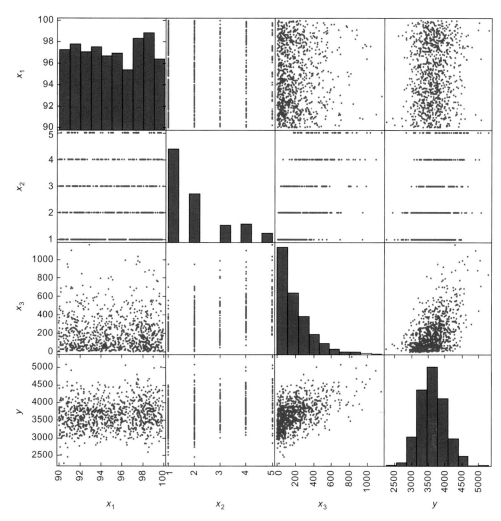

Figure 9.8 The scatter matrix for our simulated living expense data. The bottom row will be most important.

spread to the data at each value of x_2. If x_2 were the only factor, then the y values would take on only one specific value at each x_2 value. Instead, they follow at different distributions at each x_2 value.

Next, you can see the plot of x_3 and y. You can see again the data points seem to be increasing linearly (on average), but again there is a lot of noise around the trend. You can see the scatter plot is denser at smaller values of x_3. If you compare the scatter plot with the histogram for x_3, you can see that this is because most of the data points have smaller values of x_3.

Often, when people first see data like the plot of y versus x_3, they think a linear model can't possibly work. After all, if you tried to make a prediction with the linear model, you'd do a very bad job. It would just guess the average y value at each x value. Since there is so much variation around the average y value at each x value, your predictions would tend to be far from the true values.

There are two reasons why these models are still very useful. The first is that you can include many more factors than these two-dimensional plots can show. While there is still a lot of variation around the average y value at each x in these scatter plots, there will tend to be less variation if we plot the data in higher dimensions (using more of the x variables). As we include more and more independent variables, our predictions will tend to get better.

Second, predictive power isn't the only use for a model. Far more often, you're interested in learning the model parameters rather than predicting a precise y value. If I learn, for example, that the coefficient on temperature is 10, then I know that for each degree of monthly average temperature increase, there is a ten dollar increase in monthly average living expenses. If I'm working at an energy company, that information might be useful for predicting revenue based on weather forecasts!

How can we see this interpretation of this parameter? Let's look at our model again.

$$y = \beta_1 x_1 + \beta_3 x_3 \tag{9.10}$$

What happens if you increase the month's average temperature by one unit while keeping x_3 fixed? You'll see that y increases by β_1 units! If you can measure β_1 using a regression, then you can see how much temperature changes tend to increase living expenses.

Finally, you'll examine the graph for y. It looks like the distribution takes on a bell curve, but it's slightly skewed. Linear regression requires that the distribution of the errors is Gaussian, and this will probably violate that assumption. You can use a general linear model with a gamma distribution to try to do a better job, but for now let's see what you can do with the ordinary least squares model. Often, if the residuals are close enough to Gaussian, the error in the results is small. This will be the case here.

Let's actually perform the regression now. It will be clear in a minute why we've omitted x_2 from Equation (9.2). We'll use statsmodels here. Statsmodels doesn't include a y intercept, so you'll add one automatically. A y intercept is just a constant value added on to each data point. You can introduce one by adding a column of all ones as a new variable. Then, when it finds the coefficient for that variable, it's simply added to each row! For a fun exercise, try omitting this yourself, and see what happens.

```
1  X['intercept'] = 1.
2  model = OLS(X['$y$'], X[[u'$x_1$', u'$x_2$', u'$x_3$', 'intercept']],
3              data=X)
4  result = model.fit()
5  result.summary()
```

Figure 9.9 shows the results. There are a lot of numbers in this table, so we'll walk through the most important ones. You can confirm that you used the right variables by seeing the dependent variable (top of the table) is y, and the list of coefficients are for the independent variables you're regressing on.

Next, you have the R squared or R^2. This is a measure of how well the independent variables account for variation in the dependent variable. If they fully explain the variation in y, then the R^2 will be 1.

Dep. Variable:	y	R-squared:	0.214
Model:	OLS	Adj. R-squared:	0.211
Method:	Least Squares	F-statistic:	90.16
Date:	Sat, 15 Jul 2017	Prob (F-statistic):	1.28e-51
Time:	18:22:47	Log-Likelihood:	-7302.5
No. Observations:	1000	AIC:	1.461e+04
Df Residuals:	996	BIC:	1.463e+04
Df Model:	3		
Covariance Type:	nonrobust		

	coef	std err	t	P>|t|	[0.025	0.975]
x_1	10.6919	3.886	2.751	0.006	3.066	18.318
x_2	-3.5779	12.530	-0.286	0.775	-28.166	21.010
x_3	0.9796	0.082	11.889	0.000	0.818	1.141
intercept	2436.0517	370.468	6.576	0.000	1709.065	3163.039

Omnibus:	21.264	Durbin-Watson:	1.884
Prob(Omnibus):	0.000	Jarque-Bera (JB):	22.183
Skew:	0.364	Prob(JB):	1.52e-05
Kurtosis:	3.043	Cond.No.	9.34e+03

Figure 9.9 The results for the regression on all the measured dependent variables (including a y-intercept)

If they explain none of it, it will be zero (or close to zero, due to measurement error). It's important to include a y intercept for the R^2 to have a positive value and a clear interpretation. The R^2 is actually just the proportion of the variance in y that is explained by the independent variables. If you define the "residuals" of the model as the left-over part of y that isn't explained by the model,

$$r_i = y_i - \hat{y}_i \qquad (9.11)$$

then the residuals are all 0 if the model fits perfectly. The further off the prediction is, the more the residuals tend to vary around the average y value. So, the better y is explained by the data, the smaller the variance of the residuals. This leads to our intuition for the definition of R^2,

$$R^2 = \frac{SS_{total} - SS_{residual}}{SS_{total}} \qquad (9.12)$$

where $SS_{total} = \Sigma_{i=1}^N (y_i - \bar{y})^2$ is the sum of squared differences from the y values and the average y value, $\bar{y}$, and $SS_{residual} = \Sigma_{i=1}^N r_i^2$ is the sum of squared residuals. You can make this more intuitive by dividing all the sums of squares by N to get the (biased) estimate of the population variance, $R^2 = \frac{\sigma_y^2 - \sigma_r^2}{\sigma_y^2}$, so the R^2 is just the remaining variance!

You can do better than this by just dividing by the correct number of degrees of freedom to get unbiased estimates for the variances. If k is the number of independent variables (excluding the y intercept), then the variance for y has $N - 1$ degrees of freedom, and the variance for the residuals has $n - k - 1$ degrees of freedom. The unbiased variance estimates are $\hat{\sigma}_y^2 = SS_{total}/(N - 1)$ and $\hat{\sigma}_r^2 = SS_{residual}/(N - k - 1)$. Plugging these into the formula, you get the definition for the adjusted R^2.

$$R_{adj}^2 = \frac{\hat{\sigma}^2 - \hat{\sigma}_r^2}{\hat{\sigma}_y^2} \tag{9.13}$$

This is better to use in practice since the estimators for the variance are unbiased.

Next, you can see in the table of coefficients (in the middle of the figure) that the coefficients (coef column) for x_1 and x_3 are very close to the values you entered for the *beta* variables when you created our data! They don't match exactly because of all the noise from x_4 that you're not able to model (since you didn't measure it).

Instead of trying to get an estimate for the value of the coefficient, it's nicer to measure a confidence interval for the parameters! If you look to the right of the coefficients, you'll see the columns 0.025 and 0.975. These are the 2.5 and 97.5 percentiles for the coefficients. These are the lower and upper bounds of the 95 percent confidence intervals! You can see that both of these contain the true values and that x_3 is much more precisely measured than x_1. Remember that x_1 had a much weaker correlation with y than x_3, and you could hardly see the linear trend from the scatter plot. It makes sense that you've measured it less precisely.

There's another interesting problem here. In this example, x_2 causes x_3 but has no direct effect on y. Its only effect on y was by changing x_2. This may seem like a contrived example, but a less extreme version of this will happen in real data sets. In general, there might be both direct and indirect effects of x_2 on y. Notice that the measurement for the coefficient of x_2 has a very wide confidence interval! This is the problem on collinearity in independent variables: generally, if independent variables are related to each other, their standard errors (and so their confidence intervals) will be large.

In this example, there's actually a nuance that's not clear because the collinearity is so large. If the confidence interval were narrower on the x_2 coefficient, you'd see it's actually narrowed in around $\beta_2 = 0$. This is because x_3 contains all the information about x_2 that is relevant for determining y. If you drop x_3 from the regression (try it!), you'll measure a coefficient for x_2 where $80 < \beta_2 < 118$ at the 95 percent confidence level. You should proceed by dropping x_2 from the regression entirely. You'll get the final result in Figure 9.10. Notice that the confidence interval for x_3 has narrowed, but the R^2 hasn't changed significantly!

You'll use these concepts throughout the book. In particular, R^2 is a good metric for evaluating any model that has a real-valued output. Now, you'll examine your modeling assumptions. Working strictly with linear models can be too restrictive. You can do better, without having to go beyond ordinary least-squares regression.

Dep. Variable:	y	R-squared:	0.214
Model:	OLS	Adj. R-squared:	0.212
Method:	Least Squares	F-statistic:	135.3
Date:	Sat, 15 Jul 2017	Prob (F-statistic):	1.01e-52
Time:	20:42:45	Log-Likelihood:	-7302.5
No. Observations:	1000	AIC:	1.461e+04
Df Residuals:	997	BIC:	1.463e+04
Df Model:	2		
Covariance Type:	nonrobust		

	coef	std err	t	P>|t|	[0.025	0.975]
x_1	10.7272	3.882	2.763	0.006	3.109	18.346
x_3	0.9634	0.060	16.163	0.000	0.846	1.080
intercept	2428.7296	369.409	6.575	0.000	1703.821	3153.638

Omnibus:	21.411	Durbin-Watson:	1.883
Prob(Omnibus):	0.000	Jarque-Bera (JB):	22.345
Skew:	0.366	Prob(JB):	1.41e-05
Kurtosis:	3.044	Cond.No.	9.31e+03

Figure 9.10   The results for the regression on the measured dependent variables excluding x_2

9.3   Nonlinear Regression with Linear Regression

The model used for ordinary least squares regression might sound overly restrictive, but it can include nonlinear functions as well. If you'd like to fit $y = \beta x^2$ to your data, then instead of passing in x as your dependent variable, you can simply square it and regress on x^2. You can even use this approach to fit complicated functions like $cos(x)$, or nonlinear functions in several variables, like $x_1 sin(x_2)$. The problem, of course, is that you have to come up with the function you'd like to regress and compute it in order to do the regression.

Let's do an example with some toy data. As usual, we'll use numpy and pandas to work with the data, and we'll use statsmodels for the regression. The first step is to generate the data.

```
1  N = 1000
2
3  x1 = np.random.uniform(-2.*np.pi,2*np.pi,size=N)
4  y = np.cos(x1)
5
6  X = pd.DataFrame({'y': y, 'x1': x1})
```

Now, you'll plot it to see what it looks like. The cos function will make this very nonlinear. It's easy to see with a scatter plot.

```
1 X.plot(y='y', x='x1', style='bo', alpha=0.3, xlim=(-10,10),
2         ylim=(-1.1, 1.1), title='The plot of $y = cos(x_1)$')
```

This generates Figure 9.11.

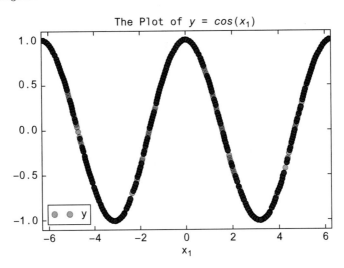

Figure 9.11   The graph of $y = \cos(x_1)$. A linear regression will fit this poorly, passing a line through the mean of the data at $y = 0$.

Without using the trick, a linear regression should try to fit this graph of $y = \beta_1 x_1$ by just fitting to the mean as well as it could. It would succeed by just finding $\beta_1 = 0$. We can confirm this by trying it.

```
1 model = OLS(X['y'], X['x1'], data=X)
2 result = model.fit()
3 result.summary()
```

You get the result in Figure 9.12.

You can see it's just a flat line with slope zero since the coefficient on x_1 is zero. Now, you can try the nonlinear version. First, you need to make a new column in the data.

```
1 X['cos(x1)'] = np.cos(X['x1'])
```

Now, you can regress on this new column to see how well it works.

```
1 model = OLS(X['y'], X[['cos(x1)']], data=X)
2 result = model.fit()
3 result.summary()
```

Dep. Variable:	y	R-squared:	0.000
Model:	OLS	Adj. R-squared:	-0.001
Method:	Least Squares	F-statistic:	0.2039
Date:	Sat, 15 Jul 2017	Prob (F-statistic):	0.652
Time:	15:16:34	Log-Likelihood:	-1073.7
No. Observations:	1000	AIC:	2149.
Df Residuals:	999	BIC:	2154.
Df Model:	1		
Covariance Type:	nonrobust		

	coef	std err	t	P>|t|	[0.025	0.975]
x_1	-0.0028	0.006	-0.452	0.652	-0.015	0.009

Omnibus:	0.106	Durbin-Watson:	2.074
Prob(Omnibus):	0.948	Jarque-Bera (JB):	94.636
Skew:	-0.025	Prob(JB):	2.82e-21
Kurtosis:	1.494	Cond.No.	1.00

Figure 9.12   The result of a linear regression on $y = \cos(x)$. Notice that the coefficient is consistent with zero. If you allowed a y-intercept in this regression, you would have found that it was zero too.

You find the result in Figure 9.13 on page 108.

Many of the metrics diverge! The R^2 is one, and the confidence interval on the coefficient is just a single point. This is because there's no noise in the function. All the residuals are zero since you've fully explained the variation in y.

9.3.1   Uncertainty

One great thing about linear regression is that we understand noise in the parameter estimates very well. If you assume the noise term, ϵ, is drawn from a Gaussian distribution (or that sample sizes are large, so the central limit theorem applies), then you can get good estimates for the coefficient confidence intervals. These will be reported by statsmodels under the 0.025 and 0.975 columns for a 95 *percent* confidence interval.

What happens if these assumptions are violated? If that happens, you can't necessarily trust the confidence intervals reported by statsmodels. The most common violations are either that the residuals are not Gaussian or that the variance of the residuals is not constant with the independent variable.

Dep. Variable:	y	R-squared:	1.000
Model:	OLS	Adj. R-squared:	1.000
Method:	Least Squares	F-statistic:	inf
Date:	Sat, 15 Jul 2017	Prob (F-statistic):	0.00
Time:	15:24:17	Log-Likelihood:	inf
No. Observations:	1000	AIC:	-inf
Df Residuals:	999	BIC:	-inf
Df Model:	1		
Convariance Type:	nonrobust		

	Coef	Std err	t	P>|t|	[0.025	0.975]
cos(x1)	1.0000	0	inf	0.000	1.000	1.000

Omnibus:	1.006	Durbin-Watson:	nan
prob(Omnibus):	0.605	Jarque-Bera (JB):	375.000
Skew:	0.000	Prob(JB):	3.71e-82
Kurtosis:	0.000	Cond. No.	1.00

Figure 9.13 The result of a linear regression on the transformed column cos(x). Now, we find the coefficient is consistent with 1, suggesting that the function is $y = 1. * cos(x)$.

You can tell if the residuals are Gaussian using some of the summary statistics reported with your regression results. In particular, the skew, kurtosis, and Jarque-Bera statistic are all good tests of Gaussian distribution; the skew is 0, and the kurtosis is 3. Significant deviations from these indicate the distribution isn't Gaussian.

The skew and kurtosis are combined to give the Jarque-Bera statistic. The Jarque-Bera test tests the null hypothesis that the data was drawn from a Gaussian distribution against the alternative that it was not. If *Prob(JB)* is large in your results, then it was likely that your distributions were drawn from a Gaussian distribution.

Another handy test is to plot a histogram of your residuals. These are stored on the resid attribute of your regression results. You can even plot them against your independent variable to check for heteroskedasticity.

If you have non-Gaussian residuals, you can use a general linear model instead of a linear model. You should plot the residuals or conditional distributions of the data to find a more appropriate distribution to describe the residuals.

A solution when you have heteroskedasticity is to use robust standard errors. In some fields (e.g., economics), this is the default choice. The result of using robust standard errors is larger confidence intervals. In the presence of homoskedasticity, this results in overly conservative estimates of standard errors. To use robust confidence intervals in statsmodels, you can set the cov_type argument of the fit method of the OLS regression object.

9.4 Random Forest

Random forests [11], as the name suggests, consists of a combination of "decision trees." In this section, you'll learn about decision trees. You'll see how they can combine to form random forests, which are a great first algorithm to try for machine-learning problems.

9.4.1 Decision Trees

You can try to fit functions using simple flow charts, or decision trees, as follows. Take a look at the function given by the blue curve in Figure 9.14.

You could try to make some simple rules to approximate the function. A rough estimate might be "If x is greater than 0.5, y should be 0.58. If x is less than 0.5, y should be 0.08." That would give the orange curve in Figure 9.14. While it's not a very good estimate, we can see that it's better than just guessing a uniform constant value! We're just using the average value of the function over each range.

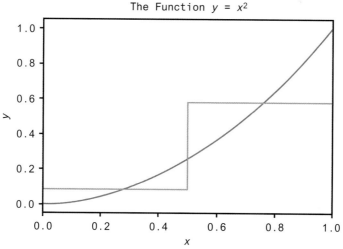

Figure 9.14   An approximation to the function $y = x^2$ on the interval [0,1] using a single decision

This is the beginning of the logic for building a decision tree. We can draw a diagram for this decision tree in Figure 9.15.

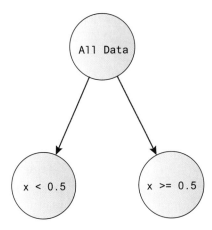

Figure 9.15   A diagram for a decision tree. You can imagine each data point falls down the tree, going along the branches indicated by the logic on each node.

Here, you start with all of the data at the top of the decision tree. Then, at the branch, you map all points with $x < 0.5$ to the left and all points with $x \geq 0.5$ to the right. The left points get one output value, 0.08, and the right points get the other 0.58.

You can make the problem more complex by adding more branches. With each branch, you can say "...and this other decision also holds." For example, making one more decision for each of these branches, you get the tree in Figure 9.16.

This tree produces a better fit to the function, because you can subdivide the space more. You can see this in Figure 9.16.

One great strength of decision trees is their interpretability. You have a set of logical rules that lead to each outcome. You can even draw the tree diagram to walk a layperson through how the decision is made!

In this example, we chose our splitting points as half the domain. In general, decision tree algorithms make a choice to minimize a loss (usually the mean-squared error) with each split. For that reason, you'd likely have finer splits when the curve is steeper and coarser splits when the curve is flatter.

Decision trees also have to decide how many split points to use. They'll keep splitting until there are very few data points left at each node and then stop. The nodes at the ends of the tree are the *terminal nodes or the leaf nodes*. After building the tree stops, the algorithm will decide which terminal nodes to cut out by trying to balance loss against the number of terminal nodes. See [12] for more details.

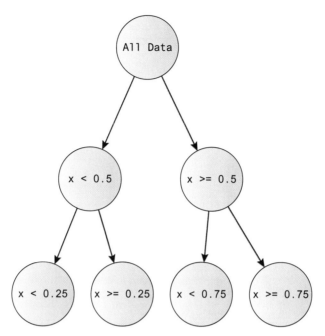

Figure 9.16 You can fit data increasingly precisely by adding more decisions. As the complexity grows, you risk overfitting. Imagine the case where each data point maps to a single node!

You can use the implementation of decision trees in the sklearn package like this:

```
1  from sklearn.tree import DecisionTreeRegressor
2
3  model = DecisionTreeRegressor()
4  model = model.fit(x, y)
5  y_decision_tree = model.predict([[xi] for xi in np.arange(0, 1,0.1)])
```

Figure 9.17 shows the result. The line is in blue, and the decision tree fit is in red. If we plot the decision tree fit as a line against this one, the overlap is too close to tell the lines apart!

This same process can be used for classification. If you have classes $i \in \{1, \ldots, K\}$, then you can talk about the proportion of data points at node k as p_{ik}. Then, the simple rule for classification at the leaf nodes would just be to output the class k at node i for which p_{ik} is the largest!

One issue with decision trees is that the split points can change substantially when you add or remove data points from your data set. The reason for that is all of the decisions that happen below a node depend on the split points above them! You can get rid of some of that instability by averaging the results of lots of trees together, which you'll see in more detail in the next section. You lose interpretability by doing this since now you're dealing with a collection of decision trees!

Another issue is that decision trees don't handle class imbalance well. If they're just looking to minimize a measure of prediction accuracy, then poor performance on a small subset of the data won't hurt the model too much. A remedy for this is to balance the classes before fitting a decision

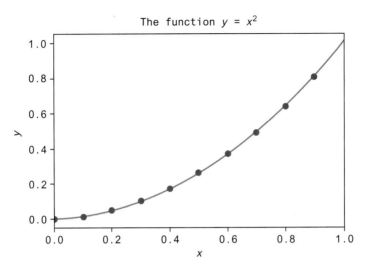

Figure 9.17   A decision tree (blue line) fit using sklearn to data (red dots) from the function $y = x^2$ on $[0, 1]$

tree. You can do that by sampling out the larger class while leaving the smaller class untouched or by drawing random samples from the smaller class (with replacement) to create a large sample that repeats data points.

Finally, because decision trees make decisions at lines of constant values of variables (e.g., the decision "$x > 0.5$"), decision boundaries tend to be rectangles or combinations of rectangles that form together as a patchwork. They also tend to be oriented along the coordinate axes.

Now, let's look at the performance increases we can get by averaging lots of decision trees together.

9.4.2   Random Forests

Random forests exploit a technique called *bootstrap aggregating*, or *bagging*. The idea is that you draw a random sample (a "bootstrap" sample) of your data with replacement and use that sample to train a decision tree. You repeat the process to train another tree, and another, and so on.

To predict the output for a single data point, you calculate the output for each decision tree. You average the results together ("aggregate" them), and that becomes the output of your model.

The hope is that you get a good sampling of the different possible trees that you can form due to the sensitivity of the decision trees to the sample, and you can average that variability by averaging over these trees.

You know that when you average random variables together, the error in the mean decreases as the number of samples increases like $\sigma_\mu^2 = \sigma^2/N$, where σ_μ^2 is the variance of the mean, and σ^2 is the variance of the output variable. That's true for independent samples, but with dependent samples, the story is a little different.

When you bootstrap, you can regard each sample of data as a random sample that leads to a random output from a decision tree (after training on that sample). If you want to understand how the variance of the random forest output decreases with the number of trees, you can similarly look at this variance formula. Unfortunately, these tree outputs are not independent: every bootstrap sample is drawn from the same data set. You can show [12] that if the tree outputs are correlated with correlation ρ, then the variance in the output is like this:

$$\sigma_\mu^2 = \rho\sigma^2 + \frac{1-\rho}{N}\sigma^2 \tag{9.14}$$

That means that as you increase the number of trees, N, the variance doesn't keep decreasing as it does with independent samples. The lowest it can get is $\rho\sigma^2$.

You can do best, then, by making sure the tree outputs are as uncorrelated as possible. One common trick is sample a subset of the input data's columns when training each tree. That way, each tree will tend to use a slightly different subset of variables!

Another trick is to try to force trees to be independent with an iterative procedure: after training each tree, have the next one predict the residuals left over from training the last. Repeat the procedure until termination. This way, the next tree will learn the weaknesses of the tree before it! This procedure is called *boosting* and can let you turn even very marginal learning algorithms into strong ones. This technique is not used in random forests but is used in many algorithms and can outperform random forests in some contexts, when enough weak learners are added.

Now, let's see how to implement random forest regression. Let's take the same data as before but add some noise to it. We'll try a decision tree and a random forest and see which has the better performance on a test set.

First, let's generate new data, adding some random noise ϵ drawn from a Gaussian distribution. This data is plotted in Figure 9.18.

Now, you can train the random forest and the decision tree on this data. You'll create test and train sets by randomly dividing your data into a training set and a test set and by training a decision tree and a random forest on the training set. You can start with just one decision tree in the random forest.

```
1  from sklearn.model_selection import train_test_split
2  from sklearn.ensemble import RandomForestRegressor
3  from sklearn.tree import DecisionTreeRegressor
4
5  x_train, x_test, y_train, y_test = train_test_split(x, y)
6
7  decision_tree = DecisionTreeRegressor()
8  decision_tree = decision_tree.fit(x_train.reshape(-1, 1), y_train)
9
10 random_forest = RandomForestRegressor(n_estimators=1)
11 random_forest = random_forest.fit(x_train.reshape(-1, 1), y_train)
```

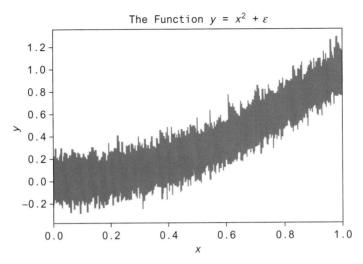

Figure 9.18   Noise added to the function $y = x^2$. The goal is to fit the average value at each x, or $E[y|x]$.

Then, you can check the model performance on the test set by comparing the R^2 of each model. You can compute the R^2 of the decision tree like this:

```
1 decision_tree.score(x_test.reshape(-1, 1), y_test)
```

and of the random forest like this:

```
1 random_forest.score(x_test.reshape(-1, 1), y_test)
```

The decision tree has an $R^2 = 0.80$, and the random forest with one tree gives $R^2 = 0.80$. They perform almost the same (smaller decimals are different). Of course, the random forest can have many more than just one tree. Let's see how it improves as you add trees. You'll want to measure the error bars on these estimates since the random forests train by bootstrapping.

```
 1 scores = []
 2 score_std = []
 3 for num_tree in range(10):
 4     sample = []
 5     for i in range(10):
 6         decision_tree = DecisionTreeRegressor()
 7         decision_tree = decision_tree.fit(x_train.reshape(-1, 1),
 8                                           y_train)
 9
10         random_forest = RandomForestRegressor(n_estimators=num_tree\
11                                           + 1)
12         random_forest = random_forest.fit(x_train.reshape(-1, 1),
13                                           y_train)
```

```
14        sample.append(random_forest.score(x_test.reshape(-1, 1),
15                                           y_test))
16    scores.append(np.mean(sample))
17    score_std.append(np.std(sample) / np.sqrt(len(sample)))
```

You can use this data to get the plot in Figure 9.19. The performance increases sharply as you go from one to two trees but doesn't increase very much after that. Performance plateaus around five or six trees in this example.

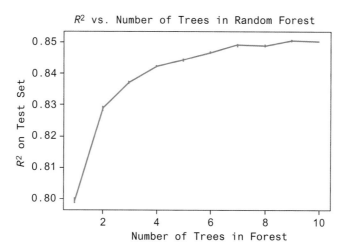

Figure 9.19   You can see here that as the complexity of the random forest (number of trees) increases, you do an increasingly good job of fitting the data (R^2 increases). There's a point of vanishing returns, and forests with more than seven trees don't seem to do much better than forests with seven trees.

You might have expected this kind of result. There's unexplainable noise in the data set because of the noise we added. You shouldn't be able to perform better than $R^2 = 0.89$. Even then, you're limited by other factors like the heuristics involved in fitting the model and the dependence between trees in the forest.

9.5   Conclusion

In this chapter, you saw the basic tools used to do regression analysis. You learned how to choose a model based on the data and how to fit it. You saw some basic examples for context and how to interpret the model parameters. At this point, you should feel relatively comfortable building basic models yourself!

Classification and Clustering

10.1 Introduction

Classification algorithms solve the problem of sorting items into categories. Given a set, N, of samples composed of features, X, and a set, C, of categories, classification algorithms answer the question "What is the most likely category for each sample?"

Clustering algorithms take a set of objects and some notion of closeness and group the objects together using some criterion. Clustering algorithms answer the question "Given a collection of objects and relationships between the objects, what is the best way to arrange them into groups, or *clusters*, to satisfy a specific objective?" That objective could be compactness of the groups, in the case of k-means clustering. It might be making sure connections fall within groups more often than not, in the case of modularity optimization.

In both cases, the range of the mapping is discrete. Both types of algorithms can handle vector input. One of the major differences is that clustering is often *unsupervised*, while classification is typically *supervised*. In the case of supervised learning, you have a set of input features and expected outputs. You tune the model so it maps each item to the expected output on the training set. This contrasts with the case of unsupervised learning. With unsupervised learning, you have the item features but no outputs for each item. Instead, you're trying to learn a mapping that most naturally groups items together based on their features. We'll cover this in a little more detail as we cover a few different algorithms.

A classification example we'll use is from medical trials. You have the value of a test result, a real number (say, the concentration of a chemical), and need to say whether a condition is present (a "positive" test result) or whether it isn't (a "negative" test result). You have a lot of past data, and you see that there's a fuzzy boundary: while higher test values tend to be positive cases, many negative cases have higher test values than positive cases. What is the best test you we can construct? How do you balance false positives (saying the test is positive when the condition isn't present) with false negatives (failing to detect the condition when it's present)?

Logistic regression will be an illustrative example. We'll walk you through this to understand the nuances at play and then cover naive Bayes, a more model-independent approach. We'll move into k-means, our the first clustering method, and go through a few more clustering methods that operate on graphs. Finally, we'll relax the concept of a category and talk about nearest-neighbor methods.

10.2   Logistic Regression

Let's look at toy data from a test you're developing to detect a medical condition. Say you measure the concentration of a chemical and plot it on the x-axis. You record whether someone had the condition and code it as a 0 if they don't and a 1 if they do. You plot this on the y-axis. You can see the data in Figure 10.1. Here, we've centered the data so that $x_1 = 0$ at the average test result.

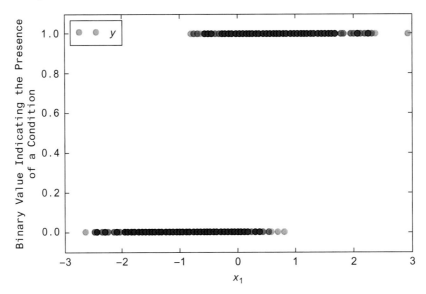

Figure 10.1   Some data from a toy medical test. The variable measured for the test is the concentration of a chemical, plotted on the x-axis. The y-axis shows whether the condition is present. You can see there's a lot of overlap around the average test outcome.

From the figure, you can see you have a choice to make. While this is a more extreme case, diagnositic tests have to worry about the same trade-off. You can say the test is positive if $x_1 > -1$ and capture all of the positive results, but then you also have many false positives. You can say it's positive if $x_1 > 1$, so you get only positive results, but then you have many false negatives. You can set the cutoff in between these values, and you get a mixture of false positives and negatives.

Wherever you set the threshold, you can calculate the number of false positives, false negatives, true positives, and true negatives. What you really need is the probabilities of these outcomes given the data you have. Then you can make an informed choice for your cutoff. In machine learning, these cutoffs are known as *decision boundaries*.

Logistic regression is a classification technique that gives the probability of an element belonging to one of two classes; let's call them P and N for positive and negative. The logistic function is given by the following:

$$logit(x) = \frac{e^x}{1 + e^x} \tag{10.1}$$

and it is always between zero and one. This is what lets us interpret the output as a probability. In general, the logistic regression is done not just on one variable but on several and is fit as a linear model. You can do this by replacing x with a more general form, such as the following, for k variables:

$$y = logit(\beta_0 + \beta_1 x_1 + \beta_2 x_2 + ... + \beta_k x_k) \tag{10.2}$$

In one dimension, the logistic (or *logit*) function is used to score the data set to give the probabilities that a data point belongs to each class. When the probability of the class passes $p = 0.5$, the assignment goes to that class. If you draw the line $p = 0.5$ on the medical data plot, it would be right at $x_1 = 0$. Let's look at the logistic function fitted to your data Figure 10.2 so you can see this.

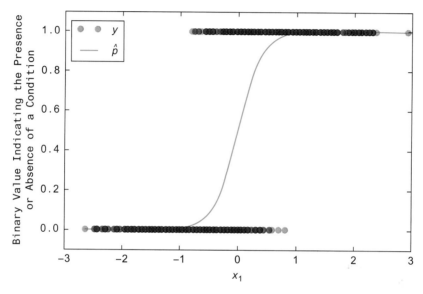

Figure 10.2   The logit function fitted to this data set. The logistic regression puts its decision function at $\hat{p} = 0.5$, but this implementation just gives you probabilities as its output. The probabilities are just the probability that $y = 1$ given the value of x_1.

On the decision boundary, the probability of an element falling into one of two classes is 0.5. If you look at the thresholds we mentioned earlier, at $x_1 = \pm 1$, you see that the logistic function nicely touches the $\hat{p} = 0$ at $x_1 = -1$ and $\hat{p} = 1$ at $x_1 = 1$. You can see that the choices you were considering just correspond to being very sure of the y value. The overlapping region in between is where the logistic function makes its transition. The width of the transition region is fitted to the data and controlled by the model parameters. If x_1 is good at predicting y values, there will be less overlap and a sharper transition.

Now, let's evaluate the model's performance. You can probably see now that more overlap between the two classes means worse prediction power. In the case where the two overlap exactly, x_1 would be useless for distinguishing the two classes: they'd be as likely to be in class P as class N.

There are some evaluation metrics that naively look useful but turn out to be deceptive. We'll call a true positive *tp* and a true negative *tn*. A false positive is *fp*, and a false negative is *fn*. Then the total correct answers are just $c = tp + tn$, and the total answer is $N = tp + fp + tn + fn$. The proportion of correct classification is called the *accuracy*, and is just c/N.

Why is accuracy deceptive? Consider the case when you have "class imbalance": 95 percent of examples in your data are positive cases, and 5 percent are negative cases. Then, if your classifier simply assigns the positive label to everything, it will have 95 percent accuracy! In our example, this is the case when the decision boundary is below the minimum value of x_1. Clearly, this classifier has learned nothing about the x values and is only using the imbalance in the y values to get high accuracy. You need a metric that can tell you when the classifier has actually learned something.

Let's think of what happens to the true positive rate ($tp/tp + fn$) and the false positive rate ($fp/fp + tn$) as you raise the decision boundary in this example. If the boundary is at $x_1 = x_{decision}$ and $x_{decision}$ is lower than all the measured x_1, then everything is classified as positive. The true positive rate is 100 percent, but the false positive rate is also 100 percent. On the opposite end, these are both 0 percent. Generally, these will vary as you increase the decision boundary from low x_1 to high x_1.

What happens if you just randomly guess "positive" with probability p? $p = 1$ or $p = 0$ gives the same results as the two cases shown earlier! $p = 0.5$ gives half of the true positives, on average, so you'll get a true positive rate of 0.5. The same happens with the false positives. You can apply this same logic for all values of p and see that a classifier that's just guessing "positive" with probability p will give a true positive rate of p, on average, and a false positive rate of p as well. If you plot the true versus false positives in a graph, you'll see a classifier that's just guessing falls along the 45-degree line from $(0, 0)$ to $(1, 1)$, as in Figure 10.3. The more area under this curve the better, where an area of 0.5 is just guessing. The name for this curve is the *receiver operator characteristic* (ROC) curve, from its history in object detection with RADAR.

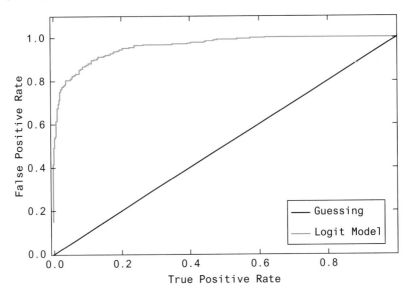

Figure 10.3 How the logistic regression model performs against guessing as you vary the decision boundary

The area under the ROC curve (auroc) has another nice interpretation. It's the probability that the classifier will assign a random positive example a higher probability of being in the positive class than a negative example. You can regard this as its ability to discriminate between positive and negative cases!

When you move into two independent variables, instead of having a point $x_1 = x_{decision}$ as your decision boundary, you have a line. All points on one side of the line have probability higher than $p = 0.5$ of being in class P, and all points on the other side of lower probability.

Just as linear regression parameters have a nice interpretation as the change in the dependent variable per unit change in an independent variable, logistic regression coefficients have a useful interpretation. Let's consider changing the value of x_1 to $x_1 + 1$. Then, you can write the predicted value of y as follows:

$$P(Y = 1|X_1 = x_1 + 1) = \frac{e^{\beta_0 + \beta_1(x_1+1)}}{1 + e^{\beta_0 + \beta_1(x_1+1)}} \tag{10.3}$$

You can look at the odds that $y = 1$ by comparing this with $P(Y = 1|X_1 = x_1)$ with $P(Y = 0|X_1 = x_1) = 1 - P(Y = 1|X_1 = x_1)$ (try the algebra yourself!).

$$\frac{P(Y = 1|X_1 = x_1)}{P(Y = 0|X_1 = x_1)} = e^{\beta_0 + \beta_1 x_1} \tag{10.4}$$

Then you can see that if you add 1 to x_1, you just increase the odds by a factor of e^{β_1}!

$$\frac{P(Y = 1|X_1 = x_1 + 1)}{P(Y = 0|X_1 = x_1 + 1)} = e^{\beta_0 + \beta_1(x_1+1)} = e^{\beta_0 + \beta_1 x_1} e^{\beta_1} = e^{\beta_1} \frac{P(Y = 1|X_1 = x_1)}{P(Y = 0|X_1 = x_1)} \tag{10.5}$$

This leads you to the interpretation: if you increase x_1 by one unit, you increase the odds that $y = 1$ by e^{β_1} units! If, for example, $e^{\beta_1} = 2$, then increasing x_1 by one unit makes it twice as likely that $y = 1$.

Logistic Regression Summary	
The Algorithm	Logistic regression predicts binary outcomes from linear combinations of features. It's useful for providing estimates of how much more likely outcomes will be given features and is best when you don't expect strong feature interactions.
Time Complexity	$O(N)$, with N data points if trained using SGD. $O(NK^2)$ per iteration with Newton's method.
Memory Considerations	The feature matrix can get large when you have sparse features! Use sparse encodings when possible.

10.2.1 Assumptions

The probability of a given class, $\mathcal{K}$, given a particular input for some dimension, $\mathcal{C}$, of the data set follows a Bernoulli distribution since the outcome is binary. The range of the classifier is the probability an element of the data set that belongs to $\mathcal{K}$. Membership in $\mathcal{K}$ is assumed to depend on $\mathcal{C}$.

10.2.2 Time Complexity

Prediction is linear. Training time complexity depends on the algorithm. With stochastic gradient descent, it's $O(N)$ for N training examples. For iteratively reweighted least squares, it uses Newton's method with $O(NK^2)$ per iteration. For maximum likelihood, it depends on the fitting method you use; see, for example, [13] for details.

10.2.3   Memory Considerations

With linear regression algorithms in general, you'll often code categorical variables as "dummy variables," where a variable with C categories will map to $C - 1$ binary variables (plus a y-intercept). With this coding, you go from N values to $(C - 1)N$. The quickly increased number of values to store are mostly zeros with this coding scheme because only one of the $C - 1$ columns are nonzero for one data point (i.e., when the categories are exclusive). For this reason, you'll usually want to use a sparse coding for the input data, as in the *scipy.sparse* module.

10.2.4   Tools

Scikit learn has an implementation at *sklearn.linear_model.LogisticRegression*. Note that this implementation regularizes by default so gives biased (shrunken) estimators for regression coefficients. Statsmodels has an implementation at *statsmodels.discrete.discrete_model.Logit*. We recommend this implementation when you want unbiased model parameters, as well as error estimates. MLPACK (www.mlpack.org/) has an implementation of logistic regression at *mlpack::regression::LogisticRegression*.

10.3   Bayesian Inference, Naive Bayes

Logistic regression is great for binary classification problems. It happens to be robust to class imbalance, and it produces interpretable results. One shortcoming might be the fact that it relies on linear decision boundaries. It trades generality for statistical efficiency and simplicity. You might want to move away from that side of the trade-off and toward methods that also lend themselves well to multiclass classification. Naive Bayes is a classic example. It's often used in spam filtering and performs well on high-dimensional feature spaces.

Basically, the probability of an element belonging to a particular class, $Y = i$, given some set of features, $\mathbf{X}$, is as follows:

$$P(Y|X) \tag{10.6}$$

Bayes' theorem states the following:

$$P(A|B) = \frac{P(B|A)P(A)}{P(B)} \tag{10.7}$$

This lets you rewrite your equation as follows for k features.

$$P(Y|X) = P(X|Y)P(Y)/P(X) \tag{10.8}$$

Then, if you make the assumption that the features are independent of each other (given Y), you can write this as follows:

$$P(Y = 1|X = \mathbf{x}) = \frac{P(Y = 1)}{P(X = \mathbf{x})} \prod_{i=1}^{k} P(X_i = x_i|Y = 1) \tag{10.9}$$

Now, you should think about a specific example to get more intuition. Using the classifier as a spam filter, then $Y = 1$ means a document is spam, and $Y = 0$ means it's not spam. The different X_i would be binary variables indicating whether a specific work appears (or not) in a document. For example, $X_{100} = 1$ means *dog* appears in the document, while $X_{100} = 0$ means *dog* does not appear.

It's easy to measure $P(X_i = 1|Y = 1)$. It's just the proportion of spam documents in the training set that contains the term X_i. It's also easy to measure the $P(Y = 1)$ term. It's just the proportion of all documents in the training set that are spam. The difficult term is $P(X = x)$. This is the proportion of documents in the training set with word vector $X = x$. Generally, no two documents will have the same word vectors, and you can't expect all word vectors to be exhausted by your limited sample of training data. For a vocabulary of just 100 words, you'd need $2^{100} = 1.3 \times 10^{30}$ data points to exhaust all combinations. That's only if they all appear just once!

Instead of estimating this term, realize that it's the same for a fixed x. If you just want to estimate the class of x, you don't actually need the probability. You just need an ordering for the classes. By just treating $P(X = x)$ as an unknown constant, you can classify x into the class that it most likely belongs to. You do this using the "likelihood" as follows:

$$\mathcal{L}(Y = y_j) = P(Y = y_j) \prod_{i=1}^{k} P(X_i = x_i|Y = y_j) \tag{10.10}$$

Notice that if you have no data for the document (because there are no words in it!), you just get $L(y_j) = P(Y = y_j)$. As you add data, each term makes a different class more or less likely by a factor of $P(X_i = x_i|Y = y_j)$. This gives a nice interpretation to these terms: they tell you how much more likely than chance a document falls into class y_j. If the term is equal to 1, it doesn't change the likelihood. If it's greater than 1, it makes class y_j more likely, and if it's less than 1 (it will always be positive), it makes the class less likely.

You can use similar evaluation strategies as logistic regression to see how well the classifier performs on each class. Instead of adjusting the cutoff probability, you can adjust the likelihood ratio between classes.

Another useful evaluation trick for multiclass models like naive Bayes is a "confusion matrix." Instead of just true or false negatives and positives, you can misclassify any class into any other class. In general, some classes will tend to be classified into others more often. This will happen in document classification, for example, if they share the same important terms.

Looking at Figure 10.4, you have the output of a hypothetical news classification problem. Along the diagonal, you see the entries where the predicted class was the true class. The more entries in the off-diagonal elements, the worse job the classifier is doing. Here, you see the classifier has

	Pred.News	Pred. Entertainment	Pred. Celebrity
True News	40	5	2
True Entertainment	3	16	10
True Celebrity	1	13	20

Figure 10.4 How the logistic regression model performs against guessing as you vary the decision boundary

trouble distinguishing celebrity articles from entertainment articles. Presumably, this is because most celebrity articles contain the names of celebrities and other features that are also important for distinguishing entertainment articles.

Naive Bayes Summary	
The Algorithm	Naive Bayes is great for classification with categorical features. Spam detection is a typical application.
Time Complexity	$O(KN)$, with N data points, and K classes.
Memory Considerations	The feature matrix can get large when you have sparse features! Use sparse encodings when possible. You will also need to maintain a large lookup table of feature counts for each class. Preprocess to minimize the number of features or classes where appropriate!

10.3.1 Assumptions

The main assumption of this model is conditional independence of the feature set given the item classification, or $P(X_i|Y, X_j) = P(X_i|Y)$ for features X_i, X_j and classification Y. Refer to later sections on Bayesian networks for more intuition on conditional independence. Note that conditional independence does not imply independence. You assume that knowing the class, each feature is independent of the others. Features can still be statistically dependent on one another!

10.3.2 Complexity

The time complexity of this model during execution is $O(c)$ for c classes, making it very fast to compute. Training takes $O(cN)$ where N is the number of sample inputs.

10.3.3 Memory Considerations

This method requires a lookup table for the probability of a given feature being assigned to a particular class. This means you should expect to store at least ck elements where k is number of features.

10.3.4 Tools

Scikit learn has a great naive Bayes module in Python at *sklearn.naive_bayes*. They include a fantastic in-depth, practical discussion of the topic in their package documentation. There are also multidimensional generalizations like *sklearn.naive_bayes.MultinomialNB*. You can train it online or offline.

Another great tool for naive Bayes is the Google project at https://code.google.com/archive/p/naive-bayes-classifier/, which can add new data at runtime.

10.4 K-Means

Naive Bayes and logistic regression are great when you're doing classification in a context where you have observed outcome data, Y. What can you do when you don't? The outcomes are your way of telling the algorithm what an example looks like so it can adjust its behavior. Learning from examples of independent and dependent variables is called *supervised learning*. When you don't have these examples and have only the independent variables, you're doing "unsupervised" learning.

In unsupervised learning, you'll often hope that any structure you discover in the data is useful for whatever your application is, but you can't generally be guaranteed that will be the case. This will be a common theme when you learn about unsupervised learning algorithms.

The first such algorithm will be a classification algorithm. The goal is to take a set of independent variables and map them into groups of similar types of points. Intuitively, you're really looking for "clusters" of points, as you might identify visually. Let's look at an example in Figure 10.5.

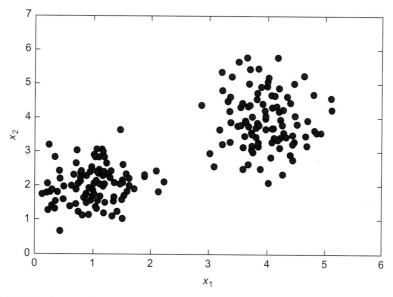

Figure 10.5   Data from a mixture of two Gaussians

This data is a mixture of two Gaussians. You'd like to be able to automatically label the points by which Gaussian they come from. You can do this well visually, but you need to make the process automatic. You'd have a lot of trouble manually labeling points in higher dimensions! You can run sklearn's KMeans model easily enough, like so:

```
from sklearn.cluster import KMeans
model = KMeans(n_clusters=2, init='k-means++', n_init=1)
model = model.fit(X[['$x_1$', '$x_2$']])
X['predicted'] = model.predict(X[['$x_1$', '$x_2$']])
```

Then, it's pretty simple to plot the result, as follows:

```
1 color = ['red' if yi else 'blue' for yi in X['predicted']]
2 X.plot(x='$x_1$', y='$x_2$', kind='scatter',
3         color=color, xlim=(0,6),
4         ylim=(0,7), legend=False); pp.ylabel('$x_2$')
```

This gives Figure 10.6. If you compare the classifications with the actual clusters, they're all correct.

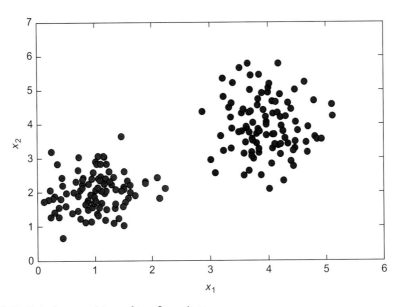

Figure 10.6   Data from a mixture of two Gaussians

To picture how k-means works, imagine placing points, k_i, randomly in the graph by centering them at random data points. You then ask, for each data point x_i, "Which of these randomly placed points is x_i closest to?" You label each of the x_i with the k_i it's closest to. You then take the average position of each of the groups by the different labels. These average positions become the new k_i, and you repeat the process until the points stop changing labels.

The random initialization is improved on with the k-means++ initialization option in many implementations. Instead of choosing initial cluster centers completely at random, they are chosen in sequence. At each step, the probability of a data point being chosen as the initial location of a cluster center increases proportionally with the distance from the other cluster centers. Intuitively, this has the effect of making sure the cluster centers start out further from each other, and it tends to decrease the number of steps you need before the algorithm converges.

K-means is great at finding clusters. It's so good that it will find clusters when there are none! Figure 10.7 shows the output of the k-means algorithm run with five cluster centers after running on Gaussian random data with no clusters.

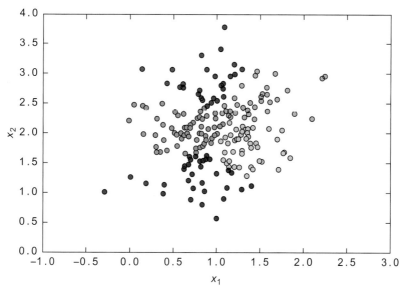

Figure 10.7   Clusters detected by k-means where there are no clusters!

This can actually be a useful quality. If you want to divide your data into discrete groups of data points that are near each other, this is a perfectly fine way to do it. This might be the case, for example, if you have article recommendations for a group of users, where the data points are different users' attributes. Instead of storing one set of recommendations for each user, you can divide them into groups of similar users and just store one recommendation set per group.

K-Means Summary	
The Algorithm	K-means is good for automatically finding clusters in clustered data. If the data doesn't have clusters, it will find somewhat arbitrary clusters.
Time Complexity	Worst case $N^{n+2/k}$, with N data points, and k features, and n clusters, average case $O(Nn)$. It can run much faster if initialized well with k-means++.
Memory Considerations	This is fairly memory efficient! You generally won't use it with categorical features (though you can), so sparsity isn't as great a concern.

10.4.1   Assumptions

The assumption is that you have a known number of distinct groups of data points. If this fails, you'll still tend to find clusters, but they won't have real meaning. If you run k-means on a Gaussian distribution, for example, you'll succeed at pixelating the Gaussian, but the clusters won't correspond to anything that you'd naturally identify as clusters from the raw data.

Further, you can assume that the data can be represented by a mixture of Gaussians. When the clusters are irregularly shaped, the algorithm can perform poorly.

10.4.2   Complexity

With n cluster centers, N data points, and k features, the average time complexity is $O(Nn)$. The worst-case complexity is $\mathcal{O}(N^{n+2/k})$[14].

10.4.3   Memory Considerations

K-means really just has to store the cluster centers, so the memory is very efficient.

10.4.4   Tools

Scikit learn has a nice implementation of k-means in the *sklearn.cluster* package, as shown in the earlier example.

10.5   Leading Eigenvalue

With k-means, there was a space of features where we had a notion of "closeness." You used this closeness to measure distances so you could assign points to different groups. What if you don't have a way to measure closeness in a feature space? What if you can say only how close pairs of points are but don't have a notion of a space of features where they reside as points? Then you can still do the initialization and assignment step in k-means, but you can't update the cluster centers. You can't run the algorithm in this setting.

What you really have is a set of objects and a set of strengths of connections between objects. This defines a graph, $G = (V, E)$, where V is the set of objects, and E is the set of connections.

To make this more concrete, we'll use an example from the network science literature [15]. Consider members of a legislative assembly, like the U.S. Senate. If two senators sponsor a piece of legislation together, we'll say their connection strength is 1. If they don't, we'll say their connection strength is 0. We'll denote the connection between senator i and senator j as A_{ij}. The total connections senator i has to the N total senators are $k_i = \sum_{j=1}^{N} A_{ij}$, and the total connections in the senate are $m = \frac{1}{2}\sum_{i=1}^{N} k_i = \frac{1}{2}\sum_{i=1}^{N}\sum_{j=1}^{N} A_{ij}$. Why the factor of $1/2$? If i is connected to j, then j is connected to i. This is just one connection, but it puts a 1 in both A_{ij} and A_{ji}. You divide by two to correct for this double-counting.

A question you might ask is "How can you arrange senators into groups such that there are the most cosponsorships within groups and the fewest between groups?" You could think of these groups as being partisan units that tend not to cooperate with each other.

This idea is called *modularity*. You're really asking how to divide Congress into partisan modules. Formally, consider the definition for modularity shown here [16]:

$$Q = \frac{1}{2m}\sum_{i=1}^{N}\sum_{j=1}^{N}\left[A_{ij} - \frac{k_i k_j}{2m}\right]\delta(c_i, c_j) \tag{10.11}$$

Here, c_i denotes the label of the cluster for senator i. $\delta(c_i, c_j)$ is the Kronecker delta. It is defined as 1 when $c_i = c_j$, and 0 otherwise.

Examining the formula, $\frac{k_i k_j}{2m}$ indicates the probability of an edge randomly occurring between i and j given that i has k_i connection, and j has k_j connections. If you broke all of each of their connections and reassigned them at random, then the expected number of connection between i and j is $\frac{k_i k_j}{2m}$. If you compare that with the actual number of edges between i and j, A_{ij}, you can see the formula is just measuring how many edges are between i and j beyond random chance.

The effect of the Kronecker delta is that these edge contrasts count only for pairs of senators who are assigned to the same clusters. Thus, the highest score for Q happens when all excess edges happen between pairs of senators who are assigned to the same groups. If you had a way to optimize Q, you'd have a way of answering the question about finding the partisan groups in Congress!

The leading eigenvalue method optimizes this quantity, producing *hierarchical* or *disjoint* communities of nodes. It does this by finding optimal splits into two groups at a time. This greedy approach can find a final result with lower modularity than the optimal one, but it's fast and works reasonably well in practice. If you have a network, like Congress, where you really only care about the two-party split, it might be exactly what you want.

We should mention that there are a few known problems with modularity optimization that are outlined well in [17] and [18]. First, there is a so-called resolution limit to the size of a cluster that is detectable. Even if you connect a fully connected graph to another large fully connected graph by a single edge, you can fail to detect the two communities because of this resolution problem. If the module contains fewer than roughly $\sqrt{2m}$ edges, then it falls below the resolution limit.

Second, modularity is not a convex function: it has many local maxima. It turns out these local maxima can all be very close together. We might hope that with small changes in modularity, the community assignments would be roughly the same. It turns out that this isn't the case. In general, a graph can have many community assignments with close to the same modularity but very different groupings of nodes.

Finally, you might hope that at least modularity is a useful metric for comparing how modular graphs are with one another. Unfortunately, it turns out that the larger a graph is, the more it will tend to the maximum value of modularity of 1. Modularity is only usefully compared between graphs with the same number of nodes.

Leading Eigenvalue Summary	
The Algorithm	Leading eigenvalue is great for finding two-way cluster splits in graphs. It performs poorly when the optimal split is odd-numbered.
Time Complexity	$O(|E|+|V|^2 S)$, where E is the set of edges in the graph and V is the set of vertices, and S is the number of splits (at most the number of vertices).
Memory Considerations	This needs to fit the adjacency matrix in memory, so it can struggle with large real-world graphs.

10.5.1 Complexity

The time complexity for the leading eigenvector method is $O(|E| + |V|^2 S)$, where E is the set of edges in the graph and V is the set of vertices. While S, the number of splits, is at most the number of vertices, in real-world networks it is typically small.

10.5.2   Memory Considerations

You should be able to store at least twice the adjacency matrix in memory at once to ensure fast computation.

10.5.3   Tools

The *igraph* package has a great implementation of this algorithm. The documentation can be found at http://igraph.org/. There are implementations in C, with bindings implementing the interface for the Python language as well as R.

10.6   Greedy Louvain

Leading eigenvector community detection is nice but doesn't give optimal results in practice. A good, scalable algorithm is the greedy Louvain method. It initializes and then operates in two steps. Initially it assigns each object to its own group.

In the first stage, the change in modularity for the community assignments is calculated if you move each node *i* from its community to one that it's connected to. After calculating this change for all neighbors, if there's a community that you can move *i* to that increases modularity the most (it must increase), then *i* is moved to that community. You run sequentially over all nodes, repeating the process for each node.

In the second stage, each community becomes a single node, and all edges within it become connections to itself. This way, you'll avoid deconstructing communities while still allowing them to aggregate into larger communities. You run the first stage again on this new network and repeat the process until no more moves happen. This algorithm has been run on millions of nodes and billions of edges.

Greedy Louvian Summary	
The Algorithm	Greedy Louvain is a great go-to algorithm for modularity optimization. It has very fast runtime and performs well on large graphs.
Time Complexity	$O(n\log(n))$ with n nodes.
Memory Considerations	This needs to fit the graph in memory, so it can struggle with large real-world graphs.

10.6.1   Assumptions

You should be able to represent the data as a weighted graph.

10.6.2   Complexity

The apparent runtime is $O(n\log n)$ for n nodes.

10.6.3 Memory Considerations

You should be able to store the graph in memory. Alternatively, you can store the graph on disk and query for neighbors and statistics of communities (total edges within and to communities).

10.6.4 Tools

This algorithm is a little hard to find in standard graph analysis packages for Python. You can find it in a module that runs on networkx, called *python-louvain*.

10.7 Nearest Neighbors

While nearest neighbors isn't a classification algorithm, it should often be used in place of clustering. We thought it was important to present it in context, which is why we're following our section on community detection with a nearest neighbor algorithm.

It's important to realize that generally your graph won't necessarily have clusters in it. If what you really want is a group of objects that are all similar to each other, you can do well by selecting one object and all of its nearest neighbors in the graph.

Nearest neighbors is generally defined on a feature space, as you were using before in k-means. The task is, for each object in the feature space, find the k closest objects to it. The brute-force approach is computationally expensive, so there are approximation methods that run much faster.

Let's say you want to find students who behave similarly in school. As the teacher, you have the average of all test scores for that student up-to-date. You also know their average score on homework assignments since the last test and the number of classes they missed since the last test.

Your vectors are, then, of the following form:

$$\vec{v} = \{\bar{T}, \bar{H}, A\} \tag{10.12}$$

Here, $\bar{T}$ is the average test score for the semester, $\bar{H}$ is the average homework score, and A is the number of times the student has been absent.

An important consideration is exactly how to determine how "close" two students are. We have a 3-D vector here, so it's pretty simple to visualize with *euclidean* distance in 3-D space, as in Figure 10.8.

There are many distance metrics we could use. Mahalanobis distance is great when your features have different units, as in this example.

If you were working without a feature space and had only object similarities, then Jaccard distance or MinHash are great metrics when dealing with sets. Levenshtein distance is a great one for *word* or *sentence* similarity. Shortest paths are a decent metric for graphs.

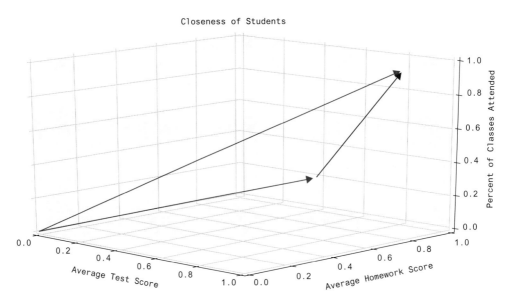

Figure 10.8   Two students represented by vectors lay in the 3-D space of their performance in class up to this point. You can measure how similar they are by measures as simple as the euclidean distance pictured in blue.

Nearest Neighbors Summary	
The Algorithm	Given a collection of data points, nearest neighbors finds the closest data points to a target point. It's great for content recommendation, matching, and other applications.
Time Complexity	For C dimensions and N data points, brute-force training runs in $O(CN^2)$. The k-d tree construction runs in $O(CNlog(N))$, and the ball tree in $O(CNlog(N))$. Brute-force querying runs in $O(CN)$, while the k-d tree provides $O(Clog(N))$ time complexity at best and worst than brute force at worst. The ball tree provides approximately $O(Clog(N))$.
Memory Considerations	The trees and neighbors need to fit in memory, so you'll typically want a fairly large in-memory data store. This algorithm is for information retrieval, so you need to store the information!

10.7.1   Assumptions

For *k-NN*, include a relationship between the features and the quantity being predicted. You also assume a relatively even spacing of elements in the feature space.

10.7.2   Complexity

The complexity of finding the nearest neighbors in an n-dimensional feature space is dramatically improved with a k-d tree.

In C dimensions with N data points, brute-force training runs in $O(CN^2)$. The k-d tree construction runs in $O(CNlog(N))$, and the ball tree runs in $O(CNlog(N))$.

Brute-forcing querying in C dimensions with N data points runs in $O(CN)$, while the k-d tree provides $O(Clog(N))$ time complexity at best and worst than brute force at worst. The ball tree provides approximately $O(Clog(N))$ [19, 20, 21].

10.7.3 Memory Considerations

The ball tree and k-d trees store elements in a `leaf` similar to a b-tree. As the leaf size grows, less memory is required. As the leaf size becomes smaller, more memory is required since more nodes are created.

The number of elements in memory is bounded by a factor of the size of the training set. It's proportional to $CN/leaf\_size$.

10.7.4 Tools

sklearn.neighbors in Python has some great nearest neighbors implementations for classification as well as regression. In classification the nearest neighbors "vote" on the class. In regression the average value of the predicted quantity is assigned to the node in question.

OpenCV also has implementations of the k-NN algorithm available in C++ with a port to Python.

ANNoy is an open source package released by Spotify with excellent performance. The intended use case is with content recommendation, which requires very fast neighbor search and allows approximate results.

10.8 Conclusion

In this chapter, you explored a few common algorithms for classification and clustering. You can get creative with these. If you can create a similarity measure, for example, you can create a graph where the edges are weighted by item similarities. Then, you can try to cluster items using that similarity measure!

With all of these methods, you'll want to plot your data to explore it and see what method is appropriate. If a scatter plot doesn't show good clustering, you probably wouldn't want to use k-means. If a feature doesn't help distinguish between a pair of categories, you probably wouldn't want to include it in a logistic regression. If a graph doesn't have obvious cluster structure when you visualize it, you probably wouldn't want to over-interpret the clusters you find from modularity optimization algorithms.

You also had a first look at Bayesian methods, with naive Bayes. You'll work with these methods in much more depth in the next two chapters, where you'll build up some intuition for the structure of Bayesian models and then look at a few specific applications.

11

Bayesian Networks

11.1 Introduction

Graphical models are a rich subject, and several excellent books focus on them. Koller and Friedman's *Probabilistic Graphical Models* covers the subject in-depth, and Murphy's *Machine Learning: A Probabilistic Perspective* uses them to teach machine learning. Graphical models provide a powerful framework for many modern algorithms for matrix factorization and text analysis.

Graphical models are what they sound like: models for systems that are described by graphs, that is, nodes and edges. Each node is a variable, and each edge represents dependence between variables. These models can be directed or undirected. Along with the graph, there is generally a list of probability distributions on each of the variables in the graph. We'll cover all these details methodically in the next sections.

The term *Bayesian network* was coined by Judea Pearl. Bayesian networks are a specific kind of graphical model and a type we'll focus on in this text. Pearl builds a science of causation on top of Bayesian networks [22], and his causal graphical models provide a powerful modern framework for causal inference. To deeply understand correlation and causation in data science, you need to understand causal graphical models. To understand causal graphical models, you need to understand Bayesian networks.

Our intent is to introduce enough information about graphical models to provide a basis for understanding causal inference. With our restricted focus, we'll gloss over many important details about graphical models and focus almost exclusively on directed, acyclic graphs. Graphical models are a subject worth exploring in their own right, and we encourage you to take a course to study them in depth or refer to one of the texts mentioned earlier.

We'll depart from the usual pedagogy for teaching Bayesian networks and start with causal Bayesian networks. Then, we'll relax the assumptions of causality and use the intuition you've developed to cover Bayesian networks more generally. We'll follow in Part IV of this text with a more thorough treatment of causality from the perspective of causal graphical models, where we'll introduce some estimators for causal effects.

11.2 Causal Graphs, Conditional Independence, and Markovity

In this section we'll lay the foundation for an understanding of Bayesian networks. You'll probably find with a few elementary examples of directed acyclic networks you'll develop an intuition quickly.

In the first section you'll see some relationships between causal graphs and conditional independence as well as a couple of rules for stating two variables are independent.

Finally, we'll discuss *dependence* and get into the types of relationships between variables. In that section, we'll address the question "If correlation doesn't imply causation, what does?"

11.2.1 Causal Graphs and Conditional Independence

Causal Bayesian networks are powerful tools for describing cause and effect. We represent each variable as a node in a graph and each causal relationship as a directed edge, pointing from cause to effect. As an example, consider a binary-valued variable, X_1, describing whether there was an accident along a person's commute to work. X_2 is an binary-valued variable saying how many hours a person is late to work, and X_3 is a real-valued variable giving the person's hourly wages on that day. Then, you could say that traffic causes people to be late to work, and being late can cause people to lose wages. Figure 11.1 represents these causal relationships.

Figure 11.1 Traffic (X_1) causes lateness (X_2), which in turn causes a loss in wages (X_3). There is no direct effect of traffic on wages other than through lateness, and there are no common causes of traffic and wages.

This graph is *directed* because it indicates the direction of cause and effect. If $A \rightarrow B \rightarrow A$, then A would cause itself. For this reason, causal graphs are also *acyclic*.

With this example, there are some interesting intuitive points you can make. First, notice that once you know whether a person is late, knowing the traffic situation tells you nothing more about the person's wages on that day. To put this in terms of probability, you can say $P(X_3|X_2, X_1) = P(X_3|X_2)$. In other words, once you know X_2, X_3 is independent of X_1. This kind of independence is called *conditional independence*. You can show (try it!) that $P(X_3|X_2, X_1) = P(X_3|X_2) \iff P(X_3, X_1|X_2) = P(X_3|X_2)P(X_1|X_2)$. In this sense, conditional independence looks more like independence (recall A and B are independent if and only if $P(A, B) = P(A)P(B)$).

How is conditional independence related to independence? They don't imply and aren't implied by each other! You can see in this example that in general X_1 and X_3 are statistically dependent: on days when there is more traffic, you will tend to get lower wages. This is true if and only if $P(X_1, X_3) \neq P(X_1)P(X_3)$. It's a little harder to see the other way, in other words, that independence doesn't imply conditional independence.

Consider another causal diagram. Here, X_1 is a binary variable indicating a student has good social skills. X_2 is a binary variable indicating that a student has good math skills. X_3 is a binary variable indicating a student was admitted to a prestigious university. This university will admit students who have good math skills or good social skills (inclusive or), and in this world, math and social skills are unrelated in the general population. Figure 11.2 shows this diagram.

Figure 11.2 Math skills (X_1) or social skills (X_2) are required for admission to a university (X_3). The two are unrelated in the general population but negatively related in the university population!

Consider choosing a student at the university (i.e., conditioning on X_3). Suppose you know that the person has poor math skills. What can you say about their social skills? You can say they have good social skills because you know they were admitted to the university. Even though these two variables are unrelated in the general population ($P(X_1, X_2) = P(X_1)P(X_2)$), they become statistically dependent (negatively) when you condition on $X_3 = 1$ ($P(X_1, X_2|X_3) \neq P(X_1|X_3)P(X_2|X_3)$). Thus, you can see that independence doesn't imply conditional independence.

11.2.2 Stability and Dependence

It's useful to see when variables in the graph are dependent. We made an argument earlier that when two variables are causally related, they should be dependent, but this technically isn't always true. Consider Figure 11.3. In this picture, X_1 causes two other variables, X_2 and X_3, which have equal and opposite effects on X_4. There is no net dependence between X_1 and X_4.

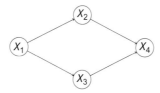

Figure 11.3 Consider if the mechanism X_2 along the path from X_1 to X_4 is aware of and tries to exactly cancel the mechanism along X_3. Then there's no dependence between X_1 and X_4, even though you might try to infer one from the graph! This is an unstable relationship.

It can be even worse: consider removing X_1 and having $X_4 = xor(X_2, X_3)$. If X_2 and X_3 are $p = 0.5$ Bernoulli random variables, then X_4 is marginally independent of X_2 and X_3 (e.g., $P(X_4, X_2) = P(X_4)P(X_2)$), but not jointly independent, as in: $P(X_4, X_2, X_3) \neq P(X_4)P(X_2)P(X_3)$.

The requirement in the first case that the cancellation be exact can happen only with finely tuned causal paths. The requirement that $p = 0.5$ is also fine-tuning. These finely tuned relationships are called *unstable*, and you can generally assume they aren't present in the causal graphs you're working with. That is, you're working only with *stable* causal graphs. When you assume stability, directed causal paths connecting variables imply statistical dependence.

Notice also that instability is a property that doesn't come from the structure of the graph itself but rather comes from the relationships that underlie the structure. That is, there can be stable causal graphs with the same structure as the ones in our example here.

You'll complete your understanding of dependence by realizing that variables can become statistically dependent in more ways than direct causal paths. This is what gives rise to the problem of misinterpreting correlative relationships as causal ones. Consider the example in Figure 11.4. Here, X_3 indicates whether it is raining on a day. X_1 indicates the amount of crime on that day, and X_2 indicates the amount of coffee sold. On rainy days, there are fewer people out, and crimes happen less often. On rainy days, people prefer not to drive to coffee shops, so there is less coffee sold.

Figure 11.4 The weather, B, is a common cause of crime, A, and coffee, C. Crime and coffee drinking will be correlated, even though they don't cause one another.

Looking only at the relationship between coffee sales and crime, you might guess (incorrectly) that the more coffee people are drinking, the more likely they are to commit crimes! This would be ridiculous. Here, there is a correlative relationship between coffee and crime but not a causal one. The dependence between crime and coffee ($P(X_1, X_2) \neq P(X_1)P(X_2)$) is because they share a common cause: the weather.

It's important to note that the two variables don't need to share a *direct* common cause to be dependent. You would see the same effect if they shared common causes anywhere upstream from both variables. You didn't explicitly represent the fact coffee sales are actually affected by the number of people driving to coffee shops, which could have been another node in the graph. You could also have explicitly represented the effect of rain on crime through another node representing the number of people outdoors.

11.3 D-separation and the Markov Property

Say you want a more general criterion to establish when a graph says variables are dependent or independent. If two variables are not connected by a causal path and don't share a common ancestor, they are independent. When are two variables conditionally independent? To understand, you'll need to develop an understanding of Markovity and a concept called *d-separation*.

11.3.1 Markovity and Factorization

Given a set of known independencies (a property of the joint distribution $P(X_1, X_2, ..., X_n)$), you would like to be able to construct a graph that is consistent with them. A necessary and sufficient condition is the following: a graph, G, and joint distribution, P, are consistent if and only if each node is independent of its nondescendants given its parents. P is said to be *Markov* relative to G.

If P is Markov relative to G, then you can factorize P in a nice way. Since P is conditionally independent of its predecessors given its parents, any conditional distribution for a node that contains both predecessors and parents can be reduced to a conditional distribution on the parents

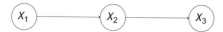

Figure 11.5   Traffic (X_1) causes lateness (X_2), which in turn causes a loss in wages (X_3). There is no direct effect of traffic on wages other than through lateness, and there are no common causes of traffic and wages.

alone! Let's return to our first example to make this more concrete. We've re-created it in Figure 11.5 for convenience.

The joint distribution for this graph is $P(X_1, X_2, X_3)$. It contains all the information about how these variables relate to one another. You could use it to derive linear regression coefficients, averages, correlations, and so on. In general, there are many graphs that can represent this distribution. You can use the chain rule for conditional probabilities, as follows:

$$P(X_1, X_2, ..., X_n) = \Pi_{i=1}^{n} P(X_i | X_{i-1}, ..., X_1) \tag{11.1}$$

to rewrite this joint distribution as $P(X_1, X_2, X_3) = P(X_3 | X_2, X_1) P(X_2 | X_1) P(X_1)$.

Note that you haven't used any knowledge about the graph structure yet! The chain rule for conditional independence applies to any joint distribution. Now, if you apply all of the conditional independence assumptions, as summarized in the graph, you get $P(X_1, X_2, X_3) = P(X_3 | X_2) P(X_2 | X_1) P(X_1)$ since $P(X_3 | X_2, X_1) = P(X_3 | X_2)$.

From this, you've arrived at something interesting. The joint distribution is factored into a form where each node depends only on its parents! You can actually write the factorization for a Bayesian network as follows:

$$P(X_1, X_2, ..., X_n) = \Pi_{i=1}^{n} P(X_i | Pa(X_i)) \tag{11.2}$$

Of course, being able to write the joint distribution like this requires you to be able to keep all predecessors and parents on the right side of the | when you apply the chain rule for conditional independence. There's a theorem that says this is possible! Such an ordering of the variables is called a *topological ordering*, and you're guaranteed one exists.

When you've factored the joint distribution like this, you go from a k-dimensional function (the joint distribution on k variables) to several lower-dimensional functions. In the case that you're using a Markov chain, where $X_1 \rightarrow X_2 \rightarrow ... \rightarrow X_k$, you have $k - 1$ two-dimensional functions. Where before factoring you were estimating a function by spreading out your data over an exponentially large (with k) space, now you estimate several two-dimensional functions! It's a much easier problem.

11.3.2   D-separation

There is a criterion called *d-separation* that tells you when two variables are conditionally independent. If they are conditionally independent given the null set, they are just independent.

Dependence flows along paths, where a cause will make its effect dependent. It subsequently makes another effect dependent, and so on. For this reason, d-separation relies heavily on the concept of a *path* in its definition. All statistical dependence happens along these paths. If two variables are statistically dependent, some of that dependence may be from causal paths between the two, while some might be because of common causes or selection bias. If you can block these latter noncausal paths, then all of the remaining statistical dependence between the two variables will be causal. You'll have removed the noncausal part of the correlation between the variables, and the remaining correlation will imply causation!

Note that the definition of *path* is a sequence of edges, where the end of one edge is the beginning of the next edge in the sequence. This definition does not require that the edges be oriented to point along the direction of the path.

You'd like the definition to be general enough to say whether variables are *jointly independent*. For this reason, it should generalize to sets of variables.

A path, p, is d-separated by a set of nodes Z if and only if one of the following criteria is satisfied:

- p contains a chain, $X_1 \rightarrow X_2 \rightarrow X_3$, or a fork of $X_1 \leftarrow X_2 \rightarrow X_3$, where the middle node is in Z.

- p contains an inverted fork $X_1 \rightarrow X_2 \leftarrow X_3$ such that the middle node is not in Z and such that no descendent of X_2 is in Z.

The set Z d-separates two sets of variables X and Y if it d-separates every path between nodes in X and nodes in Y.

Let's examine each part of this definition to understand it better. First, let's look at how to block the flow of information along a chain of causes and effects, as in Figure 11.6.

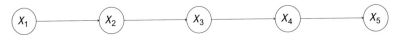

Figure 11.6 A chain graph. X_1 causes X_2, which causes X_3 and so on. These variables will end up statistically dependent.

You can factor this joint distribution like this:

$$P(X_1, X_2, X_3, X_4, X_5) = P(X_5|X_4)P(X_4|X_3)P(X_3|X_2)P(X_2|X_1)P(X_1) \tag{11.3}$$

If you look at the first part of the definition, you see that you have a chain. Let's see what happens to the dependence between the ends of this path when you condition on a variable along a chain.

You want to look at $P(X_1, X_5|X_3)$, so you're conditioning on the middle variable, X_3 (X_2 or X_4 will exhibit the same behavior; convince yourself!). Then you can write the following:

$$
\begin{aligned}
P(X_1, X_5|X_3) &= \sum_{X_2, X_4} \frac{P(X_5|X_4)P(X_4|X_3)P(X_3|X_2)P(X_2|X_1)P(X_1)}{P(X_3)} \\
&= \sum_{X_2, X_4} P(X_5|X_4)P(X_4|X_3)P(X_1, X_2|X_3) \\
&= \sum_{X_4} P(X_5|X_4)P(X_4|X_3)P(X_1|X_3) \\
&= \sum_{X_4} P(X_5, X_4|X_3)P(X_1|X_3) \\
&= P(X_5|X_3)P(X_1|X_3)
\end{aligned}
\tag{11.4}
$$

So, you can see that X_5 and X_1 are independent conditional on X_3! You can work through a similar process without conditioning on X_3 to see whether X_1 and X_5 are marginally dependent. If you do (try it!), you'll see that in general their joint doesn't separate. X_1 and X_5 are dependent, but conditionally independent given any variable along the chain in between them. So, now you can understand the first part of the definition of d-separation.

Intuitively, if you know the value of an intermediate cause, you don't need to know anything about its predecessors. The intermediate cause contains all the information about its predecessors that is necessary for determining its effects.

Next, let's look at an example with a fork, as in Figure 11.7.

Figure 11.7   Here you have a causal fork at X_3. Information about X_3 propagates along to X_1 and X_5, so they become statistically dependent. X_1 doesn't cause X_5, or vice versa.

You can factor this joint as follows:

$$
P(X_1, X_2, X_3, X_4, X_5) = P(X_1|X_2)P(X_2|X_3)P(X_3)P(X_4|X_3)P(X_5|X_4)
\tag{11.5}
$$

If you look at the dependence between X_1 and X_5 conditional on X_3, you get the following:

$$
\begin{aligned}
P(X_1, X_5|X_3) &= \sum_{X_2, X_4} \frac{P(X_1|X_2)P(X_2|X_3)P(X_3)P(X_4|X_3)P(X_5|X_4)}{P(X_3)} \\
&= \sum_{X_2, X_4} P(X_5|X_4)P(X_4|X_3)P(X_1|X_2)P(X_2|X_3) \\
&= P(X_5|X_3)P(X_1|X_3)
\end{aligned}
\tag{11.6}
$$

So, again, you can see that X_1 and X_5 are conditionally independent given the node at the fork, even though they'd be conditionally dependent without conditioning.

Finally, let's look at what happens at a collider at X_3, as in Figure 11.8.

Figure 11.8 Here you have a collider at X_3. Information about X_2 can't pass through, and neither can information about X_4 pass through to X_2. That means the left and right sides of X_3 will remain statistically independent. The collider blocks statistical dependence.

Now, you can factorize the joint as follows:

$$P(X_1, X_2, X_3, X_4, X_5) = P(X_1|X_2)P(X_2)P(X_3|X_2, X_4)P(X_5|X_4)P(X_4) \tag{11.7}$$

where you can see that by marginalizing to get $P(X_1, X_5)$, you find the two are independent! $P(X_1, X_5) = P(X_1)P(X_5)$. You can mess up this independence by conditioning on the collider, as shown here:

$$P(X_1, X_5|X_3) = \sum_{X_2, X_4} \frac{P(X_1|X_2)P(X_2)P(X_3|X_2, X_4)P(X_5|X_4)P(X_4)}{X_3} \tag{11.8}$$

Where before summing over X_3 decoupled the two sets of factors on either side of the $P(X_3|X_2, X_4)$ factor, now they're generally coupled together because of the X_2 and X_4 dependence of the middle term. So finally, you can see that including the middle node of a collider in the variables you're controlling for will end up adding extra dependence, potentially causing variables that were originally independent to become dependent.

Another intuitive word for d-separation is *blocking*. If a path is d-separated by Z, you can say that the path is *blocked* by Z. This fits with our intuition of dependence being propagated along paths and conditioning on a set Z blocking the flow of that dependence.

Finally, we can come full circle back to Markovity. If two variables are d-separated by a set Z in G and P is Markov relative to G, then they are conditionally independent in P.

11.4 Causal Graphs as Bayesian Networks

In this section you'll learn how linear regression is an example of how dependent variables are correlative but not necessarily *causal*. At the end, you should understand that edges in a directed acyclic graph are necessary but not sufficient criteria for asserting a causal relationship between two variables.

11.4.1 Linear Regression

Now, we've built up all the machinery we need to talk about Bayesian networks. You understand that you can factor joint distributions, and this might amount to simplifying estimating the distributions. Let's actually define a model by writing a graph and defining distributions over the nodes.

We'll start with something very familiar: linear regression! We'll define the distributions and then describe how they give the graph.

You'll have two independent variables X_1 and X_2 and a dependent variable Y. As usual with linear regression, you want to say Y follows a normal distribution, centered around the point you would expect from the usual regression formula, $y_i = \beta_0 + \beta_1 x_1 + \beta_2 x_2$. If you want to write down the distribution, you must have that $Y \sim \mathcal{N}(\beta_0 + \beta_1 X_1 + \beta_2 X_2, \sigma_Y)$, where the β_i and σ are parameters for you to fit.

What does the graph for this model look like? Before, we said that each variable's distribution depends on its parents in the graph. Here, you can see that the distribution for Y depends on X_1 and X_2. You can expect them to be parents of Y. To finish specifying the model, you should also describe the distributions for X_1 and X_2. We'll say they're normally distributed, $X_1 \sim \mathcal{N}(0, 1)$ and $X_2 \sim \mathcal{N}(0, 1)$. Then, the graph will be as in Figure 11.9.

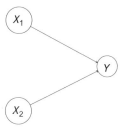

Figure 11.9   A possible network representing linear regression, where you regress Y on X_1 and X_2. You might be tempted to interpret this as a causal model, but you have to establish causation before making that interpretation. A linear regression doesn't do that!

This fully specifies a linear regression model but doesn't require that the independent variables are causes of the dependent variables. If they are causes of the dependent variable, then you are free to interpret this as a causal model. What you assume by doing so is that if you were to intervene in the system to change the value of X_1 or X_2, then Y would respond by changing a corresponding amount, $\beta_1 X_1$ or $\beta_2 X_2$. If this is not true, then the model should not be interpreted as a causal model. It is this extra interventional structure that makes a Bayesian network causal.

Even if you don't interpret the model as being causal, you have made some assumptions about how the independent variables are related. Here, because there are no directed paths between them and they have no common ancestors, you are assuming that they are independent of each other. If this were a causal network, these assumptions are that they don't cause each other and they don't share common causes, respectively. You are free to relax this assumption by making changes to the graph and making corresponding changes to the variables' distributions.

11.5   Fitting Models

Now that you have a model, you'll actually want to fit its parameters. There are many ways to do this, but you'll choose a general (but computationally expensive) class of methods: Monte Carlo methods. A complete treatment of these methods is outside the scope of this book, so we refer you to the excellent introductory treatment in [23] on p. 357.

The basic idea is that you want to estimate some expectation of a distribution, like this:

$$E[f(X_1, ..., X_k)] = \int f(x_1, ..., x_k)P(x_1, ..., x_k)dx_1...dx_k \tag{11.9}$$

Generally, evaluating these integrals can be hard, so you'll want easier ways to get answers. A trick you can use is to draw N samples, $(x_1, ..., x_k)$ from the distribution and then evaluate the following:

$$E_N[f(X_1, ..., X_k)] = \frac{1}{N}\Sigma_{i=1}^{N}f(x_1, ..., x_k) \tag{11.10}$$

for the approximation to the expected value using N data points. The expected value of this quantity is just $E[f(X_1, ..., X_k)]$, and the variance decreases with the number of samples.

Generally, the hardest part of evaluating the distribution in Equation 11.5 is evaluating the normalizing constant. For this reason, methods have been developed that let you simply evaluate an unnormalized distribution to generate samples. The metropolis-hastings algorithms is a good one for getting the feel for how they work.

You start by choosing some $(x_1, ..., x_k)$ in the domain of P. You choose a density $Q(x', x)$ over points x', e.g., a Gaussian, centered around the initial point $x = (x_1, ..., x_k)$. You choose the width of this distribution to be small compared to the domain of P. You draw a point x' from $Q(x', x)$ and then decide whether to keep it in the simulated data set or reject it. Keeping it or rejecting it depends on whether it is more or less likely under $\tilde{P}$ and $Q(x', x)$ than x. In this way, you can wander into the region of greater probability and explore the distribution P by taking many samples. You need a correction so that you can draw samples from the less probable region. If you denote the unnormalized probability distribution as $\tilde{P}$, you keep a sample if

$$\frac{\tilde{P}(x')Q(x, x')}{\tilde{P}(x)Q(x', x)} > 1 \tag{11.11}$$

If you accept the point, you append it to our list of samples. If you reject it, you re-append the old point and try again.

In this way, you generate a list of samples that starts far from the typical set of samples from the distribution (since our initialization was arbitrary) but evolves toward the typical set of samples. For this reason, you generally throw away several samples at the beginning of the process.

It's also not desirable for samples to be statistically dependent when you really want independent draws from the distribution. For this reason, you often keep only every m^{th} sample.

With these basics in place, you're ready to use a sampler provided in Python's PyMC3 package. This package is more efficient than the basic sampling approach we've described, but some of the same basic considerations apply. In particular, you might want to have a burn-in period, where you throw away early samples, and you may want to think out your data so the samples are independent and identically distributed (i.i.d.).

Let's try fitting this linear model in PyMC3. First, you'll generate some data with this model. Note that you're importing the pymc3 package and using Python 3. You'll generate a decent amount of data, with 10k data points. Note the true values of the regression parameters given here, $\beta_0 = -1$, $\beta_1 = 1$, and $\beta_2 = 2$.

```
1  import pandas as pd
2  import numpy as np
3  import pymc3 as pymc
4
5  N = 10000
6  beta0 = -1
7  beta1 = 1.
8  beta2 = 2.
9
10 x1 = np.random.normal(size=N)
11 x2 = np.random.normal(size=N)
12 y = np.random.normal(beta1 * x1 + beta2 * x2 + beta0)
```

Now that you're generated some data, you need to set priors (see the next chapter for more detail on priors) on all the parameters you'd like to estimate and encode in the Bayesian network. Here, you'll say that all of the parameters will take on normal distributions. The standard deviations are large, so you're not restrictive about the range of values they can take.

```
1  with pymc.Model() as model:
2      b0 = pymc.Normal('beta_0', mu=0, sd=100.)
3      b1 = pymc.Normal('beta_1', mu=0, sd=100.)
4      b2 = pymc.Normal('beta_2', mu=0, sd=100.)
5      error = pymc.Normal('epsilon', mu=0, sd=100.)
6
7      y_out = b0 + b1*x1 + b2*x2
8      y_var =  pymc.Normal('y', mu=y_out, sd=error, observed=y)
```

Finally, pymc3 makes it easy to run the sampling procedure. They do a lot of optimization behind the scenes and provide some nice tools to analyze the results. First, we'll run the sampler, as shown here:

```
1  with model:
2      trace = pymc.sample(3000, njobs=2)
```

The sampling process takes around 30 seconds. After, you can plot the result, as shown here:

```
1  pymc.traceplot(trace);
```

which produces the plots in Figure 11.10.

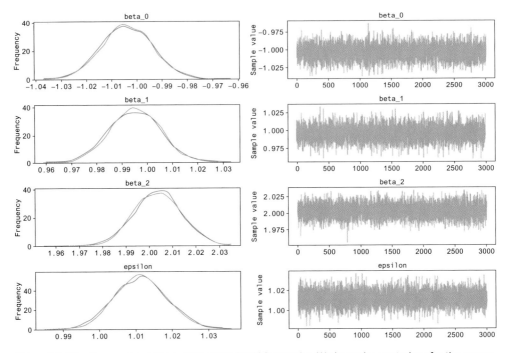

Figure 11.10 Here we have the output of the PyMC3 sampler. We have the posteriors for the parameters on the left side and the traces for the parameters on the right. These traces should be random, and any trends indicate a problem. Trends early on indicate the need of a burn-in period. The newer sampling methods are better at initializing parameters to avoid this problem.

Notice here that you went beyond just the variables in the original model, X_1, X_2, and Y. You also included distributions for the model parameters. These enter the model as random variables as well, so you should define distributions for them. The graph you really fit in this example is more like the one in Figure 11.11.

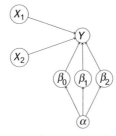

Figure 11.11 The Bayesian network for the linear regression example in PyMC3

11.6   Conclusion

Now, you have a basic idea for how to build and fit graphical models. We started with causal intuition and relaxed the assumption of causality to design more general Bayesian networks. You learned about fitting with the general (though computationally expensive) MCMC approach and went through an example where you fit linear regression.

Generally, when you use an algorithm based on a graphical model, the implementation won't be using an MCMC approach. Usually someone will have done the hard math to figure out a more efficient way to fit them. Often, there will be a fitting procedure built into an implementation.

Now that you have the basic machinery for building graphical models, you can look at a few useful models!

Dimensional Reduction and Latent Variable Models

12.1   Introduction

Now that you have the tools for exploring graphical models, we'll cover a few useful ones. We'll start with factor analysis, which finds application in the social science and in recommender systems. We'll move on to a related model, principal components analysis, and explain how it's useful for solving the collinearity problem in multiple regression. We'll end with ICA, which is good for separating signals that have blended together. We'll explain its application on some psychometric data.

One thing all of these models have in common is that they're *latent variable models*. That means in addition to the measured variables, there are some unobserved variables that underlie the data. You'll understand what this means more deeply in the context of these models.

We'll only really scratch the surface of these models. You can find a lot more detail in *Murphy's Machine Learning: A Probabilistic Perspective* [24]. Before we go into a few models, let's explore an important concept: a "prior" for a variable.

12.2   Priors

Let's talk about making a measurement of a click-through rate on a website. When you show a link to another section of the website, it's called an *impression* of that link. When a user receives an impression, they can either click the link or not click it. A click will be considered a "success" and a noisy indication that the user likes the content of the page. A nonclick will be considered a "failure" and a noisy indication that the user doesn't like the content. The click-through rate is the probability that a person will click the link when they receive an impression, $p = P(C = 1|I = 1)$. You can estimate it by looking at $\hat{p} = clicks/impressions$.

If you serve one impression of a link and the user doesn't click it, your estimate for $\hat{p}$ will be $0/1 = 0$. You'd guess that every following user will definitely not click the link! Clearly, that is a pathological result and can cause problems. What if your recommendation system was designed to remove links that performed below a certain level? You'd have some real trouble keeping content on the site.

Fortunately, there's a less pathological way to learn the click-through rate. You can take a *prior* on the click rate. To do this, you look at the distribution of all of the past values of the click rates (even better, fit a distribution to it with MCMC!). Then, having no data on a click rate, you at least know that it's drawn from that past distribution, as shown in Figure 12.1.

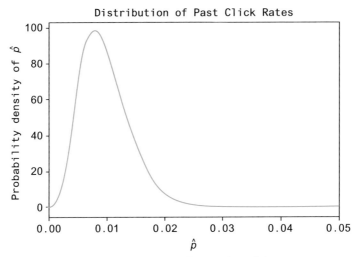

Figure 12.1   The distribution of click-through rates for past hyperlinks

This distribution represents your prior knowledge of the click-through rate, in the sense that it's what you know before you collect any data. You know here, for example, that you've never seen a link with a click rate as high as $p = 0.5$. It's extremely unlikely that the current link performs that well.

Now, as you collect data, you want to update your prior with new information. The resulting distribution will be called a *posterior* density for p. Suppose the true value is $p = 0.2$. After 20 impressions you get a posterior that looks like Figure 12.2. You can see the distribution is narrow, so you're slightly more sure that the true value lies in a smaller range. The distribution has also shifted more to the right, closer to the true value of $p = 0.2$. This represents the state of our knowledge after incorporating what you've learned from the new data with what you knew from the past data!

Mathematically, the way this works is that you say the prior, $P(p)$, takes on some distribution that you've fit using past data. In this case, it's a beta distribution with parameters to give an average value of around 0.1, with a little variance around it. You can denote this by $p \, Beta(\alpha, \beta)$, which you can read as "p is drawn from a beta distribution with parameters α and β."

Next, you need a model for the data. You can say that an impression is an opportunity for a click, and the click is a "success." That makes the clicks a binomial random variable, with success probability p and I trials: one for each impression. You can say that it takes the distribution $P(C|p, I)$ and that $C|p, I \, Bin(I, p)$. Knowing p and I, C is drawn from a binomial distribution with parameters I and p.

Let's assume impressions are a fixed parameter, I. You can say the distribution for p given I and C (our data) is $P(p|I, C) = \frac{P(C|p,I)P(p)}{P(C)} = \frac{P(C|p,I)P(p)}{\int P(C|p,I)P(p)dp}$ (by Bayes' theorem and the chain rule for

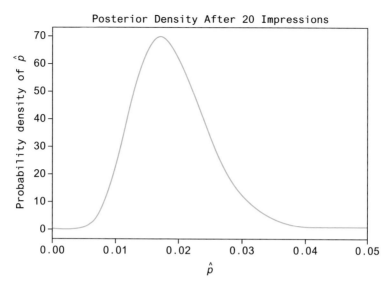

Figure 12.2   Your confidence in the click rate of the current item, given your knowledge of past click rates as well as your new data

conditional probability). You can see that the data, C and I, is used to update the prior, $P(p)$ by multiplication to get $P(p|I, C)$.

It's a fun exercise to derive this posterior and see what distribution it simplifies to!

12.3   Factor Analysis

Factor analysis tries to model N observed k-dimensional vectors, $\mathbf{x}_i$, by describing each data point with a smaller set of $f < k$ unmeasured (latent) variables. You write the data points as being drawn from a distribution, as follows:

$$p(x_i|z_i, \theta) = \mathcal{N}(\mathbf{W}\mathbf{z} + \mu, \Psi), \qquad (12.1)$$

where θ represents all of the parameters $\theta = (\mathbf{W}, \mathbf{z}, \mu)$. $\mathbf{W}$ is a k by f matrix, where there are f latent variables. μ is a global mean for the $\mathbf{x_i}$, and Ψ is the k by k covariance matrix.

The matrix $\mathbf{W}$ describes how each factor in $\mathbf{z}$ contributes to the values of the components of $\mathbf{x}_i$. It's said to describe how much the factors load on to the components of $\mathbf{x}_i$ and so is called the *factor loading matrix*. Given a vector of the values of the latent variables that correspond to a data point $\mathbf{x}$, $\mathbf{W}$ transforms $\mathbf{z}$ to the (mean-centered) expected value of $\mathbf{x}$.

The point of this is to use a model that is simpler than the data, so the major simplifying assumption that you'll make is that the matrix Ψ is diagonal. Note that this doesn't mean that the covariance matrix for $\mathbf{x}_i$ is diagonal! It's the *conditional* covariance matrix, when you know z_i, which is diagonal. This is going to mean that z_i is going to account for the covariance structure in $\mathbf{x}_i$.

Importantly, the latent factors z characterize each data point. It's a condensed representation of the information in the data. This is where factor analysis is useful. You can map from high-dimensional data down to much lower dimensional data and explain most of the variance using much less information.

You use a normal prior for the z variables in factor analysis, $z_i \sim \mathcal{N}(\mu_0, \Sigma_0)$. This makes it so it's easy to calculate the posterior for x_i. You'll denote the PDF of the normal distribution with mean μ and covariance matrix Σ as a function of x as $\mathcal{N}(x; \mu, \Sigma)$. Then, you can find the posterior for x_i as follows:

$$
\begin{aligned}
p(x_i|\theta) &= \int p(x_i|z_i, \theta) p(z_i|\theta) dz_i \\
&= \int \mathcal{N}(x_i; Wz_i + \mu, \Psi) \mathcal{N}(z_i; \mu_0, \Sigma_0) \\
&= \mathcal{N}(x_i; W\mu_0 + \mu, \Psi + W\Sigma_0 W^T)
\end{aligned}
\tag{12.2}
$$

You can actually get rid of the $W\mu_0$ term by absorbing it into the fitted parameter μ. You can also turn the Σ_0 term into I, since you're free to absorb the Σ_0 into W by defining $W' = W\Sigma_0^{-1/2}$. This lets you fix $W\Sigma_0 W^T = W'W'^T$.

From this analysis, you can see that you're modeling the covariance matrix of the x_i using this lower-rank matrix W, and the diagonal matrix Ψ. You can write the approximate covariance matrix for the x_i as follows:

$$
Cov(x_i) \cong WW^T + \Psi
\tag{12.3}
$$

Factor analysis has been applied often in the social sciences and finance. It can be good for reducing a complicated problem into a simpler, more interpretable one. An example is where x_i is the difference between the true returns on an asset from the expected returns. Then, the factors z_i are the risk factors, and the weights W determine the asset's sensitivity to the risk factors. Some of these factors might include inflation risk and market risk [25].

12.4 Principal Components Analysis

Principal components analysis (PCA) is a nice algorithm for dimensional reduction. It's actually just a special case of factor analysis. If you constrain $\Psi = \sigma^2 I$, let W be orthonormal, and let $\sigma^2 \to 0$, then you have PCA. If you let σ^2 be non-zero, then you have probabilistic PCA.

PCA is useful because it projects the data onto the *principal components* of the data set. The principal components are the eigenvectors of the covariance matrix. The first principal component is the eigenvector corresponding to the largest eigenvalue, the second component corresponds to the second largest, and so on.

The eigenvalues have a nice property in that they're uncorrelated. This results in the projected data having no covariance, so you can use this as a preprocessing step when doing regression to avoid the collinearity problem. The principal components are arranged such that the first eigenvector (principal component) accounts for the most variance in the data set, the second one, the second most, and so on. The interpretation of this is that you can look at the mapping of your data set by a few principal components to capture most of the variance (see, for example [26], pages 485–6).

It's easy to generate some multivariate normal data for an example.

```
1  import numpy as np
2  import pandas as pd
3  X = pd.DataFrame(np.random.multivariate_normal
4                  ([2,2], [[1,.5], [.5,1]], size=5000),
5                  columns=['$x_1$', '$x_2$'])
```

You can fit PCA using sklearn's implementation. Here, we just want to see the principal components of the data, so we'll use as many components as there are dimensions. Usually, you'll want to use fewer.

```
1  from sklearn.decomposition import PCA
2
3  model = PCA(n_components=2)
4  model = model.fit(X)
```

You can see the principal components in model.components_. Plotting these on top of the data results in Figure 12.3.

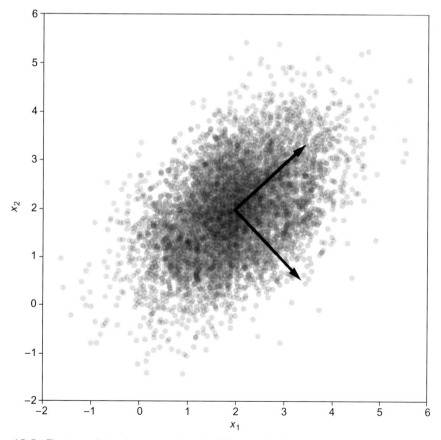

Figure 12.3 The two principal components of a 2-D gaussian data set

You can see that when you find z_i by projecting the x_i into these components, you should have no covariance. If you look at the original data, you find the covariance matrix in Figure 12.4. After transforming, you find the correlations in Figure 12.5.

```
1 | pd.DataFrame(model.transform(X), columns=['$z_1$', '$z_2$']).corr()
```

You can see that the correlations are now gone, so you've removed the collinearity in the data!

	x_1	x_2
x_1	1.000000	0.491874
x_2	0.491874	1.000000

Figure 12.4   The correlation matrix for the x_i

	z_1	z_2
z_1	1.000000	-0.045777
z_2	-0.045777	1.000000

Figure 12.5   The correlation matrix for the z_i

12.4.1   Complexity

The time complexity for PCA is $O(min(N^3, C^3))$ [27]. Assuming there are roughly as many samples as features, it's just $O(N^2)$ [28, 29].

12.4.2   Memory Considerations

You should have enough memory available to factorize your CxN matrix and find the eigenvalue decomposition.

12.4.3   Tools

This is a widely implemented algorithm. sklearn makes an implementation available at *sklearn.decomposition.PCA*. You can also find PCA implemented in C++ by the mlpack library.

12.5   Independent Component Analysis

When a data set is produced by a number of *independent* sources all jumbled together, independent component analysis (ICA) offers a technique to separate them for analysis. The largest signals can then be modeled, ignoring smaller signals as noise. Similarly, if there is a great deal of noise superimposed on a small signal, they can be separated such that the small signal isn't eclipsed.

ICA is a model that is similar to factor analysis. In this case, instead of using a Gaussian prior for the z_i, you use any non-Gaussian prior. It turns out that factor analysis varies up to a rotation! If you want a unique set of factors, you have to choose a different prior.

Let's apply this data to try to find the big five personality traits from some online data, at http://personality-testing.info/.

There are about 19,000 responses in this data to 50 questions. Each response is on a five-point scale. You can see the correlation matrix for this data in Figure 12.6. In this data, you'll notice that there are blocks along the diagonal. This is a well-designed questionnaire, based on selecting and testing

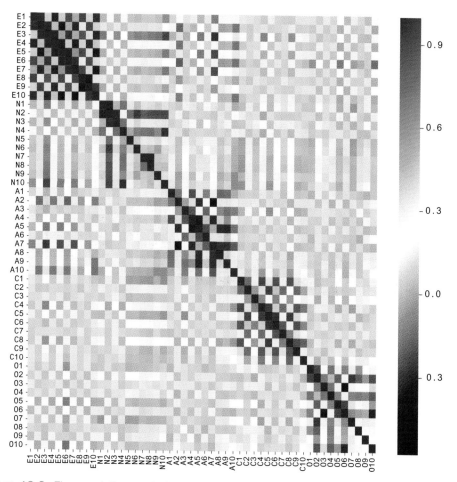

Figure 12.6 The correlation matrix for the big-five personality trait data. Notice the blocks of high and low covariance, forming checkered patterns.

questions. The test was developed using factor analysis methods to find which questions gave the best measurements of the latent factors. These questions, the x_i data, are then used to measure these factors, the z_i data, which are interpreted as personality traits. The questions that measure each factor are given in Figures 12.7.

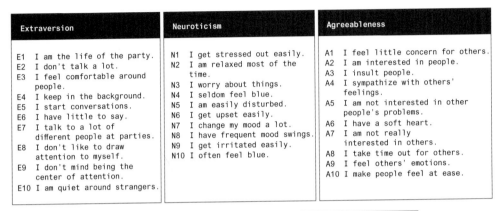

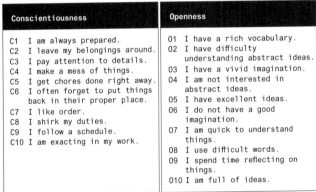

Figure 12.7   These are the questions underlying the big five personality traits. There are ten questions per trait, and they can correlate both positively and negatively with the underlying trait.

You can run the model on this data set, using sklearn's FastICA implementation, which will generate Figure 12.8.

```
1 from sklearn.decomposition import FastICA
2 model = FastICA(n_components=5)
3 model = model.fit(X[questions])
4 heatmap(model.components_, cmap='RdBu')
```

You can see in Figure 12.8 that the factors are along the y-axis, and the questions are along the x-axis. When a question is relevant for a factor, the values for the factor loadings are either low or high.

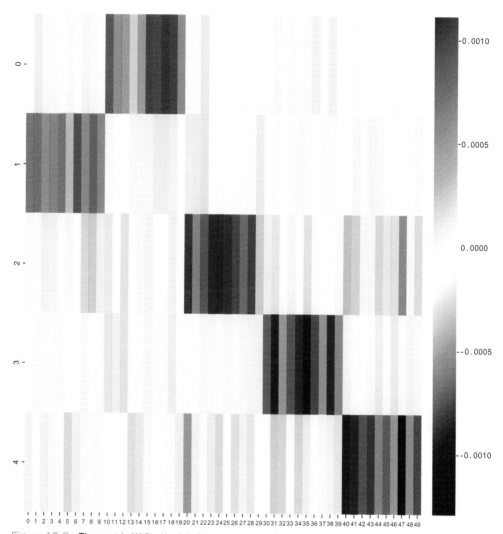

Figure 12.8   The matrix W for the big-five personality data

Finally, you can translate the sets of question responses into scores on the latent factors using the transformation in the model.

```
1 | Z = model.transform(X[questions])
```

You can histogram the columns of the Z matrix and see the distributions of the individual's scores (e.g., extraversion in Figure 12.9)!

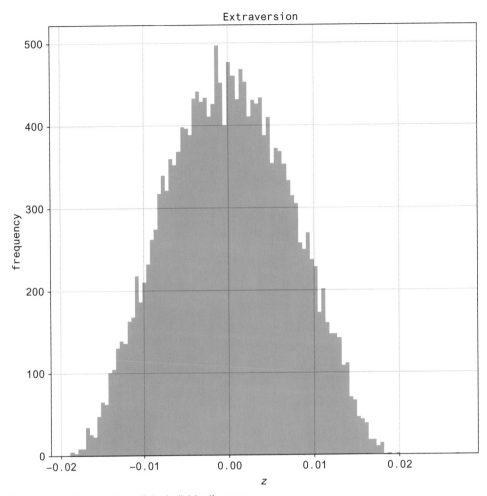

Figure 12.9   Distributions of the individual's score

12.5.1   Assumptions

The main assumption of this technique is the independence of signal sources. Another important consideration is the desire to have as many mixtures as signals (not always totally necessary). Finally, a signal being extracted can't be any more complex than the mixture it was extracted from (see, for example, pages 13–14 of [30]).

12.5.2   Complexity

There are fast algorithms for running ICA, including a fixed-point algorithm for FastICA [31] that runs quickly in practice, and a nonparametric kernel density estimation approach that runs in N log(N) time [32].

12.5.3   Memory Considerations

You should be able to fit at least $C \times N$ elements in memory.

12.5.4   Tools

ICA is another of those algorithms that seems to be implemented all over the place. FastICA is one of the more popular implementations. You can find it in scikit-learn as well as a C++ library implementing it. You'll find even more at http://research.ics.aalto.fi/ica/fastica/.

12.6   Latent Dirichlet Allocation

Topic modeling, or *latent dirichlet allocation*, is a good illustration of the power of Bayesian methods. The problem is that you have a collection of text documents that you'd like to organize into categories but don't have a good way to do it. There are too many documents to read all of them, but you're fine putting them into an algorithm to do the work.

You distill down the documents into a bag-of-words representation and often just one part of speech (e.g., nouns). Different nouns are associated at different levels with the various topics. For example, "football" almost certainly is from a sports topic, while "yard" could be referring to distance gained in a game of football or to someone's property. It might belong to both the "sports" and "homeowner" topics. Now, you just need a procedure to generate this text.

We'll describe a process that will map to a graphical model. The process will generate these bags of words. Then, you can adjust the parameters describing the process to fit the data set, and discover the latent topics associated with our documents. First, we should define some terms. We need to formalize the concept of a *topic*.

We'll describe a topic formally as a discrete probability distribution over our vocabulary. If you know a text is about one specific topic, the distribution will represent the word distribution of that document (although in practice, documents tend to be combinations of topics). In the sports topic, for example, you might find the word *football* occurring far more frequently than in other topics. It still might not be common, so it will have relatively low probability but will be much larger than it would be otherwise. In practice, sorting the words in a topic by their probability of being chosen is a good way to understand the topics you've discovered.

You also need a formal definition for a document. We mentioned that we'll represent documents as bags of words. We'll represent the topic membership of the document as a distribution over topics. If a document has a lot of weight on one topic, then any particular word from that document will likely be drawn from that topic. Now we're ready to describe our generative process.

The process will go like this:

- Draw the word distributions that define each topic.

- Draw a topic distribution for each document.

- For each word position in each document, draw a topic from the document's topic distribution and then draw a word from the topic.

In that way, you generate the whole set of documents. With this process, you can fit your documents to discover the topic distributions for each document that generate the text, as well as the word distributions for those topics. First, you have to turn the whole process into a graphical model. To do that, you have to define priors as well, so you can draw the word distributions that define your topics, and we draw topic distributions that describe your documents.

Each of these distributions is categorical: it's a normalized probability distribution over a collection of items (either topics or words). You need a probability distribution you can use to draw these distributions from! Let's think of a simpler case first: a Bernoulli distribution, or unfair coin flip.

The parameter for the Bernoulli distribution is a probability of a success. What you want to do for your word distributions is draw a probability of choosing a word. You can think of it as a higher-dimensional coin flip. To draw the coin flip probability, you need a distribution whose domain is between zero and one, and the beta distribution is a good candidate.

The beta distribution has a higher-dimensional generalization: the dirichlet distribution. Each draw from a dirichlet distribution is a normalized vector of probabilities. You can choose the dirichlet distribution as the priors for our topic distributions (documents) and word distributions (topics).

Typically people will choose uniform priors for the dirichlet distributions and leave them with relatively high variance. That allows you to have unlikely words and topics but biases slightly toward everything being equally likely.

With the priors defined, you can formalize the process a little more. For M documents, N topics, and V words in the vocabulary, you can describe it as follows:

- Draw a word distribution, t_i (a topic), from $Dir(\alpha)$ for each $i \in \{1, \ldots, N\}$.
- Draw a topic distribution, d_j (a document), from $Dir(\beta)$ for each $j \in \{1, \ldots, M\}$.
- For the kth word position in document j, draw the topic $t \in \{1, \ldots, N\}$ from d_j, and then the word from t.

It's beyond our scope to go into detail for methods to fit LDA. You should check [33].

There are some important rules of thumb to get topic modeling to work well. We'll summarize them as follows:

- Tokenize, stem, and n-gram your text into bags of words.
- Keep just the nouns from the text.
- Remove any word that occurs fewer than five times.
- Short documents (e.g., under ten words) will often have too large uncertainty for their topics to be useful.

Now, let's check out gensim [34] to see how to fit a topic model! We'll use the 20-newsgroups data set in sklearn as an example. We'll use the nltk to do the stemming and part-of-speech tagging and otherwise use gensim to do the heavy lifting. You may need to download some models for nltk, and it will prompt you with error messages if you do.

First, let's see what the part of speech tagger's output looks like.

```
1  import nltk
2  phrase = "The quick gray fox jumps over the lazy dog"
3  text = nltk.word_tokenize(phrase)
4  nltk.pos_tag(text)
```

That produces the following output:

```
[('The', 'DT'),
 ('quick', 'JJ'),
 ('gray', 'JJ'),
 ('fox', 'NN'),
 ('jumps', 'NNS'),
 ('over', 'IN'),
 ('the', 'DT'),
 ('lazy', 'JJ'),
 ('dog', 'NN')]
```

You can look up parts of speech with queries like this:

```
nltk.help.upenn_tagset('NN')
NN: noun, common, singular or mass
    common-carrier cabbage knuckle-duster Casino afghan shed thermostat
    investment slide humour falloff slick wind hyena override subhumanity
    machinist ...
```

You want just the nouns, so we'll keep the "NN" tags. Proper nouns have the "NNP" tag, and you'll want those too. See the nltk documentation for a full listing of tags to see which others you might want to include. This code will do the trick:

```
1  desired_tags = ['NN', 'NNP']
2  nouns_only = []
3  for document in newsgroups_train['data']:
4      tokenized = nltk.word_tokenize(document)
5      tagged = nltk.pos_tag(tokenized)
6      nouns_only.append([word for word, tag in tagged
7                            if tag in desired_tags])
```

Now, you want to stem the words. You'll use a language-specific stemmer, since those will do a better job.

```
1  from nltk.stem.snowball import SnowballStemmer
2
3  stemmer = SnowballStemmer("english")
4
5  for i, bag_of_words in enumerate(nouns_only):
6      for j, word in enumerate(bag_of_words):
7          nouns_only[i][j] = stemmer.stem(word)
```

Now, you want to count the words and make sure to keep words with only five or more occurrences.

```
1  word_counts = Counter()
2  for bag_of_words in nouns_only:
3      for word in bag_of_words:
4          word_counts[word] += 1
5
6  for i, bag_of_words in enumerate(nouns_only):
7      for word in enumerate(bag_of_words):
8          nouns_only[i] = [word for word in bag_of_words
9                           if word_counts[word] >= 5]
```

If you count the total words before and after stemming, you find 135,348 terms before and 110,858 after. You get rid of about 25,000 terms by stemming! Finally, you need to map your documents into the bag-of-words representation understood by gensim. It takes lists of (word, count) tuples, where the count is the number of times a word occurs in the document. To do this, you need the word to be an integer index corresponding to the word. You can make the word index mapping and use it when you create the tuples.

```
1  dictionary = {i: word for i, word in enumerate(word_counts.keys())}
2  word_index = {v:k for k, v in dictionary.items()}
3
4  for bag_of_words in enumerate(nouns_only):
5      counts = Counter(bag_of_words)
6      nouns_only[i] = [(word_index[word], count) for
7                       word, count in counts.items()]
```

Now, you can finally run the model. If you pass in the word mapping, there's a nice method to print the top terms in the topics you've discovered.

```
1  from gensim import models
2
3  model = models.LdaModel(nouns_only,
4                          id2word=dictionary,
5                          num_topics=20)
6  model.show_topics()
```

That produces the output shown here:

```
 1  [(12,
 2    '0.031*"god" + 0.030*">" + 0.013*"jesus" + 0.010*"x" + 0.009*"@"
 3    + 0.008*"law" + 0.006*"encrypt" + 0.006*"time"
 4    + 0.006*"christian" + 0.006*"subject"'),
 5   (19,
 6    '0.011*"@" + 0.011*"stephanopoulo" + 0.010*"subject"
 7    + 0.009*"univers" + 0.008*"organ" + 0.005*"ripem"
 8    + 0.005*"inform" + 0.005*"greec" + 0.005*"church"
 9    + 0.005*"greek"'),
10   (16,
11    '0.022*"team" + 0.017*"@" + 0.016*"game" + 0.011*">"
12    + 0.010*"season" + 0.010*"hockey" + 0.009*"year" + 0.009*"subject"
13    + 0.009*"organ" + 0.008*"nhl"'),
14   (18,
15    '0.056*"@" + 0.045*">" + 0.016*"subject" + 0.015*"organ"
16    + 0.011*"re" + 0.009*"articl" + 0.007*"<" + 0.007*"univers"
17    + 0.006*"nntp-posting-host" + 0.004*"comput"'),
18   (1,
19    '0.075*"*" + 0.022*"@" + 0.016*"sale" + 0.013*"subject"
20    + 0.013*"organ" + 0.011*"univers" + 0.008*"nntp-posting-host"
21    + 0.006*"offer" + 0.005*"distribut" + 0.005*"tape"'),
22   (11,
23    '0.040*"q" + 0.021*"presid" + 0.014*"mr." + 0.006*"packag"
24    + 0.006*"event" + 0.006*">" + 0.005*"handler" + 0.005*"@"
25    + 0.004*"mack" + 0.004*"whaley"'),
26   (13,
27    '0.037*"@" + 0.020*"drive" + 0.018*"subject" + 0.017*"organ"
28    + 0.011*"card" + 0.010*"univers" + 0.010*"problem" + 0.009*"disk"
29    + 0.009*"system" + 0.008*"nntp-posting-host"'),
30   (6,
31    '0.065*">" + 0.055*"@" + 0.015*"organ" + 0.014*"subject"
32    + 0.013*"re" + 0.012*"articl" + 0.007*"|" + 0.006*"univers"
33    + 0.006*"<" + 0.006*"nntp-posting-host"'),
34   (7,
35    '0.053*">" + 0.039*"@" + 0.011*"subject" + 0.010*"organ"
36    + 0.010*"re" + 0.009*"articl" + 0.006*"univers" + 0.006*"]"
37    + 0.005*"<" + 0.004*"year"'),
38   (17,
39    '0.160*"|" + 0.028*"@" + 0.015*"subject" + 0.014*"organ"
40    + 0.013*"/" + 0.008*"\\" + 0.008*"nntp-posting-host" + 0.008*">"
41    + 0.007*"+" + 0.007*"univers"')]
```

You can see a few things in these results. First, there is a lot of extra junk in the text that we haven't filtered out yet. Before even tokenizing, you should use regex to replace the nonword characters, punctuation, and markup. You can also see some common terms like `subject` and `nntp-posting-host` that are likely to occur in any topic. These are frequent terms that we should really just filter out or use term weighting to suppress. Gensim has some nice tutorials on their website, and we recommend going there to see how to use term frequency, inverse document frequency (tfidf) weighting to suppress common terms without having to remove them from the data.

You can also see that there is something discovered in the data despite the noise. The first topic has *god*, *jesus*, and *christian* in the top terms so is likely corresponding to a religion news group. You could see which newsgroups weight highly on this topic to check for yourself.

A quick way to remove bad characters is to filter everything that isn't a character or number using regular expressions. You can use the Python *re* package to do this, replacing with spaces. These will turn into nothing when they're tokenized.

```
1  filtered = [re.sub('[^a-zA-Z0-9]+', ' ', document) for document
2              in newsgroups_train['data']]
```

If you run through the same procedure again after filtering, you get the following:

```
1  [(3,
2    '0.002*"polygon" + 0.002*"simm" + 0.002*"vram" + 0.002*"lc"
3    + 0.001*"feustel" + 0.001*"dog" + 0.001*"coprocessor"
4    + 0.001*"nick" + 0.001*"lafayett" + 0.001*"csiro"'),
5   (9,
6    '0.002*"serdar" + 0.002*"argic" + 0.001*"brandei"
7    + 0.001*"turk" + 0.001*"he" + 0.001*"hab" + 0.001*"islam"
8    + 0.001*"tyre" + 0.001*"zuma" + 0.001*"ge"'),
9   (5,
10   '0.004*"msg" + 0.003*"god" + 0.002*"religion" + 0.002*"fbi"
11   + 0.002*"christian" + 0.002*"cult" + 0.002*"atheist"
12   + 0.002*"greec" + 0.001*"life" + 0.001*"robi"'),
13  (11,
14   '0.004*"pitt" + 0.004*"gordon" + 0.003*"bank"
15   + 0.002*"pittsburgh" + 0.002*"cadr" + 0.002*"geb"
16   + 0.002*"duo" + 0.001*"skeptic" + 0.001*"chastiti"
17   + 0.001*"talent"'),
18  (8,
19   '0.003*"access" + 0.003*"gun" + 0.002*"cs" + 0.002*"edu"
20   + 0.002*"x" + 0.002*"dos" + 0.002*"univers"
21   + 0.002*"colorado" + 0.002*"control" + 0.002*"printer"'),
22  (15,
23   '0.002*"athen" + 0.002*"georgia" + 0.002*"covington"
24   + 0.002*"drum" + 0.001*"aisun3" + 0.001*"rsa"
25   + 0.001*"arromde" + 0.001*"ai" + 0.001*"ham"
26   + 0.001*"missouri"'),
27  (16,
28   '0.002*"ranck" + 0.002*"magnus" + 0.002*"midi"
29   + 0.002*"alomar" + 0.002*"ohio" + 0.001*"skidmor"
```

```
30      + 0.001*"epa" + 0.001*"diablo" + 0.001*"viper"
31      + 0.001*"jbh55289"'),
32    (19,
33     '0.002*"islam" + 0.002*"stratus" + 0.002*"com"
34      + 0.002*"mot" + 0.002*"comet" + 0.001*"virginia"
35      + 0.001*"convex" + 0.001*"car" + 0.001*"jaeger"
36      + 0.001*"gov"'),
37    (0,
38     '0.005*"henri" + 0.003*"dyer" + 0.002*"zoo"
39      + 0.002*"spencer" + 0.002*"zoolog" + 0.002*"spdcc"
40      + 0.002*"prize" + 0.002*"outlet" + 0.001*"tempest"
41      + 0.001*"dresden"'),
42    (14,
43     '0.006*"god" + 0.005*"jesus" + 0.004*"church"
44      + 0.002*"christ" + 0.002*"sin" + 0.002*"bibl"
45      + 0.002*"templ" + 0.002*"mari" + 0.002*"cathol"
46      + 0.002*"jsc"')]
```

These results are pretty obviously better but still aren't perfect. There are many parameters to tune with algorithms like these, so this should put you in a good place to start experimenting.

We should mention one powerful aspect of gensim. It operates on a generator for items, instead of a batch of items. That allows you to work with very large data sets without having to load them into memory. Gensim is appropriate for, as their tutorial suggests, modeling the topics within Wikipedia and other large corpuses.

12.7 Conclusion

In this chapter, you saw how to use some Bayesian network and other methods to reduce the dimension of data and discover latent structure in the data. We walked through some examples that are useful for analyzing survey response and other categorical data. We went through a detailed example to learn topic modeling. Ideally now you're familiar with latent variable models enough to be able to use them confidently!

13

Causal Inference

13.1   Introduction

We've introduced a couple of machine-learning algorithms and suggested that they can be used to produce clear, interpretable results. You've seen that logistic regression coefficients can be used to say how much more likely an outcome will occur in conjunction with a feature (for binary features) or how much more likely an outcome is to occur per unit increase in a variable (for real-valued features). We'd like to make stronger statements. We'd like to say "If you increase a variable by a unit, then it will have the effect of making an outcome more likely."

These two interpretations of a regression coefficient are so similar on the surface that you may have to read them a few times to take away the meaning. The key is that in the first case, we're describing what usually happens in a system that we observe. In the second case, we're saying what will happen if we intervene in that system and disrupt it from its normal operation.

After we go through an example, we'll build up the mathematical and conceptual machinery to describe interventions. We'll cover how to go from a Bayesian network describing observational data to one that describes the effects of an intervention. We'll go through some classic approaches to estimating the effects of interventions, and finally we'll explain how to use machine-learning estimators to estimate the effects of interventions.

If you imagine a binary outcome, such as "I'm late for work," you can imagine some features that might vary with it. Bad weather can cause you to be late for work. Bad weather can also cause you to wear rain boots. Days when you're wearing rain boots, then, are days when you're more likely be late for work. If you look at the correlation between the binary feature "wearing rain boots" and the outcome "I'm late for work," you'll find a positive relationship. It's nonsense, of course, to say that wearing rain boots causes you to be late for work. It's just a proxy for bad weather. You'd never recommend a policy of "You shouldn't wear rain boots, so you'll be late for work less often." That would be reasonable only if "wearing rain boots" was *causally* related to "being late for work." As an intervention to prevent lateness, not wearing rain boots doesn't make any sense.

In this chapter, you'll learn the difference between correlative (rain boots and lateness) and causal (rain and lateness) relationships. We'll discuss the gold standard for establishing causality: an experiment. We'll also cover some methods to discover causal relationships in cases when you're not able to run an experiment, which happens often in realistic settings.

13.2   Experiments

The case that might be familiar to you is an AB test. You can make a change to a product and test it against the original version of the product. You do this by randomly splitting your users into two groups. The group membership is denoted by D, where $D = 1$ is the group that experiences the new change (the test group), and $D = 0$ is the group that experiences the original version of the product (the control group). For concreteness, let's say you're looking at the effect of a recommender system change that recommends articles on a website. The control group experiences the original algorithm, and the test group experiences the new version. You want to see the effect of this change on total pageviews, Y.

You'll measure this effect by looking at a quantity called the *average treatment effect* (ATE). The ATE is the average difference in the outcome between the test and control groups, $E_{test}[Y] - E_{control}[Y]$, or $\delta_{naive} = E[Y|D = 1] - E[Y|D = 0]$. This is the "naive" estimator for the ATE since here we're ignoring everything else in the world. For experiments, it's an unbiased estimate for the true effect.

A nice way to estimate this is to do a regression. That lets you also measure error bars at the same time and include other covariates that you think might reduce the noise in Y so you can get more precise results. Let's continue with this example.

```
1  import numpy as np
2  import pandas as pd
3
4  N = 1000
5
6  x = np.random.normal(size=N)
7  d = np.random.binomial(1., 0.5, size=N)
8  y = 3. * d + x + np.random.normal()
9
10 X = pd.DataFrame({'X': x, 'D': d, 'Y': y})
```

Here, we've randomized D to get about half in the test group and half in the control. X is some other covariate that causes Y, and Y is the outcome variable. We've added a little extra noise to Y to just make the problem a little noisier.

You can use a regression model $Y = \beta_0 + \beta_1 D$ to estimate the expected value of Y, given the covariate D, as $E[Y|D] = \beta_0 + \beta_1 D$. The β_0 piece will be added to $E[Y|D]$ for all values of D (i.e., 0 or 1). The β_1 part is added only when $D = 1$ because when $D = 0$, it's multiplied by zero. That means $E[Y|D = 0] = \beta_0$ when $D = 0$ and $E[Y|D = 1] = \beta_0 + \beta_1$ when $D = 1$. Thus, the β_1 coefficient is going to be the difference in average Y values between the $D = 1$ group and the $D = 0$ group, $E[Y|D = 1] - E[Y|D = 0] = \beta_1$! You can use that coefficient to estimate the effect of this experiment.

When you do the regression of Y against D, you get the result in Figure 13.1.

```
1  from statsmodels.api import OLS
2  X['intercept'] = 1.
3  model = OLS(X['Y'], X[['D', 'intercept']])
4  result = model.fit()
5  result.summary()
```

OLS Regression Results

Dep. Variable:	Y	R-squared:	0.560
Model:	OLS	Adj. R-squared:	0.555
Method:	Least Squares	F-statistic:	124.5
Date:	Sun, 08 Apr 2018	Prob (F-statistic):	3.79e-19
Time:	22:28:01	Log-Likelihood:	-180.93
No. Observations:	100	AIC:	365.9
Df Residuals:	98	BIC:	371.1
Df Model:	1		
Covariance Type:	nonrobust		

	coef	std err	t	P>|t|	[0.025	0.975]
D	3.3551	0.301	11.158	0.000	2.758	3.952
intercept	-0.1640	0.225	-0.729	0.468	-0.611	0.283

Omnibus:	0.225	Durbin-Watson:	1.866
Prob(Omnibus):	0.894	Jarque-Bera (JB):	0.360
Skew:	0.098	Prob(JB):	0.835
Kurtosis:	2.780	Cond.No.	2.78

Figure 13.1   The regression for $Y = \beta_0 + \beta_1 D$

Why did this work? Why is it okay to say the effect of the experiment is just the difference between the test and control group outcomes? It seems obvious, but that intuition will break down in the next section. Let's make sure you understand it deeply before moving on.

Each person can be assigned to the test group or the control group, but not both. For a person assigned to the test group, you can talk hypothetically about the value their outcome would have had, had they been assigned to the control group. You can call this value Y^0 because it's the value Y would take if D had been set to 0. Likewise, for control group members, you can talk about a hypothetical Y^1. What you really want to measure is the difference in outcomes $\delta = Y^1 - Y^0$ for each person. This is impossible since each person can be in only one group! For this reason, these Y^1 and Y^0 variables are called *potential outcomes*.

If a person is assigned to the test group, you measure the outcome $Y = Y^1$. If a person is assigned to the control group, you measure $Y = Y^0$. Since you can't measure the individual effects, maybe you can measure population level effects. We can try to talk instead about $E[Y^1]$ and $E[Y^0]$. We'd like $E[Y^1] = E[Y|D = 1]$ and $E[Y^0] = E[Y|D = 0]$, but we're not guaranteed that that's true. In the recommender system test example, what would happen if you assigned people with higher Y^0 pageview counts to the test group? You might measure an effect that's larger than the true effect!

Fortunately, you randomize D to make sure it's independent of Y^0 and Y^1. That way, you're sure that $E[Y^1] = E[Y|D = 1]$ and $E[Y^0] = E[Y|D = 0]$, so you can say that $\delta = E[Y^1 - Y^0] = E[Y|D = 1] - E[Y|D = 0]$. When other factors can influence assignment, D, then you can no longer be sure you have correct estimates! This is true in general when you don't have control over a system, so you can't ensure D is independent of all other factors.

In the general case, D won't just be a binary variable. It can be ordered, discrete, or continuous. You might wonder about the effect of the length of an article on the share rate, about smoking on the probability of getting lung cancer, of the city you're born in on future earnings, and so on.

Just for fun before we go on, let's see something nice you can do in an experiment to get more precise results. Since we have a co-variate, X, that also causes Y, we can account for more of the variation in Y. That makes our predictions less noisy, so our estimates for the effect of D will be more precise! Let's see how this looks. We regress on both D and X now to get Figure 13.2.

Dep. Variable:	Y	R-squared:	0.754
Model:	OLS	Adj. R-squared:	0.749
Method:	Least Squares	F-statistic:	148.8
Date:	Sun, 08 Apr 2018	Prob (F-statistic):	2.75e-30
Time:	22:59:08	Log-Likelihood:	-151.76
No. Observations:	100	AIC:	309.5
Df Residuals:	97	BIC:	317.3
Df Model:	2		
Covariance Type:	nonrobust		

	coef	std err	t	P>|t|	[0.025	0.975]
D	3.2089	0.226	14.175	0.000	2.760	3.658
X	1.0237	0.117	8.766	0.000	0.792	1.256
intercept	0.0110	0.170	0.065	0.949	-0.327	0.349

Omnibus:	2.540	Durbin-Watson:	1.648
Prob(Omnibus):	0.281	Jarque-Bera (JB):	2.362
Skew:	-0.293	Prob(JB):	0.307
Kurtosis:	2.528	Cond. No.	2.81

Figure 13.2   The regression for $Y = \beta_0 + \beta_1 D + \beta_2 X$

Notice that the R^2 is much better. Also, notice that the confidence interval for D is much narrower! We went from a range of $3.95 - 2.51 = 1.2$ down to $3.65 - 2.76 = 0.89$. In short, finding covariates that account for the outcome can increase the precision of your experiments!

13.3   Observation: An Example

Let's look at an example of what happens when you don't make your cause independent of everything else. We'll use it to show how to build some intuition for how observation is different from intervention. Let's look at a simple model for the correlation between race, poverty, and crime in a neighborhood. Poverty reduces people's options in life and makes crime more likely. That makes poverty a cause of crime. Next, neighborhoods have a racial composition that can persist over time, so the neighborhood is a cause of racial composition. The neighborhood also determines some social factors, like culture and education, and so can be a cause of poverty. This gives us the causal diagram in Figure 13.3.

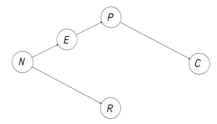

Figure 13.3   The neighborhood is a cause of its racial composition and poverty levels. The poverty level is a cause of crime.

Here, there is no causal relationship between race and crime, but you would find them to be correlated in observational data. Let's simulate some data to examine this.

```
1  N = 10000
2
3  neighborhood = np.array(range(N))
4
5  industry = neighborhood % 3
6
7  race = ((neighborhood % 3
8
9          + np.random.binomial(3, p=0.2, size=N))) % 4
10
11 income = np.random.gamma(25, 1000*(industry + 1))
12
13 crime = np.random.gamma(100000. / income, 100, size=N)
14
15 X = pd.DataFrame({'$R$': race, '$I$': income, '$C$': crime,
16
17                  '$E$': industry, '$N$': neighborhood})
```

Here, each data point will be a neighborhood. There are common historic reasons for the racial composition and the dominant industry in each neighborhood. The industry determines the income levels in the neighborhood, and the income level is inversely related with crime rates.

If you plot the correlation matrix for this data (Figure 13.4), you can see that race and crime are correlated, even though there is no causal relationship between them!

	C	E	I	N	R
C	1.000000	-0.542328	-0.567124	0.005518	-0.492169
E	-0.542328	1.000000	0.880411	0.000071	0.897789
I	-0.567124	0.880411	1.000000	-0.005650	0.793993
N	0.005518	0.000071	-0.005650	1.000000	-0.003666
R	-0.492169	0.897789	0.793993	-0.003666	1.000000

Figure 13.4   Raw data showing correlations between crime (C), industry (E), income (I), neighborhood (N), and race (R)

You can take a regression approach and see how you can interpret the regression coefficients. Since we know the right model to use, we can just do the right regression, which gives the results in Figure 13.5.

Generalized Linear Model Regression Results

Dep. Variable:	C	No. Observations:	10000
Model:	GLM	Df Residuals:	9999
Model Family:	Gamma	Df Model:	0
Link Function:	inverse_power	Scale:	1.53451766278
Method:	IRLS	Long-Likelihood:	-68812.
Date:	Sun, 06 Aug 2017	Deviance:	15138.
Time:	22:43:02	Pearson chi2:	1.53e+04
No. Iterations:	7		

	coef	std err	z	P>|z|	[0.025	0.975]
1/I	123.0380	1.524	80.726	0.000	120.051	126.025

Figure 13.5   Regression for crime against the inverse of income

```
1 from statsmodels.api import GLM
2 import statsmodels.api as sm
3
4 X['$1/I$'] = 1. / X['$I$']
5 model = GLM(X['$C$'], X[['$1/I$']], family=sm.families.Gamma())
6 result = model.fit()
7 result.summary()
```

From this you can see that when $1/I$ increases by a unit, the number of crimes increases by 123 units. If the crime units are in crimes per 10,000 people, this means 123 more crimes per 10,000 people.

This is a nice result, but you'd really like to know whether the result is causal. If it is causal, that means you can design a policy intervention to exploit the relationship. That is, you'd like to know if people earned more income, everything else held fixed, would there be less crime? If this were a causal result, you could say that if you make incomes higher (independent of everything else), then you can expect that for each unit decrease in $1/I$, you'll see 123 fewer crimes. What is keeping us from making those claims now?

You'll see that regression results aren't necessarily causal; let's look at the relationship between race and crime. We'll do another regression as shown here:

```
1  from statsmodels.api import GLM
2  import statsmodels.api as sm
3
4  races = {0: 'african-american', 1: 'hispanic',
5          2: 'asian', 3: 'white'}
6  X['race'] = X['$R$'].apply(lambda x: races[x])
7  race_dummies = pd.get_dummies(X['race'])
8  X[race_dummies.columns] = race_dummies
9  model = OLS(X['$C$'], race_dummies)
10 result = model.fit()
11 result.summary()
```

Figure 13.6 show the result.

Here, you find a strong correlative relationship between race and crime, even though there's no causal relationship. You know that if we moved a lot of white people into a black neighborhood (holding income level constant), you should have no effect on crime. If this regression were causal, then you would. Why do you find a significant regression coefficient even when there's no causal relationship?

In this example, you went wrong because racial composition and income level were both caused by the history of each neighborhood. This is a case where two variables share a common cause. If you don't control for that history, then you'll find a spurious association between the two variables. What you're seeing is a general rule: when two variables share a common cause, they will be correlated (or, more generally, statistically dependent) even when there's no causal relationship between them.

Another nice example of this common cause problem is that when lemonade sales are high, crime rates are also high. If you regress crime on lemonade sales, you'd find a significant increase in crimes per unit increase in lemonade sales! Clearly the solution isn't to crack down on lemonade stands. As it happens, more lemonade is sold on hot days. Crime is also higher on hot days. The weather is a common cause of crime and lemonade sales. We find that the two are correlated even though there is no causal relationship between them.

The solution in the lemonade example is to control for the weather. If you look at all days where it is sunny and 95 degrees Fahrenheit, the effect of the weather on lemonade sales is constant. The

Dep. Variable:	C	R-squared:	0.262
Model:	OLS	Adj. R-squared:	0.262
Method:	Least Squares	F-statistic:	1184.
Date:	Sun, 06 Aug 2017	Prob (F-statistic):	0.00
Time:	22:59:47	Log-Likelihood:	-65878.
No. Observations:	10000	AIC:	1.318e+05
Df Residuals:	9996	BIC:	1.318e+05
Df Model:	3		
Covariance Type:	nonrobust		

	coef	std err	t	P>|t|	[0.025	0.975]
african-american	411.9718	3.395	121.351	0.000	405.317	418.626
asian	155.0682	3.020	51.350	0.000	149.149	160.988
hispanic	248.8263	3.066	81.159	0.000	242.817	254.836
white	132.0232	6.909	19.108	0.000	118.479	145.567

Omnibus:	2545.693	Durbin-Watson:	1.985
Prob(Omnibus):	0.000	Jarque-Bera (JB):	7281.773
Skew:	1.335	Prob(JB):	0.00
Kurtosis:	6.217	Cond. No.	2.29

Figure 13.6   Statistics highlighting relationships between race and crime

effect of weather and crime is also constant in the restricted data set. Any variance in the two must be because of other factors. You'll find that lemonade sales and crime no longer have a significant correlation in this restricted data set. This problem is usually called *confounding*, and the way to break confounding is to control for the confounder.

Similarly, if you look only at neighborhoods with a specific history (in this case the relevant variable is the dominant industry), then you'll break the relationship between race and income and so also the relationship between race and crime.

To reason about this more rigorously, let's look at Figure 13.3. We can see the source of dependence, where there's a path from N to R and a path from N through E and P to C. If you were able to break this path by holding a variable fixed, you could disrupt the dependence that flows along it. The result will be different from the usual observational result. You will have changed the dependencies in the graph, so you will have changed the joint distribution of all these variables.

If you intervene to set the income level in an area in a way that is independent of the dominant industry, you'll break the causal link between the industry and the income, resulting in the graph in Figure 13.7. In this system, you should find that the path that produces dependence between race and crime is broken. The two should be independent.

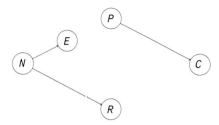

Figure 13.7 The result of an intervention, where you set the income level by direct intervention in a way that is independent of the dominant industry in the neighborhood

How can you do this controlling using only observational data? One way is just to restrict to subsets of the data. You can, for example, look only at industry 0 and see how this last regression looks.

```
1  X_restricted = X[X['$E$'] == 0]
2
3  races = {0: 'african-american', 1: 'hispanic',
4          2: 'asian', 3: 'white'}
5  X_restricted['race'] = X_restricted['$R$'].apply(lambda x: races[x])
6  race_dummies = pd.get_dummies(X_restricted['race'])
7  X_restricted[race_dummies.columns] = race_dummies
8  model = OLS(X_restricted['$C$'], race_dummies)
9  result = model.fit()
10 result.summary()
```

This produces the result in Figure 13.8.

Now you can see that all of the results are within confidence of each other! The dependence between race and crime is fully explained by the industry in the area. In other words, in this hypothetical data set, crime is independent of race when you know what the dominant industry is in the area. What you have done is the same as the conditioning you did before.

Notice that the confidence intervals on the new coefficients are fairly wide compared to what they were before. This is because you've restricted to a small subset of your data. Can you do better, maybe by using more of the data? It turns out there's a better way to control for something than restricting the data set. You can just regress on the variables you'd like to control for!

```
1  from statsmodels.api import GLM
2  import statsmodels.api as sm
3
4  races = {0: 'african-american', 1: 'hispanic',
5          2: 'asian', 3: 'white'}
6  X['race'] = X['$R$'].apply(lambda x: races[x])
7  race_dummies = pd.get_dummies(X['race'])
8  X[race_dummies.columns] = race_dummies
9
10 industries = {i: 'industry_{}'.format(i) for i in range(3)}
11 X['industry'] = X['$E$'].apply(lambda x: industries[x])
```

Dep. Variable:	C	R-squared:	0.001
Model:	OLS	Adj. R-squared:	0.000
Method:	Least Squares	F-statistic:	1.109
Date:	Sun, 06 Aug 2017	Prob (F-statistic):	0.344
Time:	23:19:14	Log-Likelihood:	-22708.
No. Observations:	3334	AIC:	4.542e+04
Df Residuals:	3330	BIC:	4.545e+04
Df Model:	3		
Covariance Type:	nonrobust		

	coef	std err	t	P>|t|	[0.025	0.975]
african-american	415.1116	5.260	78.914	0.000	404.798	425.425
asian	421.3615	12.326	34.185	0.000	397.194	445.529
hispanic	421.3907	6.239	67.536	0.000	409.157	433.624
white	484.8838	40.816	11.880	0.000	404.856	564.911

Omnibus:	538.823	Durbin-Watson:	1.947
Prob(Omnibus):	0.000	Jarque-Bera (JB):	943.390
Skew:	1.038	Prob(JB):	1.40e-205
Kurtosis:	4.575	Cond. No.	7.76

Figure 13.8 A hypothetical regression on race indicator variables predicting crime rates, but controlling for local industry using stratification of the data. There are no differences in expected crimes, controlling for industry.

```
12  industry_dummies = pd.get_dummies(X['industry'])
13  X[industry_dummies.columns] = industry_dummies
14
15  x = list(industry_dummies.columns)[1:] + list(race_dummies.columns)
16
17  model = OLS(X['$C$'], X[x])
18  result = model.fit()
19  result.summary()
```

Then, you get Figure 13.9 shows the result.

Here, the confidence intervals are much narrower, and you see there's still no significant association between race and income level: the coefficients are roughly equal. This is a causal regression result: you can now see that there would be no effect of an intervention to change the racial composition of neighborhoods. This simple example is nice because you can see what to control for, and you've measured the things you need to control for. How do you know what to

Dep. Variable:	C	R-squared:	0.331
Model:	OLS	Adj. R-squared:	0.331
Method:	Least Squares	F-statistic:	988.5
Date:	Sun, 06 Aug 2017	Prob (F-statistic):	0.00
Time:	23:29:24	Log-Likelihood:	-65483.
No. Observations:	10000	AIC:	1.310e+05
Df Residuals:	9994	BIC:	1.310e+05
Df Model:	5		
Covariance Type:	nonrobust		

	coef	std err	t	P>|t|	[0.025	0.975]
industry_1	-215.1618	4.931	-43.638	0.000	-224.827	-205.497
industry_2	-278.9783	5.581	-49.984	0.000	-289.919	-268.038
african-american	415.2042	3.799	109.306	0.000	407.758	422.650
asian	418.0980	5.203	80.361	0.000	407.900	428.296
hispanic	423.5622	4.216	100.464	0.000	415.298	431.827
white	422.1700	6.530	64.647	0.000	409.369	434.971

Omnibus:	2493.579	Durbin-Watson:	1.991
Prob(Omnibus):	0.000	Jarque-Bera (JB):	7156.219
Skew:	1.306	Prob(JB):	0.00
Kurtosis:	6.218	Cond. No.	4.56

Figure 13.9 Statistics highlighting the relationship between race and industry from an OLS fit

control for in general? Will you always be able to do it successfully? It turns out it's very hard in practice, but sometimes it's the best you can do.

13.4 Controlling to Block Non-causal Paths

You just saw that you can take a correlative result and make it a causal result by controlling for the right variables. How do you know what variables to control for? How do you know that regression analysis will control for them? This section relies heavily on d-separation from Chapter 11. If that material isn't fresh, you might want to review it now.

You saw in the previous chapter that conditioning can break statistical dependence. If you condition on the middle variable of a path $X \rightarrow Y \rightarrow Z$, you'll break the dependence between X and Z that the path produces. If you condition on a confounding variable $X \leftarrow Z \rightarrow Y$, you can break the dependence between X and Y induced by the confounder as well. It's important to note that statistical dependence induced by other paths between X and Y is left unharmed by this conditioning. If, for example, you condition on Z in the system in Figure 13.10, you'll get rid of the confounding but leave the causal dependence.

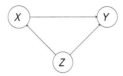

Figure 13.10   Conditioning on Z disrupts the confounding but leaves the causal statistical dependence between X and Y intact

If you had a general rule to choose which paths to block, you could eliminate all noncausal dependence between variables but save the causal dependence. The "back-door" criterion is the rule you're looking for. It tells you what set of variables, Z, you should control for to eliminate any noncausal statistical dependence between X_i and X_j. You should note a final nuance before introducing the criterion. If you want to know if the correlation between X_i and X_j is "causal," you have to worry about the direction of the effect. It's great to know, for example, that the correlation "being on vacation" and "being relaxed" is not confounded, but you'd really like to know whether "being on vacation" causes you to "be relaxed." That will inform a policy of going on vacation in order to be relaxed. If the causation were reversed, you couldn't take that policy.

With that in mind, the back-door criterion is defined relative to an ordered pair of variables, (X_i, X_j), where X_i will be the cause, and X_j will be the effect.

Definition 13.1. Back-Door Conditioning

It's sufficient to control for a set of variables, Z, to eliminate noncausal dependence for the effect of X_i on X_j in a causal graph, G, if

- No variable in Z is a descendant of X_i, and
- Z blocks every path between X_i and X_j that contains an arrow into X_i.

We won't prove this theorem, but let's build some intuition for it. First, let's examine the condition "no variable in Z is a descendant of X_i." You learned earlier that if you condition on a common effect of X_i and X_j, then the two variables will be conditionally dependent, even if they're normally independent. This remains true if you condition on any effect of the common effect (and so on down the paths). Thus, you can see that the first part of the back-door criterion prevents you from introducing extra dependence where there is none.

There is something more to this condition, too. If you have a chain like $X_i \rightarrow X_k \rightarrow X_j$, you see that X_k is a descendant of X_i. It's not allowed in Z. This is because if you condition on X_k, you'd block a causal path between X_i and X_j. Thus, you see that the first condition also prevents you from conditioning on variables that fall along causal paths.

The second condition says "Z blocks every path between X_i and X_j that contains an arrow into X_i." This part will tell us to control for confounders. How can you see this? Let's consider some cases where there is one or more node along the path between X_i and X_j and the path contains an arrow into X_i. If there is a collider along the path between X_i and X_j, then the path is already blocked, so you just condition on the empty set to block that path. Next, if there is a fork along the path, like the path $X_i \leftarrow X_k \rightarrow X_j$, and no colliders, then you have typical confounding. You can condition on any node along the path that will block it. In this case, you add X_k to the set Z. Note that there can be no causal path from X_i to X_j with an arrow pointing into X_i because of the arrow pointing into X_i.

Thus, you can see that you're blocking all noncausal paths from X_i to X_j, and the remaining statistical dependence will be showing the causal dependence of X_j on X_i. Is there a way you can use this dependence to estimate the effects of interventions?

13.4.1 The G-formula

Let's look at what it really means to make an intervention. What it means is that you have a graph like in Figure 13.11.

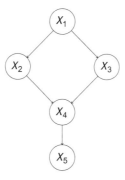

Figure 13.11   A pre-intervention causal graph. Data collected from this system reflects the way the world works when we just observe it.

You want to estimate the effect of X_2 on X_5. That is, you want to say "If I intervene in this system to set the value of X_2 to x_2, what will happen to X_5? To quantify the effect, you have to realize that all of these variables are taking on values that depend not only on their predecessors but also on noise in the system. Thus, even if there's a deterministic effect of X_2 on X_5 (say, raising the value of X_5 by exactly one unit), you can only really describe the value X_5 will take with a distribution of values. Thus, when you're estimating the effect of X_2 on X_5, what you really want is the distribution of X_5 when you intervene to set the value of X_2.

Let's look at what we mean by *intervene*. We're saying we want to ignore the usual effect of X_1 on X_2 and set the value of X_2 to x_2 by applying some external force (our action) to X_2. This removes the usual dependence between X_2 and X_1 and disrupts the downstream effect of X_1 on X_4 by breaking the path that passes through X_2. Thus, we'll also expect the marginal distribution between X_1 and X_4, $P(X_1, X_4)$ to change, as well as the distribution of X_1 and X_5! Our intervention can affect every variable downstream from it in ways that don't just depend on the value x_2. We actually disrupt other dependences.

You can draw a new graph that represents this intervention. At this point, you're seeing that the operation is very different from observing the value of $X_2 = x_2$, i.e., simply conditioning on

$X_2 = x_2$. This is because you're disrupting other dependences in the graph. You're actually talking about a new system described by the graph in Figure 13.12.

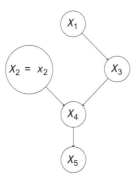

Figure 13.12   The graph representing the intervention $do(X_2 = x_2)$. The statistics of this data will be different from that in from the system in Figure 13.11

You need some new notation to talk about an intervention like this, so you'll denote $do(X_2 = x_2)$ the intervention where you perform this operation. This gives you the definition of the intervention, or *do-operation*.

Definition 13.2. Do-operation

We describe an intervention called the *do() operation* in a system described by a DAG, G as an operation where we do X_i by

- Delete all edges in G that point into X_i, and

- Set the value of X_i to x_i.

What does the joint distribution look like for this new graph? Let's use the usual factorization, and write the following:

$$P_{do(X_2=x_2)}(X_1, X_2, X_3, X_4, X_5) = P(X_5|X_4)P(X_4|X_2, X_3)P(X_3|X_1)\delta(X_2, x_2)P(X_1) \tag{13.1}$$

Here we've just indicated $P(X_2)$ by the δ-function, so $P(X_2) = 0$ if $X_2 \neq x_2$, and $P(X_2) = 1$ when $X_2 = x_2$. We're basically saying that when we intervene to set $X_2 = x_2$, we're sure that it worked. We can carry through that $X_2 = x_2$ elsewhere, like in the distribution for $P(X_4|X_2, X_3)$, but just replacing X_2 with $X_2 = x_2$, since the whole right-hand side is zero if $X_2 \neq x_2$.

Finally, let's just condition on the X_2 distribution to get rid of the weirdness on the right-hand side of this formula. We can write the following:

$$P_{do(X_2=x2)}(X_1, X_2, X_3, X_4, X_5|X_2) = P(X_5|X_4)P(X_4|X_2 = x_2, X_3)P(X_3|X_1)P(X_1) \tag{13.2}$$

However, this is the same as the original formula, divided by $P(X_2|X_1)$! To be precise,

$$P_{do(X_2=x2)}(X_1, X_2, X_3, X_4, X_5|X_2 = x_2) = \frac{P(X_1, X_2 = x_2, X_3, X_4, X_5)}{P(X_2 = x_2|X_1)} \tag{13.3}$$

Incredibly, this formula works in general. We can write the following:

$$P(X_1, ..., X_n | do(X_i = x_i)) = \frac{P(X_1, ..., X_n)}{P(X_i | Pa(X_i))} \qquad (13.4)$$

This leads us to a nice general rule: the parents of a variable will always satisfy the back-door criterion! It turns out we can be more general than this even. If we marginalize out everything except X_i and X_j, we see the parents are the set of variables that control confounders.

$$P(X_j, Pa(X_i) | do(X_i = xi)) = \frac{P(X_j, X_i, Pa(X_i))}{P(X_i | Pa(X_i))} \qquad (13.5)$$

It turns out (we'll state without proof) that you can generalize the parents to any set, Z, that satisfies the back door criterion.

$$P(X_j, Z | do(X_i = xi)) = \frac{P(X_j, X_i, Z)}{P(X_i | Z)} \qquad (13.6)$$

You can marginalize Z out of this and use the definition of conditional probability to write an important formula, shown in Definition 13.3.

Definition 13.3. Robins G-Formula

$$P(X_j | do(X_i = x_i)) = \sum_z P(X_j | X_i, Z) P(Z)$$

This is a general formula for estimating the distribution of X_j under the intervention X_i. Notice that all of these distributions are from the *pre*-intervention system. This means you can use observational data to estimate the distribution of X_j under some hypothetical intervention!

There are a few critical caveats here. First, the term in the denominator of Equation 13.4, $P(X_i | Pa(X_i))$, must be nonzero for the quantity on the left side to be defined. This means you would have to have observed X_i taking on the value you'd like to set it to with your intervention. If you've never seen it, you can't say how the system might behave in response to it!

Next, you're assuming that you have a set Z that you can control for. Practically, it's hard to know if you've found a good set of variables. There can always be a confounder you have never thought to measure. Likewise, your way of controlling for known confounders might not do a very good job. You'll understand this second caveat more as you go into some machine learning estimators.

With these caveats, it can be hard to estimate causal effects from observational data. You should consider the results of a conditioning approach to be a provisional estimate of a causal effect. If you're sure you're not violating the first condition of the back-door criterion, then you can expect that you've removed some spurious dependence. You can't say for sure that you've reduced bias.

Imagine, for example, two sources of bias for the effect of X_i on X_j. Suppose you're interested in measuring an average value of X_j, $E_{do(X_i=x_i)}[X_j] = \mu_j$. Path A introduces a bias of $-\delta$, and path B introduces a bias of 2δ. If you estimate the mean without controlling for either path, you'll find $\mu_j^{(biased)} = \mu_j + 2\delta - \delta = \mu_j + \delta$. If you control for a confounder along path A, then you remove its contribution to the bias, which leaves $\mu_j^{(biased,A)} = \mu_j + 2\delta$. Now the bias is twice as large! The problem, of course, is that the bias you corrected was actually pushing our estimate back toward its correct value. In practice, more controlling usually helps, but you can't be guaranteed that you won't find an effect like this.

Now that you have a good background in observational causal inference, let's see how machine-learning estimators can help in practice!

13.5 Machine-Learning Estimators

In general, you won't want to estimate the full joint distribution under an intervention. You may not even be interested in marginals. Usually, you're just interested in a difference in average effects.

In the simplest case, you'd like to estimate the expected difference in some outcome, X_j, per unit change in a variable you have control over, X_i. For example, you'd might like to measure $E[X_j|do(X_i = 1)] - E[X_j|do(X_i = 0)]$. This tells you the change in X_j you can expect on average when you set X_i to 1 from what it would be if X_i were set to 0.

Let's revisit the g-formula to see how can measure these kinds of quantities.

13.5.1 The G-formula Revisited

The g-formula tells you how to estimate a causal effect, $P(X_j|do(X_i = xi))$, using observational data and a set of variables to control for (based on our knowledge of the causal structure). It says this:

$$P(X_j|do(X_i = x_i)) = \sum_Z P(X_j|X_i, Z)P(Z) \tag{13.7}$$

If you take expectation values on each side (by multiplying by X_j and summing over X_j), then you find this:

$$E(X_j|do(X_i = x_i)) = \sum_Z E(X_j|X_i, Z)P(Z) \tag{13.8}$$

In practice, it's easy to estimate the first factor on the right side of this formula. If you fit a regression estimator using mean-squared error loss, then the best fit is just the expected value of X_j at each point (X_i, Z). As long as the model has enough freedom to accurately describe the expected value, you can estimate this first factor by using standard machine-learning approaches.

To estimate the whole left side, you need to deal with the $P(Z)$ term, as well as the sum. It turns out there's a simple trick for doing this. If your data was generated by drawing from the observational joint distribution, then your samples of Z are actually just draws from $P(Z)$. Then, if you replace the $P(Z)$ term by $1/N$ (for N samples) and sum over data points, you're left with an estimator for this sum. That is, you can make the substitution as follows:

$$E_N(X_j|do(X_i = x_i)) = \frac{1}{N} \sum_{k=1}^{N} E(X_j|X_i^{(k)}, Z^{(k)}), \tag{13.9}$$

where the (k) index runs over our data points, from 1 to N. Let's see how all of this works in an example.

13.5.2   An Example

Let's go back to the graph in Figure 13.11. We'll use an example from Judea Pearl's book. We're concerned with the sidewalk being slippery, so we're investigating its causes. X_5 can be 1 or 0, for slippery or not, respectively. You've found that the sidewalk is slippery when it's wet, and you'll use X_4 to indicate whether the sidewalk is wet. Next, you need to know the causes of the sidewalk being wet. You see that a sprinkler is near the sidewalk, and if the sprinkler is on, it makes the sidewalk wet. X_2 will indicate whether the sprinkler is on. You'll notice the sidewalk is also wet after it rains, which you'll indicate with X_3 being 1 after rain, 0 otherwise. Finally, you note that on sunny days you turn the sprinkler on. You'll indicate the weather with X_1, where X_1 is 1 if it is sunny, and 0 otherwise.

In this picture, rain and the sprinkler being on are negatively related to each other. This statistical dependence happens because of their mutual dependence on the weather. Let's simulate some data to explore this system. You'll use a lot of data, so the random error will be small, and you can focus your attention on the bias.

```
1  import numpy as np
2  import pandas as pd
3  from scipy.special import expit
4
5  N = 100000
6  inv_logit = expit
7  x1 = np.random.binomial(1, p=0.5, size=N)
8  x2 = np.random.binomial(1, p=inv_logit(-3.*x1))
9  x3 = np.random.binomial(1, p=inv_logit(3.*x1))
10 x4 = np.bitwise_or(x2, x3)
11 x5 = np.random.binomial(1, p=inv_logit(3.*x4))
12
13 X = pd.DataFrame({'$x_1$': x1, '$x_2$': x2, '$x_3$': x3,
14                   '$x_4$': x4, '$x_5$': x5})
```

Every variable here is binary. You use a logistic link function to make logistic regression appropriate. When you don't know the data-generating process, you might get a little more creative. You'll come to this point in a moment!

Let's look at the correlation matrix, shown in Figure 13.13. When the weather is good, the sprinkler is turned on. When it rains, the sprinkler is turned off. You can see there's a negative relationship between the sprinkler being on and the rain due to this relationship.

There are a few ways you can get an estimate for the effect of X_2 on X_5. The first is simply by finding the probability that $X_5 = 1$ given that $X_2 = 1$ or $X_2 = 0$. The difference in these probabilities tells you how much more likely it is that the sidewalk is slippery given that the sprinkler was on. A simple way to calculate these probabilities is simply to average the X_5 variable in each subset of the data (where $X_2 = 0$ and $X_2 = 1$). You can run the following, which produces the table in Figure 13.14.

```
1  X.groupby('$x_2$').mean()[['$x_5$']]
```

	X_1	X_2	X_3	X_4	X_5
X_1	1.000000	-0.405063	0.420876	0.200738	0.068276
X_2	-0.405063	1.000000	-0.172920	0.313897	0.102955
X_3	0.420876	-0.172920	1.000000	0.693363	0.255352
X_4	0.200738	0.313897	0.693363	1.000000	0.362034
X_5	0.068276	0.102955	0.255352	0.362034	1.000000

Figure 13.13 The correlation matrix for the simulated data set. Notice that X_2 and X_3 are negatively related because of their common cause, X_1.

X_2	X_5
0	0.861767
1	0.951492

Figure 13.14 The naive conditional expectation values for whether the grass is wet given that the sprinkler is on, $E[X_5|X_2 = x_2]$. This is not a causal result because you haven't adjusted for confounders.

If you look at the difference here, you see that the sidewalk is $0.95 - 0.86 = 0.09$, or nine percentage points more likely to be slippery given that the sprinkler was on. You can compare this with the interventional graph to get the true estimate for the change. You can generate this data using the process shown here:

```
1  N = 100000
2  inv_logit = expit
3  x1 = np.random.binomial(1, p=0.5, size=N)
4  x2 = np.random.binomial(1, p=0.5, size=N)
5  x3 = np.random.binomial(1, p=inv_logit(3.*x1))
6  x4 = np.bitwise_or(x2, x3)
7  x5 = np.random.binomial(1, p=inv_logit(3.*x4))
8
9  X = pd.DataFrame({'$x_1$': x1, '$x_2$': x2, '$x_3$': x3,
10                   '$x_4$': x4, '$x_5$': x5})
```

Now, X_2 is independent of X_1 and X_3. If you repeat the calculation from before (try it!), you get a difference of 0.12, or 12 percentage points. This is about 30 percent larger than the naive estimate!

Now, you'll use some machine learning approaches to try to get a better estimate of the true (0.12) effect strictly using the observational data. First, you'll try a logistic regression on the first data set. Let's re-create the naive estimate, just to make sure it's working properly.

```
1  from sklearn.linear_model import LogisticRegression
2
3  # build our model, predicting $x_5$ using $x_2$
4  model = LogisticRegression()
5  model = model.fit(X[['$x_2$']], X['$x_5$'])
6
7
8  # what would have happened if $x_2$ was always 0:
9  X0 = X.copy()
10 X0['$x_2$'] = 0
11 y_pred_0 = model.predict_proba(X0[['$x_2$']])
12
13 # what would have happened if $x_2$ was always 1:
14 X1 = X.copy()
15 X1['$x_2$'] = 1
16 y_pred_1 = model.predict_proba(X1[['$x_2$']])
17
18 # now, let's check the difference in probabilities
19 y_pred_1[:, 1].mean() - y_pred_0[:,1].mean()
```

You first build a logistic regression model using X_2 to predict X_5. You do the prediction and use it to get probabilities of X_5 under the $X_2 = 0$ and $X_2 = 1$ states. You did this over the whole data set. The reason for this is that you'll often have more interesting data sets, with many more variables changing, and you'll want to see the average effect of X_2 on X_5 over the whole data set. This procedure lets you do that. Finally, you find the average difference in probabilities between the two states, and you get the same 0.09 result as before!

Now, you'd like to do controlling on the same observational data to get the causal (0.12) result. You perform the same procedure as before, but this time you include X_1 in the regression.

```
1  model = LogisticRegression()
2  model = model.fit(X[['$x_2$', '$x_1$']], X['$x_5$'])
3
4  # what would have happened if $x_2$ was always 0:
5  X0 = X.copy()
6  X0['$x_2$'] = 0
7  y_pred_0 = model.predict_proba(X0[['$x_2$', '$x_1$']])
8
9  # what would have happened if $x_2$ was always 1:
10 X1 = X.copy()
11 X1['$x_2$'] = 1
12
13 # now, let's check the difference in probabilities
14 y_pred_1 = model.predict_proba(X1[['$x_2$', '$x_1$']])
15 y_pred_1[:, 1].mean() - y_pred_0[:,1].mean()
```

In this case, you find 0.14 for the result. You've over-estimated it! What went wrong? You didn't actually do anything wrong with the modeling procedure. The problem is simply that logistic regression isn't the right model for this situation. It's the correct model for each variable's parents to predict its value but doesn't work properly for descendants that follow the parents. Can we do better, with a more general model?

This will be your first look at how powerful neural networks can be for general machine-learning tasks. You'll learn about building them in a little more detail in the next chapter. For now, let's try a deep feedforward neural network using keras. It's called *deep* because there are more than just the input and output layers. It's a *feedforward* network because you put some input data into the network and pass them forward through the layers to produce the output.

Deep feedforward networks have the property of being "universal function approximators," in the sense that they can approximate any function, given enough neurons and layers (although it's not always easy to learn, in practice). You'll construct the network like this:

```
1  from keras.layers import Dense, Input
2  from keras.models import Model
3
4  dense_size = 128
5  input_features = 2
6
7  x_in = Input(shape=(input_features,))
8  h1 = Dense(dense_size, activation='relu')(x_in)
9  h2 = Dense(dense_size, activation='relu')(h1)
10 h3 = Dense(dense_size, activation='relu')(h2)
11 y_out = Dense(1, activation='sigmoid')(h3)
12
13 model = Model(input=x_in, output=y_out)
14 model.compile(loss='binary_crossentropy', optimizer='adam')
15 model.fit(X[['$x_1$', '$x_2$']].values, X['$x_5$'])
```

Now do the same prediction procedure as before, which produces the result 0.129.

```
1  X_zero = X.copy()
2  X_zero['$x_2$'] = 0
3  x5_pred_0 = model.predict(X_zero[['$x_1$', '$x_2$']].values)
4
5  X_one = X.copy()
6  X_one['$x_2$'] = 1
7  x5_pred_1 = model.predict(X_one[['$x_1$', '$x_2$']].values)
8
9  x5_pred_1.mean() - x5_pred_0.mean()
```

You've done better than the logistic regression model! This was a tricky case. You're given binary data where it's easy to calculate probabilities, and you'd do the best by simply using the g-formula directly. When you do this (try it yourself!), you calculate the true result of 0.127 from this data. Your neural network model is very close!

Now, you'd like to enact a policy that would make the sidewalk less likely to be slippery. You know that if you turn the sprinkler on less often, that should do the trick. You see that enacting this policy (and so intervening to change the system), you can expect the slipperiness of the sidewalk to decrease. How much? You want to compare the pre-intervention chance of slipperiness with the post-intervention chance, when you set sprinkler = off. You can simply calculate this with our neural network model like so:

```
1 | X['$x_5$'].mean() - x5_pred_0.mean()
```

This gives the result 0.07. It will be 7 percent less likely that the sidewalk is slippery if you make a policy of keeping the sprinkler turned off!

13.6   Conclusion

In this chapter, you've developed the tools to do causal inference. You've learned that machine learning models can be useful to get more general model specifications, and you saw that the better you can predict an outcome using a machine learning model, the better you can remove bias from an observational causal effect estimate.

Observational causal effect estimates should always be used with care. Whenever possible, you should try to do a randomized controlled experiment instead of using the observational estimate. In this example, you should simply use randomized control: flip a coin each day to see whether the sprinkler gets turned on. This re-creates the post-intervention system and lets you measure how much less likely the sidewalk is to be slippery when the sprinkler is turned off versus turned on (or when the system isn't intervened upon). When you're trying to estimate the effect of a policy, it's hard to find a substitute for actually testing the policy through a controlled experiment.

It's especially useful to be able to think causally when designing machine-learning systems. If you'd simply like to say what outcome is most likely given what normally happens in a system, a standard machine learning algorithm is appropriate. You're not trying to predict the result of an intervention, and you're not trying to make a system that is robust to changes in how the system operates. You just want to describe the system's joint distribution (or expectation values under it).

If you would like to inform policy changes, predict the outcomes of intervention, or make the system robust to changes in variables upstream from it (i.e., external interventions), then you will want a causal machine learning system, where you control for the appropriate variables to measure causal effects.

An especially interesting application area is when you're estimating the coefficients in a logistic regression. Earlier, you saw that logistic regression coefficients had a particular interpretation in observational data: they describe how much more likely an outcome is per unit increase in some independent variable. If you control for the right variables to get a causal logistic regression estimate (or just do the regression on data generated by control), then you have a new, stronger interpretation: the coefficients tell you how much more likely an outcome is to occur when you intervene to increase the value of an independent variable by one unit. You can use these coefficients to inform policy!

Advanced Machine Learning

14.1 Introduction

We've covered the basics of machine learning but only scratched the surface of what there is to know. In this chapter, we'll give a small glimpse of what else is out there. Our goal is to provide enough information to get you started and to help you find the search terms to learn more on your own.

Neural networks make nice examples for a few reasons. They can reduce to familiar models, like linear regression, in special cases. They have many parameters that you can adjust to show what happens as a simple model becomes more complex. This lets you see how generalization performance behaves as you move from simpler models to more complex models. You can also see that simple models have trouble representing complicated functions.

Neural networks' complexity will require you to introduce regularization methods. These are methods that let you keep the expressive power of a complex model (so you can fit complicated functions) but recover some of the efficiency and generalization power of smaller models. These methods can also be used on simple models, like linear regression.

Finally, neural networks can require massive amounts of data. To fit them, you take an approach that scales to large data sets.

We'll start by framing machine learning problems as an optimization problem. Then, we'll introduce neural networks and explore capacity, model expressiveness, and generalization. Finally, we'll note that this approach can scale to large data sets.

14.2 Optimization

You've seen linear regression, where you minimize the mean-squared error of a linear model. In that context, you had two model parameters, β the slope, and a y-intercept. You changed those parameters to minimize the error, which gave you a line that best fit the data.

You can go further and choose a much more complex model with many more parameters. You can proceed in the same way, by writing the model output as a function of the model's parameters and adjusting the value of the parameters to minimize a "loss," producing better and better outputs. There are also many other metrics, losses you might like to minimize. These losses can have complicated shapes, where they can be smooth or irregular, like that in Figure 14.2. When the surface is smooth, like in Figure 14.1, it's easy to find the minimum. When it's irregular, it's much harder. To see why you need to understand how you find minima.

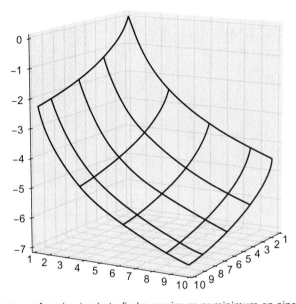

Figure 14.1   A convex surface is simple to find a maximum or minimum on since you can follow the gradient

You can find the minima or maxima of these surfaces using *gradient descent*. To find a minimum with this method, you pick a point at random to start. You look at the slope at that point and follow it downhill toward a minimum. You do this by taking a small step in the downhill direction and then repeating the process.

To find the downhill direction for the 1-dimensional loss $f(x)$ at the point x_0, you look at the slope at that point. The slope is just given by the derivative. To calculate the step you should take, you compute the following:

$$\delta x = -\epsilon \frac{df}{dx}\Big|_{x=x_0} \tag{14.1}$$

where ϵ is an adjustable parameter. ϵ can be 1 and can vary to fine-tune the performance of the optimization. Then, to compute the new x value, you just update $x_{new} = x_0 + \delta x$. You repeat this process until the slope gets to be zero. The derivative is 0 when you're at a minimum, so the step distance will naturally go toward zero as you're getting close.

This process can run into trouble if there are many minima. A local minimum is a point where no matter what direction you go (for small distances), the value of the function increases. That doesn't have to mean it's the lowest value of the function overall. You can go over a hill and end up on a much longer downslope. The true lowest point is called the *global minimum*.

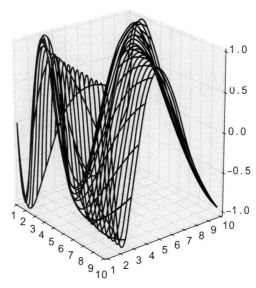

Figure 14.2   On irregular surfaces, it's much harder to find global extrema since there can be many local maxima and minima

It's easy to visualize these functions in one or two dimensions, when they're either curves or surfaces. It's harder when they are higher dimensional, but the same basic concepts apply. You can have local or global extrema, and you can apply the same procedures for finding local extrema.

If you happen to initialize into an area where you're close to a local minimum but far from the global minimum, you can settle into a local minimum without realizing it. There are many approaches to try to avoid this, but none of them works in all cases. Some problems have the nice property that there is a single unique minimum, so a local minimum is guaranteed to be a global minimum. Other problems are harder. This is a problem you have to deal with when you're fitting parameters for neural networks. Generally, there are many local minima, and you hope to start out close enough to a good one that it's easy to find your way toward it.

14.3   Neural Networks

Neural networks have shown state-of-the-art performance in a variety of tasks that have traditionally been hard for computers to solve. These include object recognition in images, text translation, and audio transcription.

Neural networks are powerful because they can fit general types of functions. In the examples we've mentioned, these functions can map an image to a probability distribution over objects (in the case of object recognition). They can map an English sentence into its French translation. They can map a recording of spoken words into a string of text.

In every case, the networks are designed not to be completely general. Their structure is specific for the task they are to perform. For images, they apply a series of filters (called *convolutions*) over the images. For text translation and audio transcription, they have a recurrent structure that respects the fact that their inputs have a specific ordering to them. Limiting the freedom in these functions lets us fit them much more efficiently and can make tasks tractable that weren't tractable before.

It's beyond our scope to go into complete detail on the zoology of neural networks. We'll stop at introducing deep feedforward networks, using them to illustrate how a neural network can fit a general function and how the architecture of the network relates to its capacity to fit a broad class of functions.

14.3.1 Layers

Deep feedforward networks consist of a few layers of *neurons*. Each neuron is a cell where an operation is performed. We'll consider some simple neurons. We'll consider a vector of inputs for the neuron, $\mathbf{x}$. The neurons' knowledge is represented by a vector of weights, $\mathbf{w}$. The neuron, when passed some inputs, will compute an activation that it can pass on to the next neuron in the next layer. The activations here will be the product between the weight vector and the inputs, plus some bias, b. These will all be passed into some function, $f()$, that will produce the activation, a. Altogether, $a = f(\mathbf{w}\mathbf{x} + b)$.

Several neurons can be activated at the same time from an input. You can compute a whole vector of activations by stacking their weight vectors together in a matrix, $\mathbf{W}$, and computing the vector of activations $\mathbf{a} = f(\mathbf{W}\mathbf{x} + \mathbf{b})$, where the bias is now also a vector, and now the function is operating element-wise.

You can stack many of these layers together, where the output of one layer becomes the input of the next. This kind of stacking gives you a deep neural network. A deep neural network is just a network with one or more layers beyond the input and output layers.

If you look at the most basic version of this network, you can have the function $f()$ simply be the identity function, which maps its input to its output. Then, you'll just have a single output neuron, whose activation is computed directly from the input data as $a = \mathbf{w}\mathbf{x} + b$. This should look familiar: you're just doing linear regression!

Let's see what happens when you add another layer between the input and output. Now, you should compute a new vector of activations in the middle layer and again compute a single output activation at the end. Then you compute the first set of activations from the input, $\mathbf{h} = \mathbf{W}_1\mathbf{x} + \mathbf{b}_1$, and the final output is $a = \mathbf{w}_2\mathbf{h} + b_2$. If you compose these together, you get the following:

$$a = \mathbf{w}_2\mathbf{h} + b_2 \tag{14.2}$$

$$= \mathbf{w}_2(\mathbf{W}_1\mathbf{x} + \mathbf{b}_1) + b_2 \tag{14.3}$$

$$= \mathbf{w}_2\mathbf{W}_1\mathbf{x} + \mathbf{w}_2\mathbf{b}_1 + b_2 \tag{14.4}$$

This is just a new linear model, where the new weight vector is $\mathbf{w}_2\mathbf{W}_1$ and the new intercept is $\mathbf{w}_2\mathbf{b}_1 + b_2$. Adding a new layer didn't give you any new expressive power but did greatly increase the number of parameters. This is a bad situation since this new model is worse than linear regression! Where did we go wrong?

The problem here was that the activation used was calculated with the identity function. Generally, a neural network will use a nonlinear function like tanh to compute the activation.

That makes it so the next layer doesn't simply compose linear transformations on the input data, and you can gain new expressive power.

14.3.2 Capacity

Let's look at an example where a neural network is fit to a very nonlinear function but doesn't have the capacity, or expressive power, to fit it very well. Let's look at the function $y = sin(2\pi x)sin(3\pi x)$. Let's generate some data for it.

```
1  import numpy as np
2
3  N = 15000
4  X = np.random.uniform(-2 * np.pi, 2*np.pi, size=N)
5  Y = np.sin(2*np.pi*X)*np.sin(3*np.pi*X)
```

You can plot this data in Figure 14.3, and see that it's very nonlinear!

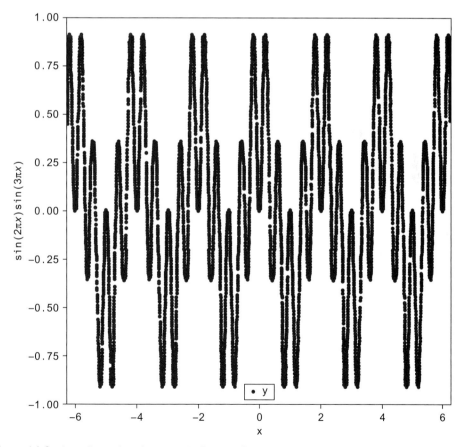

Figure 14.3   A nonlinear function, $y = sin(2\pi x)sin(3\pi x)$

Let's try fitting a neural network to it. Keras implements the layers we've talked about so far. The input layer is simply the one that reads in your data, and the Dense layer is the type we described with weights, bias, and an activation function.

```
1  from keras.layers import Dense, Input
2  from keras.models import Model
3
4  dense_size = 64
5
6  x = Input(shape=(1,))
7  h = Dense(dense_size, activation='tanh')(x)
8  y = Dense(1, activation='linear')(h)
```

Then you tell the model to train it by minimizing mean-squared error:

```
1  model = Model(input=x, output=y)
2  model.compile(loss='mean_squared_error', optimizer='adam')
3  model.fit(X, Y, epochs=10)
```

When you fit this model, you get a pretty poor result, as shown in Figure 14.4.

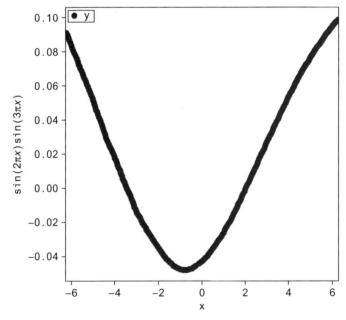

Figure 14.4 A poor fit to $y = sin(2\pi x)sin(3\pi x)$, using one hidden layer and only 64 units in the hidden layer

The problem here is that you don't have enough expressive power in the network to fit the function properly. You can do much better by adding extra nonlinearity. It's easier to achieve this by adding depth to the network. Experiment a little yourself: try adding the same number of neurons to the first layer as you're using to create the second layer. Can you reach a similar level of expressiveness? You'll add in the second layer as shown here:

```
1  from keras.layers import Dense, Input
2  from keras.models import Model
3
4  dense_size = 64
5
6  x = Input(shape=(1,))
7  h1 = Dense(dense_size, activation='tanh')(x)
8  h2 = Dense(dense_size, activation='tanh')(h1)
9  y = Dense(1, activation='linear')(h2)
10
11 model = Model(input=x, output=y)
12 model.compile(loss='mean_squared_error', optimizer='adam')
13 model.fit(X, Y, epochs=100)
```

You run this for many epochs, and you find a much better fit to the data, as shown in Figure 14.5. You can see that it's matching the finer structure in the middle but can only fit the broader part of the structure toward the outside. Still, that's pretty good! You can see that it probably just doesn't have the expressive power to fit all of this structure. Try adding one more layer yourself, and see what it can do!

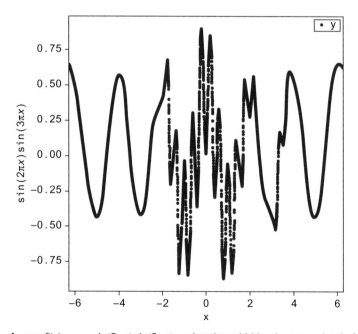

Figure 14.5 A poor fit to $y = sin(2\pi x)sin(3\pi x)$, using three hidden layers and only 64 units in the hidden layers

You'll find you keep doing better as you increase the network size. You can't do this indefinitely. At some point the network will have too much capacity and will start memorizing specific data points instead of measuring the function well. Let's examining this problem, called *overfitting*.

14.3.3   Overfitting

In the worst case, overfitting happens when your model learns specific data points in your training data. If you would like the model to generalize to novel data collected from the same system, it's unlikely that an overfit model will do a good job.

You can overfit our neural network in the previous example. You just reduce the number of training data points to, say, 10, and run the model for a large number of epochs, say 2000. When you do this, you find the fit shown in Figure 14.6, where you see that the fit line (in blue) looks nothing like our original function, in Figure 14.3. If you were to include more data points from the original function, you'd see they fall far from this fit line.

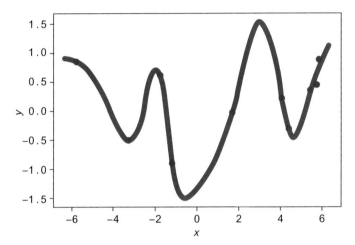

Figure 14.6   A poor fit to $y = sin(2\pi x)sin(3\pi x)$, using three hidden layers and 512 units in the hidden layers. There are only 10 data points (shown in red), so the model has far more expressive power than can be learned from this data set!

How can you check for overfitting when you're training a model? This is where model validation can be useful. The key is that if you overfit, new data won't match the function you've fit. If you had some data the model has never seen before (in the sense that it wasn't used for training), you could check the fit on that extra data and see how well the model does. You could do this periodically while you're training a model to see how well it might generalize. You can do this by looking at the loss function. If the loss is small on the training data but large on the held-out data, then you can see the parameters you've learned to minimize the loss aren't working on new data. This probably means the parameters are bad.

In practice, when training a model, you'll split your data into three sets. The largest will be the "training set" and includes 80 to 90 percent of the data. Next, you'll have a validation set. This is data the model never sees directly but that you might use to test and adjust parameter settings (like the number of layers in a neural network, or the number of neurons in each layer). The model does learn about this data indirectly, through your parameter changes. This data will help you control overfitting within a training run. You'll periodically check the validation error and make sure it continues to decrease as the training error decreases.

Finally, you have a test data set. Once you've done your parameter tuning, you'll test your model out on a final data set you've held out. This is supposed to give you an idea of how well your model will perform out in the real world, on data it has never seen before. Of course, assuming that the data you'll encounter in practice behaves statistically like your test data is a strong assumption, and you should try to make as realistic a test data set as you can. This might mean splitting your data across time, so your test set is just the most recent data, and you've trained and validated the model on past data.

Let's see how this works in practice. You'll generate a new data set with some noise added. You'll use a simpler function to generate the data, $f(x) = sin(2\pi x)$. If the model discovers the function exactly, the remaining loss will be from the noise alone. The noise has a variance of $\sigma^2 = 0.25$, so the mean squared error when the function is fit perfectly would be 0.25. If the model starts fitting to random noise around this function, then you'll see the training loss drop below 0.25. The validation loss is 0.25 in the best case (except for random error working in our favor), so you'll expect it to end up higher than 0.25 in the case you overfit. This is because in order to overfit, the model has to deviate from the true underlying function. That deviation will lead to error on the validation set. You can create our data set like this:

```
1  import numpy as np
2
3  N = 500
4  X = np.random.uniform(-np.pi, np.pi, size=N)
5  Y = np.sin(2*np.pi*X) + 0.5*np.random.normal(size=N)
6  X_valid = np.random.uniform(-np.pi, np.pi, size=1000)
7  Y_valid = np.sin(2 * np.pi * X_valid)
8              + 0.5*np.random.normal(size=1000)
9
10 from keras.layers import Dense, Input
11 from keras.models import Model
12
13 dense_size = 512
14
15 x = Input(shape=(1,))
16 h1 = Dense(dense_size, activation='relu')(x)
17 h2 = Dense(dense_size, activation='relu')(h1)
18 h3 = Dense(dense_size, activation='relu')(h2)
19 h4 = Dense(dense_size, activation='relu')(h3)
20
21 y = Dense(1, activation='linear')(h4)
22
23 model = Model(input=x, output=y)
24 model.compile(loss='mean_squared_error', optimizer='adam')
25 model.fit(X, Y, epochs=500, batch_size=128,
26             validation_data=(X_valid, Y_valid))
```

You can see in Figure 14.7 that the training loss drops below the validation loss. At the final epochs in the plot, the training error is at 0.20, and the validation error is 0.30. This is consistent with what you should expect with overfitting. You've fit the model to the noise in the data set, and you've lost some power to generalize to data the model hasn't seen. Around epoch 340, the validation error was around 0.26. This suggests a strategy where you stop early, when the generalization error is good, even though you can still minimize training loss. What you really want is generalization power.

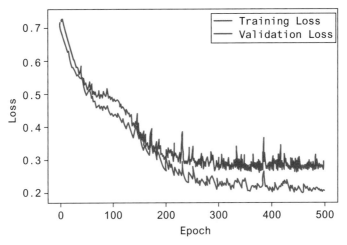

Figure 14.7   In a network with a lot of capacity and not enough data, you end up fitting some of the noise at the cost of generalization error

There are many ways to attempt to reduce generalization error without reducing training error. These methods are generally called *regularization*. If you'd like to keep the classes of functions your network can describe general enough, without letting the space of functions get too large, you can try constraining the parameters. One way of doing this is to penalize parameters that get too large. You can do this simply by adding a penalty to the loss function. For mean-squared error, your loss function is $J(\mathbf{W}, \mathbf{b}) = \frac{1}{N} \sum_{i=1}^{N} \left(y_i - y_i^{(predicted)} \right)^2 = \frac{1}{N} \sum_{i=1}^{N} \left(y_i - y_i^{(predicted)} \right)^2$. If you want to penalize weights that get too large, you can add the sum of squares of the weights to this loss. For the case of a single-layer neural network, this looks like $J_2(\mathbf{W}, b) = \frac{1}{N} \sum_{i=1}^{N} \left(y_i - y_i^{(predicted)} \right)^2 + \alpha \sum_{k,l} W_{kl}^2$. There's a natural generalization to deeper networks, where you add the sum of squares of the weights of each layer. Now, the larger the magnitudes of the weights, the more loss. This is called L^2 regularization, since you're using the sum of squares, or L^2 norm, of the weights. The benefit is that you keep the benefits of deep neural networks, modeling very nonlinear functions, while not providing quite as much capacity as we would if you left the weights unconstrained. If you add L^2 regularization to the weights from the previous example, you find the losses in Figure 14.8. Here, the final training error is around 0.32, and the validation error is 0.36 with $\alpha = 0.002$. You might try increasing the model size and fine-tuning the regularization parameter α to get the validation error down even more.

You can find a similar curve where validation error decreases, plateaus, and then increases again as a function of model capacity. The underfit regime is where the validation error is decreasing. As

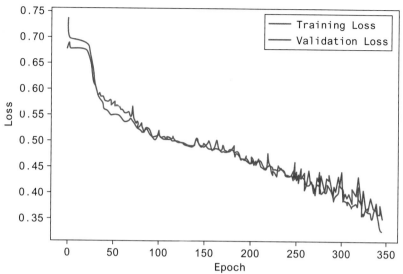

Figure 14.8   When you regularize a network, you can see the generalization gap close a little

model complexity grows, you underfit less and less. You reach a bottom at the right capacity for your data. As you continue increasing capacity, you begin to overfit, and the validation error starts growing again. An important nuance is that the level of capacity where you plateau depends on the size of your data set. Small data sets can be noisy and can be easy to overfit with high-capacity models. As your data set grows, you can introduce more and more capacity without overfitting. If you have a complex problem, you might need a large data set to fit a model!

14.3.4   Batch Fitting

If you need to fit a model to a large data set, you might not be able to fit all the data in memory on a single machine. You need a new strategy from what you're used to for fitting these kinds of models. Fortunately, there's a nice trick you can use.

If you go back to our optimization methods, you minimize loss by taking steps in increments like $\delta x = -\epsilon \frac{df}{dx}\big|_{x=x_0}$. If you can compute these steps using only a subset of the data, then you can take these steps and hope that you're wandering closer to a minimum without having to do any calculations using the whole data set.

The procedure you generally use is to take a sample of the data, compute $\frac{df}{dx}$ on the sample, and compute the step. You take the step and then choose another sample and repeat the process. As long as the samples are large enough to give reasonable approximations to the derivative, then you can hope that you're stepping in the right direction.

The fact that you estimate the derivative of the loss with respect to the parameters on only a sample of the data, instead of the whole data set, means that you have a noisy approximation of these derivatives over the whole data set. This "stochasticity" is the reason for the name *stochastic gradient descent*.

There are some other benefits to this procedure. You can get much better computational speed per step by running over small amounts of data. The individual steps can be noisy, so if the loss function isn't convex, there's a better chance that you'll wander away from a local minimum toward a better local minimum.

This approach can also be appropriate when you're training a model on a data stream. The data comes in one or a few points at a time. You can accumulate points into a batch and then compute a step to train the model on the batch.

14.3.5   Loss Functions

We should say something about loss functions before we finish. Previously, we picked mean squared error (MSE) as a nice measurement for how far our model is from estimating our function, and then minimized it to make our model fit our function well. We didn't have to choose MSE, though; we could have chosen any function with the same qualitative behavior, like mean absolute error (MAE). If $f(x_i)$ is our model's prediction for the point x_i, then we can write the MAE loss function as

$$\mathcal{L} = \sum_{i=1}^{N} |y_i - f(x_i)| \tag{14.5}$$

What effect does changing the loss function have, if they both force our model to approach our function? It turns out that when you have noisy data, these two loss functions can have very different results.

In *Elements of Statistical Learning* (§2.4), Hastie et al. show that the function that minimizes the MSE loss is the conditional expectation, or $f(x_i) = E[Y|X = x_i]$! That means the loss function will be minimized when our model has converged to estimate the conditional expected value of Y given X. Applying the same procedure to the MAE loss function, above, you find that the function that minimizes the loss is $f(x_i) = Median(Y|X = x_i)$, the conditional median!

The median is especially useful when your data contains many extreme values. The median doesn't change, even when you multiply an extreme value ten-fold. Contrast that with the mean, which can change drastically. Analogously, the MSE loss function (which gives us estimators for a conditional mean) is very sensitive to extreme values, since it depends quadratically on the distance between our model, $f(x_i)$, and the true y_i. Compare this with the MAE loss above, which only depends linearly on extreme values. This makes the MAE loss much less sensitive to extreme values.

The downside to robustness to extreme values is that MAE loss is also less statistically efficient. There's a loss function that lets you interpolate between MSE loss and MAE loss, which is called the *Huber loss*. While the deviation, $a = |f(x_i) - y_i|$, is less than the value δ, the loss is given by

$$\mathcal{L}_\delta = \frac{1}{2} \left(f(x_i) - y_i \right)^2 \tag{14.6}$$

which is proportional to the MSE loss. When the deviation is greater than δ, the loss is given by

$$\mathcal{L}_\delta = \frac{1}{2} \delta \left(|f(x_i) - y_i| - \frac{1}{2} \delta \right) \tag{14.7}$$

which is proportional to the MAE loss! What this accomplishes is that for small deviations, the loss function acts like MSE and so it keeps its statistical efficiency. For large deviations (greater than δ), we want to get rid of the sensitivity of the quadratic loss, so we replace the loss function with MAE at these deviations. We keep more statistical power, but also keep some of the robustness to error.

The parameter δ is something you're free to vary. When $\delta = 0$, the Huber loss becomes the MAE loss. When δ is larger than your largest deviation, the loss becomes the MSE loss. You can choose a value of δ that works well for your application.

14.4   Conclusion

In this chapter, you saw some basic concepts in machine learning illustrated with deep feedforward neural networks. You saw how to optimize an objective like loss and learned the difference between nonconvex and convex objectives. You saw how you need to balance the generality of your model with the desire not to overfit the data. This is a matter of giving up capacity that you don't need (e.g., models with large weights, in the case of L^2 regularization) to close the gap between training error and generalization error. You saw that you might need large data sets to fit complex models.

If your data set is too large, you have to use training approaches that iterate over the data set. These perform the same stepwise minimization strategy as you mentioned before, but only use a subset of the data to compute each step. They are implemented in machine-learning libraries like TensorFlow and scikit-learn and are often called *batch fitting methods*, or *partial fitting*.

III

Bottlenecks and Optimizations

Chapter 15, "Hardware Fundamentals," runs through basic bottlenecks in hardware and includes a brief discussion of the components that make up modern computers.

In Chapter 16, "Software Fundamentals," we discuss some fundamentals of software design as it relates to quickly and reliably processing data. We'll take a look at IO efficiency as well as guarantees related to consistency.

Chapter 17, "Software Architecture," contains a higher-level overview of architectural patterns used in distributed systems.

Chapter 18, "The CAP Theorem," goes into the trade-offs between availability, consistency, and partition tolerance.

Finally, Chapter 19, "Logical Network Topological Nodes," provides a toolkit. It describes the various nodes you will commonly find in a network that you can use to build your data pipeline or recommender system.

15

Hardware Fundamentals

15.1 Introduction

To get the most out of your machines, it is important to understand the capabilities and limitations of them both physically and abstractly. In this chapter, we will go over several core hardware concepts. With an adequate understanding of these concepts, you can use your resources as effectively as possible, avoiding common (and uncommon) pitfalls.

15.2 Random Access Memory

Random access memory exists on the vast majority of, if not all, modern computers. It's fast to access, so it's commonly used as scratch paper when processes are performing tasks. In algorithm work, this is commonly referred to as *working memory*, or *working tape*.

From the perspective of the data scientist or engineer, there are two major characteristics that are important to understand: access and volatility.

15.2.1 Access

The ideal rule of RAM is that, given an address, it takes the same amount of time to access any element of memory as any other. It doesn't matter how that memory is stored or whether it is contiguous or fragmented.

Practically speaking, on bare-metal machines there is a memory hierarchy. Many types of RAM exist, though the acronym RAM is usually used to refer to them all. Operating systems usually provide access to them from fastest to slowest. This causes there to be thresholds at which memory performs faster as each type of RAM is used up.

RAM used by CPU caches/registers, for example, will be faster than the dynamic memory typically used by applications. Swap memory (which is an abstraction over memory that actually resides on disk) will perform slower than both.

Allocating and accessing RAM for working processes is not without its own characteristics of degradation under heavy load. The specific implementation of the `malloc` function varies from one library to the next. Normally, though, to protect access in multithreaded applications, memory allocation data structures are subject to mutexes. Contention on those mutexes can cause minor slowdowns when there are many `frees` and `mallocs` at the same time.

Contention on the hardware memory management unit (MMU) can also serve as a bottleneck for multithreaded applications accessing shared memory. When two threads make a request for the same resource, those events are put on a queue. A memory arbiter decides which process to allow access to first. If many processes request that same memory, all those events must be appended to the queue, and decisions have to be made about the order.

Normally memory management hardware does a great job of resolving this type of contention, and the result is negligible total time waiting on volatile IO resources. When lots of threads are accessing the same shared memory, that is when problems arise.

Although uncommon, it's entirely possible for RAM to serve as the bottleneck to a process.

15.2.2   Volatility

There is a downside to the speed and general reliability of accessing RAM with the same performance regardless of storage location. This downside is volatility. That is, when a machine powers down, everything stored in RAM will be lost. For this reason, anything that must be stored for a long period of time should be written to disk.

There are a few fundamental electronic components used to store information in RAM. The most common is a capacitor combined with a transistor. The transistor provides control, while the capacitor maintains a state of being charged or not, predictably. When power is shut off, the capacitor's charge is allowed to drain.

In general you should consider things stored in memory gone when power is lost.

The problem of volatility requires a secondary storage mechanism for important data. This is also known as *persistent*, *nonvolatile*, or *robust* storage.

15.3   Nonvolatile/Persistent Storage

When storage is required to persist, there are two common solutions. The first is a hard disk drive (HDD), also known as a *spinning disk*. The second is a solid-state drive, where information is stored on semiconductors. Spinning disk drives are becoming less common. It's cost effective and, in some ways, less error prone to store data on a solid-state drive.

These are commonly both referred to as *disk*. Reading from and writing to disk, compared to RAM, is very slow. Commonly there are issues of latency, as well as imperfectly efficient retrieval of data from the device itself. To understand how these factors occur, you have to know a little more about the hardware itself.

15.3.1   Hard Disk Drives or "Spinning Disks"

Spinning disk drives are composed of a flat ferromagnetic disk that spins at a high rate of speed underneath a mechanical arm with a delicate tip, capable of reading and generating magnetic fields.

As the disk spins, the arm moves the tip along the radius of the disk to sense the polarity of magnetic fields in each of many small regions. Each of these tiny regions has a field with the direction either up or down, representing a single bit of information.

When information is deleted, the operating system simply forgets the address of the deleted information on disk. The underlying charges still exist in the regions to which they were written. They are overwritten as new information is assigned the addresses of the old information.

15.3.2   SSDs

Solid-state drives have no moving parts. This makes them more durable compared to HDDs, especially when a laptop is carried around in a backpack, for example. SSDs provide faster access and lower latency than HDDs. Combine that with the cheapness of very high-density SSDs, and HDDs are losing popularity relatively (though not absolutely yet).

15.3.3   Latency

Latency, in general, is the amount of time required for a storage media to start returning information from the time that information is requested. This is one of the factors that affects the performance of reading to and writing from disk.

In the case of SSD, latency tends to be very low. This is related to the time the embedded processor takes to address the storage and the response time of the underlying transistors and capacitors that implement the physical storage.

Latency for the HDD is considerably higher. This is largely because of the mechanical nature of the device. HDDs store information not dissimilar to how a music record stores information. Bits are written along the circumference of the disk at even or uneven intervals as the disk spins by the tip of the mechanical arm. When two bits are far apart, the disk must spin farther to retrieve them both. When bits are stored on different tracks, the arm must move to retrieve them. Each of these adds time to the latency.

As you might imagine, HDDs benefit from storing information contiguously since they can read it all in a row, requiring minimal mechanical action. In fact, there is a second reason, called *paging*, for storing information contiguously from which both types of storage media benefit.

15.3.4   Paging

There is a layer of abstraction provided to applications that separate the lowest-level semantics of accessing memory. Disks are composed of physical blocks of constant size that have on them pages of (usually) a constant size.

Since pages have constant sizes, it's unusual for a given amount of information to take an integer number of pages. The last page is usually not completely filled up. This means two things. The first is that there is some amount of memory wasted since the entire page is allocated to store the information in question. Second, when that page is paged into memory, it requires the effort of loading an entire page of information even though it is possible for the majority of the page to be unused.

15.3.5 Thrashing

When RAM fills up, some pages must be released from memory to make way for others to be loaded. This is known as *swapping* or *thrashing*. The CPU will spend considerable time loading and unloading pages, taking away from the available CPU to do the work a program is intended to do. Swapping prevents memory errors but comes with a typically severe performance degradation.

15.4 Throughput

Throughput in reference to the transfer of information is the measure of how much information is able to be moved from one point to another. For a program to perform quickly, it must both be able to quickly read and write the information it requires to proceed and be able to process that information quickly. There are a few circumstances where throughput is especially worthy of consideration.

15.4.1 Locality

The discussion of the arrangement of information on disk and the benefits of contiguous storage lead nicely into the general concept of locality. Simply put, *locality* refers to the concept of storing information together that is typically accessed together. You already heard why and how this works for physical storage media, but there are other means by which information is commonly transferred.

Locality, simply and abstractly, can be considered to exist in a hierarchy. There is locality in storage media, locality in a single application space, locality in a local area network, and locality in a wide area network. To understand the benefits of processing data in one way or another, these must each be understood, at least in passing. Since we have already discussed locality on storage media, let's move on to locality in the memory space of an application.

15.4.2 Execution-Level Locality

Applications on modern operating systems have a level of abstraction known as *threads* that allow their time on the CPU to be allocated in turn. The common case on Linux operating systems is that the amount of time the CPU allocates for a given process is proportionate to the amount of time requested by that process versus the amount of time already allocated to it.

Many processes run in a single thread (like the Python interpreter) by default but can run in many threads if a threading interface (like Posix threads) is implemented. Between two threads, RAM can be shared and is referenced by the same address space. Between two processes, however, memory spaces are isolated.

Having two threads access the same RAM provides the benefit that if a given page is needed by both threads, it needs to be paged from disk only once. If it is needed by two processes, however, it must be paged twice. For the data to be transferred from one process to the other, it must be sent through a pipe or socket, which, ultimately, writes to disk.

15.4.3   Network Locality

Two nodes on a LAN are subject to a different bottleneck than RAM or disk. Between each of these nodes exists any number of routers, switches, and buses. The speed of these components adds to the total time it takes to transfer data from one node to the next.

With components one after the other (in serial), the time to get a piece of information from one end of the network to the other is considerably long. With components connected in parallel, this decreases as the number of connections increases. This explains why a wide area of network has longer data transfer rates than a local area network. There are simply more network components between them.

When it takes more time to process a batch of data than to distribute it across a network, it makes sense to parallelize the processing. When the opposite holds true (and redundancy is not required), it can be more beneficial to process the data on a single node.

15.5   Processors

The last hardware bottleneck we'll discuss is the CPU, or processor. As you most likely already know, the processor is responsible for sending instructions to load and unload data to and from working memory (RAM) and disk as well as conducting various operations on that data. How fast it is able to conduct those operations depends on a few things. Among them is the frequency of the CPU clock, threading, and the effectiveness of branch prediction.

15.5.1   Clock Rate

Usually measured in gigahertz, clock rate is colloquially considered the speed of a processor. It's used largely in marketing to convey to consumers how fast a computer is overall. This isn't wholly inaccurate.

For two processors with all other things the same, a 10 percent difference in clock speed would result in a 10 percent increase in the number of instructions per second that CPU is able to execute.

Clock rate is determined by the frequency of an oscillating crystal built into the CPU architecture. It serves as a timer for the CPU instructions to stay in sync. If you have a faster oscillating crystal, you have a faster rate at which you're able to execute a given instruction.

What makes this story a little more complicated is the idea of an instruction set. This is the language a CPU uses to do work. Two instruction sets can be more complex and, hence, require more instructions to perform the same work.

Register and cache availability also play a role in CPU throughput, but we touched on those earlier.

15.5.2   Cores

As more computing resources are required on a single machine than the CPU speed alone can provide, we scale by increasing the number of threads of execution. This is done at the hardware level by adding more CPU cores. At the most basic level, a computer is able to run as many concurrent tasks as it has cores. There is, however, a case where it is able to do more.

If a CPU supports hyper-threading, it is able to use idle time on a CPU core that is assigned to another process. This means the CPU is able to execute a concurrent number of processes equal to the number of hyper-threads per CPU core times the number of CPU cores.

If you are running a large number of processes, you will probably want to invest in a CPU with many cores. If that CPU also supports hyper-threading, even better.

Now we've talked about running many processes in parallel on a CPU, but there is a way to increase the parallelization of a single process.

15.5.3   Threading

By default one process can use at most one CPU at a time during its execution. We touched on threading when we talked about shared memory earlier. Threading can also be used to increase the number of CPUs used by a running process.

Threading is often preferred to running a separate process because of the savings in memory allocation and access as well as the speed of communication between threads.

There are a few pitfalls. First, concurrency techniques have to be used. If you're using atomic operations such incrementing or decrementing, it is safe for two threads to modify a single variable without regard to each other. If you're reading and setting a value, though, as in Figure 15.1 have to implement locking (also known as a *latch* when it occurs in RAM) to prevent race conditions.

Each time a thread has to wait for a lock to be released before it can do work, you're serializing a parallel application. This negates the benefit of parallel execution. For this reason, the more concurrency management required by a process, the worse of a candidate it is for parallelization.

15.5.4   Branch Prediction

Lastly, there is a really interesting optimization implemented by modern CPUs. When a control flow statement is encountered (e.g., if/else), the CPU attempts to predict the result. It then computes what it imagines the result will be so it can be used if the prediction was correct. If the prediction is incorrect, the computed value is reverted, and execution picks up in the correct branch. This requires some additional computational overhead.

To make this idea more concrete, consider separating a list of numbers into those greater than a particular value and those less than a particular value.

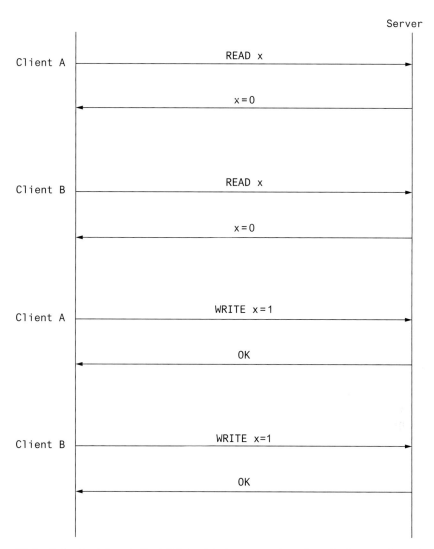

Figure 15.1 Both client A and client B intend to increment the value of x by one. Since they both read before either of them wrote, client B overwrote client A's increment. The result is the value of x is off by 1.

When this list is sorted, the first numbers up to the threshold value will fall into the first category, while the numbers after that value will fall into the second. If the if block puts the numbers into the first bin and the else block the second, then the if branch will be taken many times in a row for the numbers before the threshold, while the else will be taken for the rest. Since this is predictable, you can make great use of branch prediction.

Now consider when this list is completely random. Each time a value is encountered (assuming the threshold value is the median), it will have a 50 percent chance of an incorrect branch prediction. This can add considerable overhead. A quick benchmark on my machine shows an approximate 20 percent improvement in performance when the list is sorted, with the overhead to sort the list being only a 10 percent performance hit.

Naturally this is going to depend on a number of factors, including the randomness of the list and the sorting algorithm used, but it's pretty illustrative. You can consider the case where you're sending the same list to many processes at once to do a similar operation. Sorting beforehand saves the overhead in each process.

15.6   Conclusion

In this chapter, you learned that accessing RAM across lots of threads at once can lead to unforeseen slowdowns. You also learned that volatile storage is much faster than persistent storage but that it is not resistant to events like a process being killed. We went over the concept of latency from a hard disk perspective and a network perspective, with the takeaway that you should minimize the number of "hops" from one piece of hardware to the next to minimize latency. An understanding of paging leads to an effective but complex optimization to accessing elements that are referenced frequently. Thrashing is the negative outcome of using too much memory where pages of memory that would be volatile are accessed from the persistent store instead. We touched on parallel computation and finally branch prediction as a method to speed up processing by breaking work into little bits and a means of dishing out inputs to upstream processes.

With these concepts together, one has the building blocks to effectively design both local and distributed applications. Next you'll look into software fundamentals to reinforce and build on what you've learned.

Software Fundamentals

16.1 Introduction

We just went over a number of hardware bottlenecks you should take into account while you work on applications and data science pipelines. In this chapter, we'll talk about important bottlenecks at the software level with regard to how data is stored.

Each of the following topics is an additional consideration to make as you're designing your pipeline. Looking at your use case as it relates to these concepts will help you choose a more optimal storage engine as it relates to your specific use case.

16.2 Paging

In Chapter 15 we touched on how the inefficient storage of information on disk relates to overhead in retrieving that data. But how does that affect your application? Page/block size is well beyond normal consideration when designing most application. That doesn't mean you shouldn't consider them at all or that no one has done it on your behalf.

For many applications, such as databases, the primary concerns are storage and retrieval. These applications often do consider the efficiency of paging and access when they lay out information. One special example is the graph project, graphchi.

Graphchi lays out adjacent nodes on a network graph adjacently on disk, as roughly illustrated in Figure 16.1. This is for a pretty simple reason: nodes that are adjacent are frequently accessed together. If you query for one node and its neighbors, graphchi makes it simple to return them all by reading a single page.

This results in remarkable performance in traversals and operations that implement propagation across the network.

The point of this discussion is to encourage you to consider how your data is accessed before choosing a database management system as well as how to organize the data in that system.

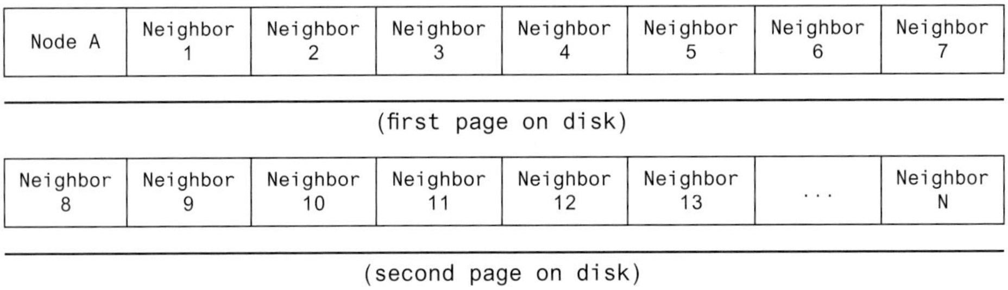

Node A	Neighbor 1	Neighbor 2	Neighbor 3	Neighbor 4	Neighbor 5	Neighbor 6	Neighbor 7

(first page on disk)

Neighbor 8	Neighbor 9	Neighbor 10	Neighbor 11	Neighbor 12	Neighbor 13	. . .	Neighbor N

(second page on disk)

Figure 16.1   Each node takes a fraction of a page on disk. Since each page is read when any node in it is recalled, the neighbors are efficiently paged from disk.

16.3   Indexing

Storing data on disk without some way of finding it would require lots of scanning and paging. In most RDBMSs, the time complexity to read data from the database would be linear in the number of records stored. The first bottleneck you'll see in most database applications that don't have indexes is related to the processes' lack of indexes.

You can think of a database index much in the same way as the index of a book. It contains a search term associated with the location of the record you're trying to find. Just as the index of a book requires a search term, most database indexes require a column name to index. The values of that column are analogous to the search terms you would use in a book index.

When there is a column that requires frequent querying, you should create an index with which to query that column more quickly. There are two common kinds. The first is a binary tree, and the second is a hash index.

Binary trees essentially traverse down a tree, dividing the number of possible entries left to search by roughly 2 with each traversal. This results in $O(\log(N))$ time complexity.

Hash indexes use a hash function to map the column value to an offset. By inputting a column value to search by, the offset can be computed again, and the record can be looked up with $O(1)$ time complexity.

While indexes improve read performance, it's at the cost of write performance. Each time a new entry is added to the database, it has to be added to the index. The more columns that are indexed, the more detriment to write performance.

16.4   Granularity

Consumer-facing applications and those that generate granular event logs are capable of generating a lot of data. Storing each record at its highest level of granularity in financial applications can be colloquially referred to as *ledger format*. Computing the statistics individually and storing only those summaries is referred to as *aggregation*.

When you query averages, sums, and other statistics, the granularity of storage is important to consider. Let's look at both of these approaches in turn. They each have many benefits and drawbacks. Many of those drawbacks have decent workarounds.

If reporting on your event data requires only outputting summary statistics, aggregating that data as it comes in provides the most efficient means of storing and querying it. The time complexity of querying aggregated data is basically the time complexity of the index that refers to the record.

One downside of storing aggregated data is the fact that it requires some infrastructure to process as it comes in. This is necessary overhead apart from the database management system itself, which often has built-in facilities to compute summary statistics. The additional infrastructure means development time, compute resources, and network overhead that would be avoided at least in part by sticking to database writes alone.

Online algorithms are capable of processing one event after the other to form a statistic. As statistics become more complex, only approximations are available. Hence, aggregated data isn't guaranteed to be 100 percent accurate in many cases. This can be fine for many applications, but when statistics are used in later computations, errors compound.

The online approach presents a problem when a new statistic needs to be added to a report. Not only does a new implementation have to be put in place to implement the online portion of the calculation (and the query mechanism), but the old data has to be processed to backfill that statistic for past reports. If your application has been around a while and older reports are still relevant, this can mean some additional lead time before the features launch (since all the old data would need to be reprocessed).

Storing ledger-style records or event logs allows data to be processed a number of ways. As new statistics are required, they can be incorporated as easily as adding a new query to aggregate them. Storing an unbounded amount of data in a database, though, can become pretty expensive.

Some databases, like Amazon's RDS, have a limit to the amount of storage they allow. As table sizes grow beyond what a 32bit ID will allow, expensive data migrations have to take place. Databases that store a working set in RAM of frequently used records can experience thrashing. There are some reasons storing unbounded data for fast access or on-the-fly aggregation can be a problem.

There are cheaper alternatives to storing data than a database. Storing data on a distributed file system, for example, allows fast processing for large amounts of data and very cheap storage. MapReduce or frameworks built on top of these file systems speed the development time to produce these queries. If your use case doesn't require an immediate view of the requested data, distributed storage solutions are a good approach.

When statistics are calculated for a large data set, the overhead of computing the statistic becomes part of the overhead for the query. Querying a lot of statistics this way means a lot of computational overhead. This overhead is the major downside, apart from storage space, of storing granular event data.

16.5   Robustness

The last consideration we'll discuss in choosing how to store information for processing is robustness. This is the general concept of having that data around even after problems arise. There are two factors that contribute to the robustness of a data set. The first is persistence, and the second is redundancy.

Persistence means your data is written to disk. As we discussed earlier, when data is written to disk, it means if the database process or the computer itself is killed, the data is safe. For your data to persist, there's no other way than to encounter the slow operation of actually writing it to an SSD or a spinning disk. When persistence is a requirement, the application will be necessarily slower.

Persistent data is safe in the event of a loss of power, for example, but if the disk it resides on becomes unrecoverable, it is gone forever. This is why redundancy is another important concept for robustness. Writing to multiple backup disks in multiple data centers ensures your data stays available even in the event of a data-center-wide outage.

Redundancy, in general, is not a replacement for persistence. However, if the data you're retrieving is not all that costly to lose (for example, a cached web page), it's often fine to simply implement redundancy over persistence. In the case of the cached web page, it simply means the origin servers will have to do a little more work.

16.6   Extract, Transfer/Transform, Load

One category of processes that combines the concepts of the last few sections is extract transfer/transform, and load (ETL). This refers to three steps that characterize the process. ETLs are usually ad hoc processes, so they're usually not daemonized. They're usually run by a process like cron or another task scheduler.

Generally, these processes take some granular data from a data source (extract), manipulate it or move it across a network in some way (transfer/transform), and then load it into another data store (load). Storing more granular data allows a broader range of statistics to be derived by ETLs, while less granular data can make processes faster.

16.7   Conclusion

In this chapter, we talked about how to organize your data for fast access. We also touched on the idea of granularity as it relates to the speed of aggregation and analysis. Finally, we talked about storing data resiliently.

These concepts are especially important for extract, transfer/transform, load processes, also known as ETL processes. ETLs are one of many types of processes that run in a distributed ecosystem. In the coming chapter, we'll talk about many other process types and how they relate to and communicate with each other over a network.

17

Software Architecture

17.1 Introduction

If you consider the total cost of building and running a given application or data pipeline, you'll realize there are two major factors. The first is the cost of research and development. Building the application itself is essentially human power. The second is the cost of hosting the application, i.e., infrastructure costs. How much does it cost to store the data? How much does it cost to run the servers that respond to queries or build models?

Your understanding of hardware bottlenecks from Chapter 15 is useful in predicting infrastructural costs because avoiding different bottlenecks will have different impacts. What about the cost of development? Besides administrative, managerial, and procedural practices, software architecture can help alleviate some of the cost of production and balance the readability and organization of code with hardware bottlenecks.

There are many software architectures to choose from that result in different levels of granularity or modularity of an application. Each one has trade-offs, balancing savings in cognitive overhead with savings in infrastructure costs. Several of these are discussed in the following sections.

17.2 Client-Server Architecture

In the most basic client-server application, there are two components: the client and the server. The client sends requests to the server, and the server listens for and responds to those requests.

In the vast majority of applications, communication between the client and the server takes place on a socket. There are many types of sockets, but the most common you'll have experience with are the UNIX domain socket and the Internet socket.

UNIX sockets communicate by writing and reading information to and from operating system buffers on a single node. Internet sockets read and write information from a network interface. Sockets are APIs over lower-level operating system functions, which are themselves APIs to hardware functionality.

Some examples of clients that use Internet sockets are your favorite web browser, a peer-to-peer download tool like Napster, your OpenSSL client you use to log into remote machines, or your database client you use to interact with remote databases from an API host.

A few web servers you're probably familiar with are nginx, apache, and lighttpd. A few database servers are mysqld, postgresql, and mongod. There are many other servers, such as OpenVPN, openssh-server, and nsqd, to name a few.

You may notice that many servers end with a *d*. This is short for *daemon*, which is a long-running process that is intended to (almost) never be stopped for as long as the application is run. Exceptions to this are related to maintenance, such as when updating the server software, updating the host hardware, or reloading configurations after a change. Generally speaking, most, if not all, servers are daemons.

Clients, on the other hand, are typically short-lived processes. They open connections to sockets servers listen on and close those connections when they are finished. Take your browser, for example. When you request a web page from a web server, the browser establishes a connection on port 80 (HTTP) or an encrypted connection on 443 (HTTPS). It sends a request to the server for the data that makes up the web page and displays it to you. When you close your browser, the client is shut down, but the server continues to run.

To complete a request, the client must first send it to the server. Once the server has received the request, it must process it and then send a response. This is pictured in Figure 17.1. The amount of time it takes for the request to arrive at the server and be sent back is referred to as *latency*.

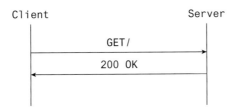

Figure 17.1 A simple client-server interaction

Since clients and servers tend to use sockets, they are subject to the hardware and/or network bottlenecks that impact latency, as we discussed in the previous chapter.

17.3 N-tier/Service-Oriented Architecture

A more complicated version of the basic server-client architecture is the n-tier or service-oriented architecture. The tier is intended to indicate there are many levels of servers and clients, each potentially serving as well as sending requests. Tiers can be third-party services, or they can be services run in the local network.

An example is the typical web application, where a browser sends a request to a web server, and the underlying database client sends a request to a database server to fulfill that request. This complicates the basic server-client interaction by adding a layer of interaction that must be fulfilled serially. Now you don't just have the round-trip (and resulting latency) from the client to the server and back. You have a round-trip between both clients and servers.

Since the database result is required to fulfill the client request, it usually has to happen before the server can begin responding to the request. This is pictured in Figure 17.2.

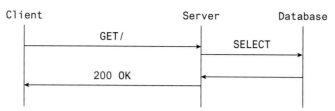

Figure 17.2   A client-server interaction backed by a database

As you can see, the latency between the client and server at each tier adds a layer of latency to the application since the requests happen serially. This can be a major drawback to service-oriented architectures, especially when there are many dependent requests happening serially.

Typically services are partitioned by some concern. For example, you may have one service responsible for basic interactions with user records (name, address, email, etc), while another third-party service could be responsible for providing demographic information about those users.

If you wanted to populate a web page with that user and their demographics, your web application would have to query both the User service and the Demographics service. Since the Demographics service is a third-party service, it uses a different lookup key than your application stores. For this reason, you have to look up the user record before querying the third party.

Since there can be many third-party services your application uses, it's usually not a reasonable solution to update your application to use the third-party user ID. There are a few ways, still, to make this process faster.

Realizing most of the latency in the application is spent waiting to read on a socket, you can implement asynchronous requests for the user and demographics data. Now the total latency is roughly the greater of the two, rather than the sum.

The second approach to making this faster is to decompose the two services into one. Rather than querying the third party for demographic data, you could make that request once for all your users and query it along with the user record in your database. This makes what were two requests into one with the overhead of additional storage (Figure17.3).

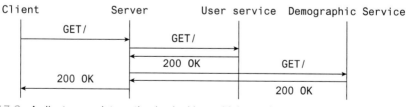

Figure 17.3   A client-server interaction backed by multiple services

17.4   Microservices

Microservices are similar to n-tier architectures, except that they're not strictly tiered. Services can interact with whichever services they need, with whichever interdependencies are required. Figure 17.4 depicts an example network diagram.

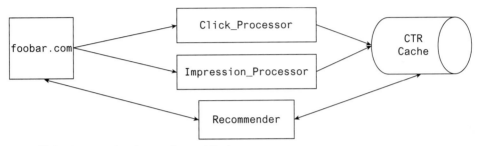

Figure 17.4   An example microservice architecture

Microservice software architectures are typically organized as a large set of individual applications, each running as independently from the other as possible. Code is laid out at a root directory either for all the applications (when the code base isn't prohibitively large) or by product concern.

With hundreds or even thousands of small applications, the most common complaints with microservice software architectures are maintainability and readability. This method of code organization stands in contrast to monolithic architectures.

17.5   Monolith

If microservices are the smallest possible applications, decomposed to separate their business concerns from each other, a monolithic architecture is close to the opposite in terms of organization.

There is an ease of development when boilerplate, or repeated code, can be avoided in favor of implementing a new feature in the existing code base. This is one reason monolithic architectures are so popular and also a natural reason they're adopted.

One of the problems with monolithic architectures comes when a deeply nested dependency needs to change its function signature. Either all code implementing that feature has to be updated to match the signature or a bridge has to be built to make the legacy code compatible. Neither of these outcomes is desirable.

On one hand, code in a monolithic architecture can be organized according to objects and functional utility (e.g., user objects, authentication, database routing), making it easy to find and extend. On the other hand, having all the tools you might need right in front of you can result in the yo-yo problem of having to climb up and down the call stack to figure out bugs or add new features, which add a lot of cognitive overhead.

17.6   Practical Cases (Mix-and-Match Architectures)

Depending on the application you're building, one or the other architecture might be most appropriate for you.

If your code base has clear product separations, a microservice architecture as is might be best.

If your application is expected to reuse many common data-access components for a common, complex product purpose, you may choose a monolithic architecture.

If both these things are true, you may choose a combination of architectures, as shown in Figure 17.5. To the left you can see components of a web page, and to the right is a diagram of the services serving those components.

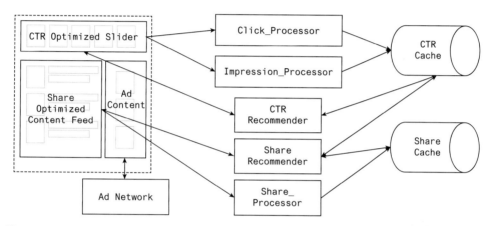

Figure 17.5   An example polyglot architecture

17.7   Conclusion

In this chapter, we discussed several software architectures that can help you organize your code as your application grows. Each has a few benefits and drawbacks. Regardless of your choice of architecture, it should be a choice. The default is typically a monolith, which is not suitable for every occasion.

Knowing the difference between n-tier, microservices, monoliths, and basic client-server applications, your choice of architecture is sure to be well-informed.

18

The CAP Theorem

18.1 Introduction

Now that we've talked a little about software architectures and hardware bottlenecks, we can talk a little bit about a more advanced issue you can run into while building distributed systems.

Any distributed system has three properties, of which any two exclude the third. Those properties are consistency, availability, and partition tolerance. This is most commonly known as the CAP theorem but also carries the name Brewer's theorem.

Luckily, most technologies will make default choices with respect to these issues for you already. Your choice in building a distributed system, then, is choosing the technology that meets your own CAP requirements, or "tuning" a technology away from its defaults.

In the following sections, we'll get into mechanisms for implementing each of these. We will also discuss a common use case where the particular property may be a requirement.

18.2 Consistency/Concurrency

Proper consistency ensures that a piece of data is updated consistently from the perspective of all parts of an ecosystem. Issues of consistency are some of the most common you'll find in any real-world application over the course of its development.

Here is the classic example. Imagine you have a record in a SQL database. To make things concrete, let's say it's MySQL. Your record has two columns. The first is a primary key to look up the record, and the second is a value that will be routinely incremented from its current value.

A common first approach to this is to read the value, increment it in memory, and write the result to the database.

The problem comes into play, when this process is distributed. As soon as a second process comes into play, a race condition is introduced. Both processes read the value from the database at roughly the same time. Both processes increment the value in memory, and then each process in turn writes the updated value back to the database. The final result will be missing the increment from whichever process writes first. See Figure 18.1.

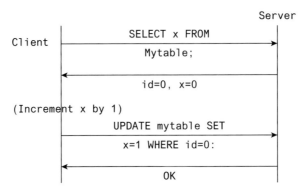

Figure 18.1   Don't do this. This is how to increment a record the wrong way.

MySQL offers two approaches to correcting this problem. The first is to use SELECT FOR UPDATE. This locks the record so that other processes can't update it. When the connection issuing the SELECT FOR UPDATE command finishes with the record, other processes are then allowed to modify it.

The second approach MySQL offers to solve this problem is to issue an UPDATE statement with an increment from whatever the current value is. MySQL will lock in a way that is invisible to the client during the update, ensuring consistency to all clients involved.

An example of this syntax is as follows:

```
UPDATE record SET value = value + 1 WHERE id = 1;
```

One problem with this approach happens when a single value is updated at an extremely high rate. Contention results for the record because many clients end up in line waiting to update the resource. For this reason, MySQL is a poor out-of-the-box choice for highly contentious aggregation.

Now you've seen the downside of locking for consistency. But it's not the only approach! A second method of ensuring consistency of a record in a highly contentious environment is to implement a conflict-free data type. This is a form of eventual consistency.

18.2.1 Conflict-Free Replicated Data Types

Conflict-free data types are those that can be updated consistently across many nodes in a way that is completely reproducible. With rules for resolving conflicts like the one pictured in Figure 18.1, this approach to consistency allows us to "toss writes over the fence." It's simple to write "increment the current value by 1" or "decrement the current value by 2." Rules of incrementing and decrementing are simple to resolve without coordination between nodes.

At a very low level, it is easy to take the implication that "conflict-free" means zero locking. Locking is generally still used for even a simple increment/decrement operation. The concern is that an event, such as an interrupt, can be encountered during access/modification of the integer. This can result in a race condition between two threads. While the C programming language, for example, notes that `int` data types are usually atomic to modify, it's not guaranteed. For more details on particular implementations, take a look at `__atomic_add_fetch` and `__sync_add_fetch` `built-ins`.

Since locking alone has a lot of overhead and since locking effectively serializes writes anyway, it makes sense in some cases to make writes occur in a single thread of execution. This is the approach the Redis data store takes when operating on a single node. Each write is applied sequentially, and performance is very high. Redis also implements CRDTs in the clustered environment.

18.3   Availability

Availability is the general concept that when a request to a service is made, the service is available to produce and send a response. There are various measurements of service availability that can be used, at least as a proxy, to gauge the availability of a service. Uptime, specific error rates (such as timeouts and connection errors), and "health checks" are all examples. You may hear organizations talk about achieving "4 nines." That is a reference to 99.99 percent availability of the service.

There are many components to a highly available system. We'll talk about some of them in the following sections.

18.3.1   Redundancy

Operating on a single node is a no-no. This is a common pitfall. The justification is often given that "servers rarely fall over." Unless multitenancy is used on that machine, there is no way to do a deploy without downtime. This alone is a compelling reason to have redundancy, especially in your application layer.

Redundancy allows you to avoid having a single point of failure, that is, a single component whose demise ensures the demise of the system as a whole. There are a couple approaches to this. They vary depending on the particular role of the node in the network.

18.3.2   Front Ends and Load Balancers

When you have redundant hosts, it becomes necessary to route requests to them in a sensible way so as not to overload a single host. This is where load balancing becomes important. Clients send a query to the load balancer, and the load balancer forwards that request to one of many available hosts. There are two techniques most commonly used for routing these requests. The first is leveraging the Domain Name System (DNS), "the poor man's load balancer," and the second is to use an app server that handles this specifically, such as nginx.

The public-facing side of any service addressed over the Internet can use the publicly available domain name system through a registered provider (such as Amazon's Route 53, GoDaddy, etc). You simply register an IP address to an "at" record, once for each host. When a client application queries your domain name, a shuffled list of your registered IP addresses will be returned. Figure 18.2 shows a network diagram of this setup.

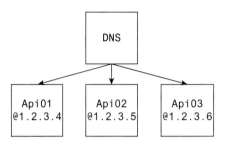

Figure 18.2   Load balancing with DNS. The domain name server points to each of three API nodes. Each node has its own IP address, 1.2.3.4-6.

It is a problem if one of your hosts becomes unhealthy. Clients can still be routed to the unhealthy hosts and experience connection errors or other problems. You can implement retries on clients, but it's generally a bad practice to expect service consumers to do this. Route 53 offers health checks to determine when a host should be removed from a domain configuration. When a health check fails for a host, it is removed from the shuffled list of IP addresses returned to the client until the check passes again. The following is a dig request on the subdomain foo of the domain titfortat.io.

Notice how in the ANSWER section the domain is listed twice, and to the far right is an IP address. These are the IP addresses of two API hosts:

```
$ dig foo.titfortat.io

; <<>> DiG 9.8.3-P1 <<>> foo.titfortat.io
;; global options: +cmd
;; Got answer:
;; ->>HEADER<<- opcode: QUERY, status: NOERROR, id: 7144
;; flags: qr rd ra; QUERY: 1, ANSWER: 2, AUTHORITY: 0, ADDITIONAL: 0

;; QUESTION SECTION:
;foo.titfortat.io.   IN   A

;; ANSWER SECTION:
foo.titfortat.io.   300 IN A 54.213.178.5
foo.titfortat.io.   300 IN A 54.201.109.161

;; Query time: 56 msec
;; SERVER: 209.18.47.62#53(209.18.47.62)
;; WHEN: Thu May  3 06:44:03 2018
;; MSG SIZE  rcvd: 66
```

Amazon makes this easily configurable with Route 53. Figure 18.3 shows the Route 53 console.

There can still be downtime when only active health checks are used. Since health checks don't run continuously. This, coupled with the fact that DNS responses are heavily cached, makes DNS an

Figure 18.3   Amazon Route 53 console for configuring two AT records for the domain foo.titfortat.io

undesirable technique if you want to get as close to 100 percent availability as possible. This is where using an app server for load balancing becomes a good idea.

nginx also implements both passive and active health checks to decide whether to stop forwarding requests to a host. Passive checks in nginx monitor transactions between the load-balancing host and upstream servers it routes requests to. If a transaction fails some number of times, as specified by its configuration, the load balancer stops forwarding requests there. Figure 18.4 shows a basic diagram of an API balanced behind nginx.

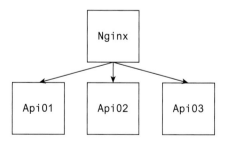

Figure 18.4   Load balancing with nginx

This discussion of redundancy from the perspective of the load balancer would not be complete if we did not address the fact that the load balancer itself can serve as a single point of failure. To address this issue, the Common Address Redundancy Protocol (CARP) is implented by agents such

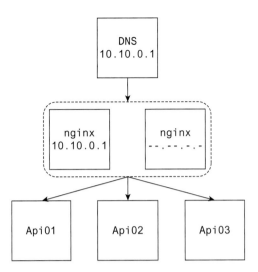

Figure 18.5 Load balancing with nginx and IP virtualization with CARP, for example

as uCARP to share IP addresses across hosts (such as one serving as a load balancer). If a single host becomes unhealthy, the shared IP is assigned to a healthy host, as shown in Figure 18.5.

18.3.3 Client-Side Load Balancing

On the other end, you can implement client-side load balancing for your services. In the configuration for the client, you specify the complete list of possibly available hosts. The client can then implement logic to choose one at random or in a cycle. Upon some failure, it can remove the host from its rotation for a time and try another host.

More advanced client-side load balancing allows the client to query a domain name for available hosts. Elasticsearch is one example. The Elasticsearch service provides an endpoint for clients to find a node in the mesh network. Clients can (and do in the official Python driver) establish connection pools to these nodes and send requests to them in turn. Unhealthy nodes are removed from ElastiCache's service discovery endpoint.

18.3.4 Data Layer

In the data layer of your application, the most common approach to redundancy is a primary/replica (also known as *master-slave* configuration), as pictured in Figure 18.6. In this mode of operation, one node is responsible for receiving both writes and reads from clients, while the second is responsible only for reads. In the case of MySQL and PostgreSQL, the replica (also known as the *secondary*) receives data from the primary in a compressed binary format.

Typically writes to the replica lag slightly behind what can be found on the primary node. This is known as *replication lag*. For use cases that require 100 percent accurate up-to-date data, the primary

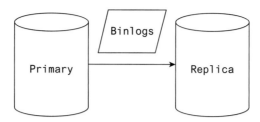

Figure 18.6   Basic primary/secondary replication

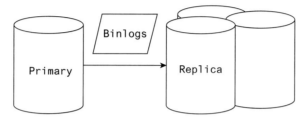

Figure 18.7   Replication with multiple secondaries

node will be both read from and written to. Otherwise, it's usually more resource-efficient to do as many reads as possible on the replicas. Reads are scaled by adding replicas (Figure 18.7).

In the case that vertical scaling is no longer viable and a single cluster has reached its maximum capacity, it can be desirable to use multiple primary nodes. Multiprimary configurations allow writes to be scaled horizontally. The downside is that this requires partitioning the data. To achieve effectively distributed writes, some should be routed to one primary node, while the rest are routed to the other. This is normally handled by the application with at least an implicit approach to sharding.

Sharding, as shown in Figure 18.8, is a general abstraction allowing data to be treated separately in blocks with desirable characteristics. If you want to save infrastructure costs by avoiding replica overhead, you can replicate by placing data on a single shard, which is replicated across multiple hosts. Figure 18.9 shows a common scheme for achieving this. If data is partitioned into disjoint shards 0, 1, and 2, those shards are replicated by hosting 0 and 1 on host A, 1 and 2 on host B, and 2 and 0 on host C. This is known as colloquially as *A/B replication*.

Shard data structures provide a useful mechanism for maintaining facts about a set of data. Attributes a shard might include are hostname, index range, indexed column, and the shard state (e.g., operational, migrating, etc.).

There is a lot to take into account when choosing an approach to sharding. A good choice of index or shard key is essential since this ultimately determines what the load on each shard (and hence host) will be. Complex approaches to sharding allow ranges of indexes to be rebalanced between shards in the event they become uneven. Commonly, though, you're stuck with manually migrating shards that become unbalanced over time.

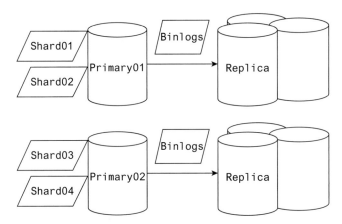

Figure 18.8   Multimaster replication

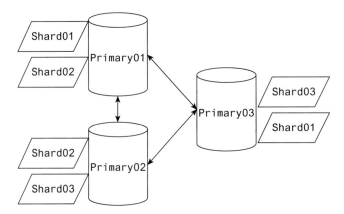

Figure 18.9   A/B replication, where shards are shared across hosts for redundancy

18.3.5   Jobs and Taskworkers

Redundancy in scheduled jobs and taskworker processes is simple. You just create more processes, run them on more machines, and implement retries when there are failures.

18.3.6   Failover

In any redundant configuration, you have to have a plan for when there is a failure. In the case there is a failure in your load balancer, it implements the procedures of active and passive health checks and then stops routing to that node. This means the fallback or approach to failover is simply to rely on the rest of the network.

For databases there are other approaches to failover. A simpler case is when a replica or primary node fails in MySQL. A secondary node is simply promoted to master and interaction with the database proceeds normally.

In ElastiCache, for example, shards from the failed node are routed to other nodes in the cluster and continue to support reading and writing.

18.4   Partition Tolerance

The last feature of networks that can cause major headaches is the idea of a partition in the network. This means one portion of the network over which a cluster of data nodes is distributed cannot reach another portion of the network. This is also known as a *split brain*. Let's take a look at RabbitMQ for an example of what happens in this type of scenario.

18.4.1   Split Brains

Let's say you have two nodes in a network of RabbitMQ servers, as in Figure 18.10. One is on the East Coast, and one is on the West Coast. Let's also imagine you have two clients, also one on the East Coast and one on the West Coast. Each of these nodes is receiving ordered messages from a client, starting at 0 and going up to n. For the sake of this discussion, let's just assume the messages arrive in order. Figure 18.11 shows the network.

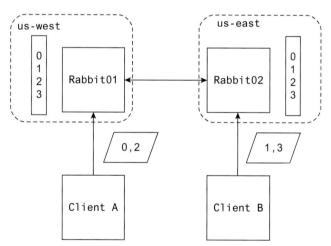

Figure 18.10   A synchronized two-node RabbitMQ cluster

So, now the West Coast client sends message 0 to the West Coast RabbitMQ node. It receives that message and replicates it to the node on the East Coast. Now the East Coast node receives message 1 from the East Coast client, and it replicates message 1 on the West Coast. Consumers on either coast can receive messages 0 and 1 from their respective RabbitMQ host.

Now let's imagine there's a break in the network. The East Coast and West Coast nodes are no longer reachable from each other. The way RabbitMQ handles this situation is by essentially

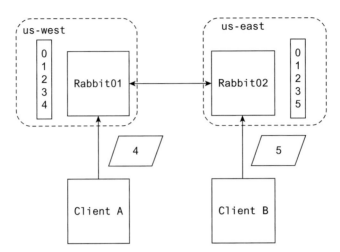

Figure 18.11   A split-brain RabbitMQ cluster

treating the queues on each side of the network separately. This means consumers on the East Coast will receive both messages 0 and 1, while those on the West Coast also receive messages 0 and 1. After they finish processing, 0 and 1 will have been processed twice. This is depicted in Figure 18.11.

If a publisher writes a new message on the East Coast, the message will be written only to the East Coast node, and a new message on the West Coast will be written only to the West Coast node. This approach is not very tolerant to partitions, but depending on the application this is fine. As long as consumers are able to deduplicate messages or repeated processing is inconsequential, there is no problem.

To make the network partition tolerant, it comes either at the sacrifice of availability as the process blocks new requests until network issues are resolved or at the expense of consistency, as the previous example illustrates.

18.5   Conclusion

We've talked, now, about several approaches to balancing the C, the A, and the P of the CAP theorem. In most modern systems, options are provided to balance the various trade-offs to suit the needs of your application. With these hyperbolic examples of real-world issues, you can decide the needs of your application from the perspective of both the end user and the project maintainers.

Logical Network Topological Nodes

19.1 Introduction

This chapter covers network topological nodes. We won't get into specific network hardware components such as routers and switches but will focus on the parts more relevant to designing and architecting a hearty application layer.

19.2 Network Diagrams

Network diagrams are a useful way to articulate an architectural design to colleagues. Being able to sketch components on the board allows you to summarize a complicated network clearly, concisely, and efficiently.

Several applications support drawing network diagrams. There are lots of flavors of edges and nodes, but they share commonalities. For the sake of this chapter, we'll choose a few icons necessary to represent the components we'll be discussing. Google Drive makes many icons available using the drawing dialog.

Hosts, compute instances, and *worker machines* are all terms referring to a computer on a network. They can host server applications, implement mapreduce, host daemonized processes like crond, or host a queue listener such as an nsq or a kafka client as well as any number of other tasks. We'll represent these with the icon shown in Figure 19.1, where "Hostname" represents the name of the host in the network.

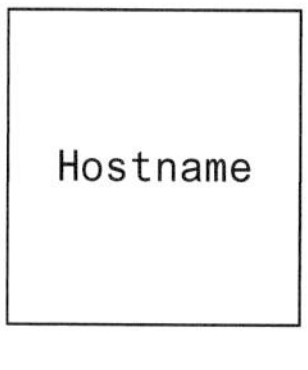

Figure 19.1 A common representation of a single host computer in a network

The Internet is usually represented with a cloud icon, as shown in Figure 19.2. It represents any type of possible traffic. This has a number of implications. First, any sort of request could come through. If there are types of traffic you would like to accept or reject, the Internet icon serves as a reminder that input should be filtered to only the sort of traffic desired. Further, it comes with the implication that potentially malicious traffic could be encountered, so inputs should be sanitized. These are two basic building blocks and the minimum required for a complete public-facing application (though the application wouldn't be terribly resilient). Let's get into some components that offer more robustness.

Figure 19.2   A common representation of the Internet

19.3   Load Balancing

Earlier we discussed using load balancers for the purpose of redundancy and distributing load to hosts of heavily used applications. The case we described earlier was for load balancing requests to an API. Figure 19.3 illustrates a simple network.

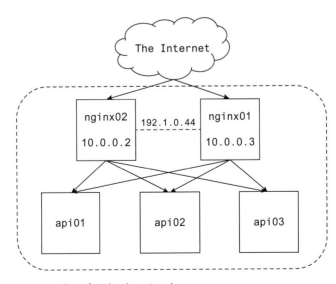

Figure 19.3   A representation of a simple network

There are several things to note here. First, the border around the nginx and api nodes indicates they are on the same network or behind the same gateway, which is the door to the Internet. The gateway is not pictured in Figure 19.3 since it's out of the scope of our discussion. For our purposes, you can consider this boundary a convenient way to group nodes in your network.

Next, you should note there are two nginx hosts receiving requests from the Internet. Each of these has its own IP, but they also have a virtual IP, which is shared between them by CARP. This allows one to take over for the other in the event there is a node failure.

Finally, there are three api nodes, and each can receive requests from each nginx node. These are drawn as a full directional mesh, but it's worth noting a lot of people prefer to draw an API layer to cut down on busy details like lots of arrows.

Most cloud providers make a reliable load balancer available to you. They take care of these little details so you don't have to. It is still a good idea to know how to do them yourself.

There are a few great use cases for load balancers. The most common is the one pictured in Figure 19.3. A second one, though, is as a means of implementing multitenancy. Many applications are single-threaded (Python and Redis, for example). To make the most use of the CPU cores on larger machines, it's common to run several of these processes at once, each listening on a different port.

Figure 19.4 shows how you might diagram multitenancy on a single API node.

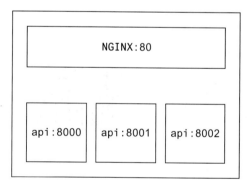

Figure 19.4   Multitenancy pictured on an API node

The colon indicates what port each process is listening to on that host. Here it's understood from the context that nginx is routing requests to/from the API processes on this machine. You could make it more explicit, though, by drawing arrows.

19.4   Caches

Caches serve a few common purposes. There are many types of caches and many ways to use each one. We'll discuss a few next.

19.4.1   Application-Level Caching

What makes a cache so fast? There is a short answer: it usually stores all your data in RAM. RAM is fast!

Caching in the application is appealing sometimes, especially when the application is small. In general, though, if you wanted to speak strictly, this violates the separation of concerns between processes. You should have one process for caching and another for handling requests. The 12-factor standard for application development supports this with the assertion that state should not be maintained in a 12-factor application. Something sitting in the cache represents the state of that cached object at that time.

If you insist on application-level caching, be aware of some important caveats: processes don't typically share memory. This means a cache on one process will not be visible to another; hence, invalidating an object on write in that cache will not invalidate it in other application caches. Effective caching requires a memory management/eviction strategy. If you don't have a process in place for removing elements from the cache, you have effectively created a memory leak. Each time your application reboots (normal deploys, for example), the origin of your cached resource will see burst traffic. This can become a bigger concern as your application becomes more popular. Shared resources between requests, especially those that require authentication, should be a big red flag. Making it possible to share state across requests opens your application to many dangers, including accidentally revealing an access token (or worse) for one user to another user.

Now, if you still insist on application-level caching, allow us to give two use cases, one of which is totally fine and another that can cause major headaches.

19.4.1.1   The Case for Static Content

The first case is when you have only a few processes that receive API requests, which commonly need to translate IDs into static content. Let's imagine you've built a recommender system that maintains a mapping of IDs to content features it takes into account. When the recommender has generated some optimal results for a user, it ends up with a list of these content IDs. Now it's faced with the task of sending the client back the content representation itself.

This is typically done by making a database call for the content through another API, joining those results to the recommender results, and sending the whole package back to the user. If you use an application cache, you can store the content mapped to each ID and avoid ever having to make the request. This would be a big time-saver. Since the content is pretty static, it's no big deal if one application's version goes stale for a while.

You might notice in this case content that is currently popular stays popular for a while and then makes way for new popular content. In this case, a "least recently used" eviction policy would be pretty appropriate. As content becomes less often used, it will fall off the end of the cache. This ensures the number of external API calls for the static content is at a minimum.

19.4.1.2   The Case to Avoid Locally Caching Sensitive Information

Let's say you have a complicated process of checking a user ID against a number of subroutines to validate their eligibility to use a particular feature. Since each of these are well-encapsulated and all of them require the complete user record, it might be appealing to store the user account information in the application cache. You might think that if you encapsulate all the cached data per request, other users won't be able to see it since it will be gone after the current user has been served.

This seems sound at a glance. However, it assumes there is no shared state between requests. In app servers that allow for coroutines and other asynchronous code, these objects can still persist as other requests are being served since one request can be paused while waiting on IO and another request resumed. If, in your subroutines, you use a globally defined method to reference the request, you will inevitably end up with the wrong user information in the request.

19.4.2   Cache Services

The most common of these is memcached and Redis. Redis seems to be eclipsing memcached at the moment for a couple reasons. It offers types, and it happens to be faster when it's implemented right (using multitenancy or multiple master nodes).

In Figure 19.5 you can find a typical interaction between the API layer, the application cache, and the database. The cache usually serves two purposes in this context. The first is a response cache. The second is an object cache.

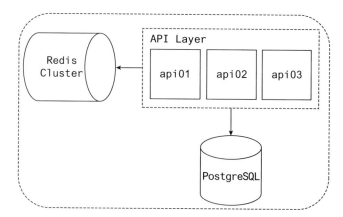

Figure 19.5   An API with a caching layer backed by a database

Caching responses that can be reused allows the API to save a ton of time. What might be a series of template computations and API and database calls turns into an $O(1)$ lookup and a simple transfer of data.

Object caches allow the API to say "Have I requested this recently?" and in the case it has, it says, "Okay, I'll take it from the cache instead of the database."

19.4.3   Write-Through Caches

The process of aggregating statistics can be heavy. Further, if you have many applications doing the aggregation, they often need some form of concurrency control. There are a few ways to achieve this. A cache is one possible solution.

One of the simplest ways to manage applications that are aggregating concurrently is to use the incr/decr methods made available by Redis. If the statistics are not business critical in the sense that they absolutely cannot disappear, a cache is a good choice to aggregate them and serve them from.

When you do need that persistence layer, a database will usually do. If the rate of incoming updates becomes too high, though, you may consider techniques for batching them. There are two approaches to using a write-through cache to do this that come to mind.

The first involves a write-through cache in the application. As your taskworker receives messages from your queueing system, it saves them for a moment. If it encounters more than one update for a single record, it combines them. When those updates are successfully communicated to the database, the taskworker signals it has completed the update.

The second approach to managing a write-through cache takes into account that a user will continue sending events related to their session until the session times out. Imagine taskworkers each register a user session in the cache upon receipt of the first message from a given user. If the session already exists, the taskworker can increment its reference count. If a taskworker already has an active session (meaning they have incremented the session by 1), each additional message for the session is simply written to the cache as it arrives. This allows you to track how many taskworkers have an active reference to a given session at any time during the session. When that initial create session or increment operation occurs, a timer can be started on the taskworker. A new message coming in extends the time. No messages coming in allows the clock to run out. When the clock runs out for a given taskworker, it decrements the reference count to the session. The last taskworker to decrement its reference count deletes the session from the cache and writes the aggregate data to the database.

19.5   Databases

There are so many databases out there! Depending on which one you're running, there are a handful of standard approaches to ensuring the resilience of your data. We'll go through a few of them here.

19.5.1   Primary and Replica

Lots of databases use this approach to replication. MySQL, PostgreSQL, Redis, and MongoDB are a few. Figure 19.6 pictures the standard interactions between an API and a primary-replica database configuration.

The gist of it is that only one node accepts database writes. That node is responsible for communicating the data it receives to the replica, secondary, or slave as you prefer. Usually this is

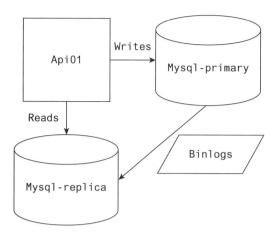

Figure 19.6   An API implementing reads from a replica and writes to a primary node

done by transferring a binary log of the writes to the secondary node. This allows the two to stay in sync for the most part.

Replica lag is the phenomenon associated with the latency between the primary and replica nodes. It takes a bit of time to sync the binlogs from the primary to the replica, so data on the replica isn't immediately available after writing to the master. Common replica lag is in milliseconds.

This is an important caveat to take into account. If you need a strong guarantee the value you're reading is completely up-to-date, you will have to do that read on the primary node. A common method for scaling at the early stage, though, is reading from the replica wherever possible. This phenomenon is what decides what reads can be done where.

Naturally with this configuration your writes go to one node, and to the best of your ability you send the reads to another. If your application is more read-heavy, you can keep adding replica nodes with little consequence in terms of syncing binlogs. But what if it's more write-heavy?

19.5.2   Multimaster

There are a couple cases where it makes sense to use multiple master nodes. One case is to scale database writes. There are two approaches to this. The first is the more standard approach, using two master nodes and backing up to the same slave. Each master will have a partition of the data, but the replica will have all of it. The second approach is to route objects in the application to a master based on some characteristic of the object. With this approach each master is typically backed up to its own replica (Figure 19.7).

But it simplifies reading from your database to have them write to the same replica.

In the first approach, clients can choose what primary node to write to at random and distribute objects pretty effectively. There are some important caveats to this approach. As long as reads are sent to the replica, it's simple to return a complete result. If reads are sent to either primary node, the results will be missing the data stored on the parallel primary node. The second important

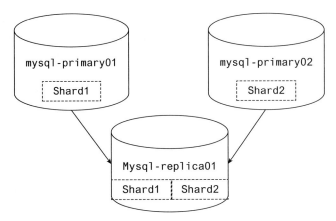

Figure 19.7 Two primary nodes in a multimaster configuration writing to the same replica

caveat involves avoiding conflicting data on the replica. If your keys are set to auto-increment on both master nodes, two objects sent to the replica can and will have matching primary keys, which violates the unique constraint of a primary key. A simple solution is to increment on both masters by 2 and give one an offset of 1.

19.5.3   A/B Replication

Figure 19.8 shows two primaries writing to a single replica; this is the simplest case of A/B replication. In this scenario, data is conceptually partitioned into separate distinct shards. It is then replicated at least once for each shard.

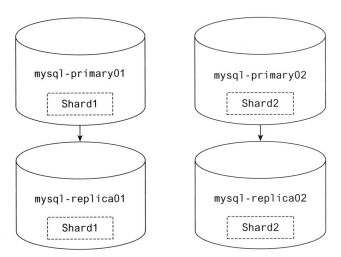

Figure 19.8 Two primary nodes in a multimaster configuration writing to their own replicas

This approach makes a lot of sense in terms of storage. If you have a 100-node cluster, for example, each containing a complete record of your database, that is a lot of space! By copying each shard twice, you save a lot of room. Many databases take this approach to replicating data. Elasticsearch, MongoDB, and Cassandra are a few.

Figure 19.9 shows a slightly more complicated approach to sharding. Elasticsearch manages its data in this way. If one node disappears for whatever reason, it begins copying the missing copy of whichever shards were on that node to another available host. If two nodes disappear with the only copy of a shard, that data is lost forever.

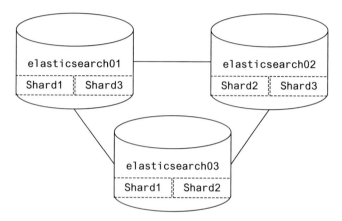

Figure 19.9   A more complete example of a basic sharded database

19.6   Queues

There are many use cases for queues. In essence, they allow for asynchronous event handling. This enables parallel execution as well as the management of "who does what." In this section, we will talk about scheduling dependent tasks, remote procedure calls, and API buffering.

19.6.1   Task Scheduling and Parallelization

Sometimes it's necessary to run tasks every so often. When the task is a one-off, it's simple. You can just run it as a `crond` task. As infrastructure becomes more complex, though, and as one-off scheduled tasks become to depend on each other, it becomes more necessary to use a queue.

Why might you use a queue instead of just running the tasks synchronously, one after the other? I'm glad you asked. There is a single case where it makes sense to do that. That is in the case your dependency has no branches, as shown in Figure 19.10. We start with the event, A. The result of A is sent to process B, and the result of B is sent to process C. Executing this on one node would have about the same benefit as using a queue since they have to execute serially.

When you have multiple tasks dependent on a single result, the case for a queue becomes clear. By having each dependent process subscribe to the queue for the process on which it depends, they

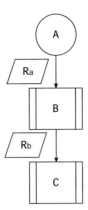

Figure 19.10   Cascading scheduled tasks, originating at A and ending at C

can all be relayed the result to process independently. Further, if there are tasks dependent on them, they can be triggered in the same way. In Figure 19.11, B and C both depend on the result of A. D, E, and F depend on the result of B, while G depends on the result of C.

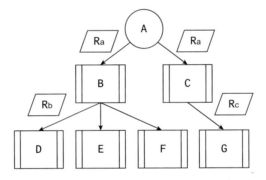

Figure 19.11   Cascading scheduled tasks, forming a complex tree of tasks

The benefit of this approach is parallelization. Assuming there exist four processes to do the execution, D, E, F, and G can all be executed at the same time. Distributing workload in this way ensures computational resources are used as efficiently as possible since those processes that are not busy are listening for work to do.

19.6.2   Asynchronous Process Execution

When a user-facing client sends a request, it's usually desirable for them to see an immediate result. If there's a lot of work to do, it makes sense to respond to the client and kick off a job to do that work asynchronously.

One great example of this is when a user signs up to a social network and you want to find all their friends on that network and make it available for them to interact with those friends. In this case, you'll send an event indicating contacts should be synced and then allow the user to proceed to the next dialog.

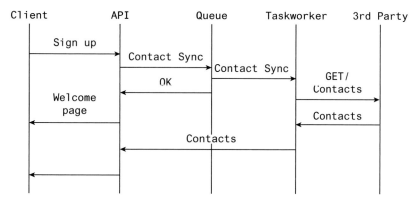

Figure 19.12   Tasks firing outside the critical path of the user to provide a seamless experience

This could look something like what is pictured in Figure 19.12.

In other words, the client signs up for a service to the API. The API sends a message to a queue indicating contacts should be synced for that user. A taskworker, listening to that queue, receives the message and queries a third party. It then relays those results to the API upon receipt, making them available to the user.

19.6.3   API Buffering

Sometimes applications can see burst traffic far out of bounds from what is typical for the application. When this happens, the application has to either scale or space out requests to a level that is acceptable. Concretely, if an application designed to handle 100 requests per second receives 500 requests in a second, it could find itself inundated to the extent that application errors result or it times out. A five-second delay on a request isn't fatal from a user perspective; it's a degradation for sure but not a failure.

Queues provide a great way to space out incoming requests to a rate the API can handle. If writes are written to a horizontally scaled queue, they can be inserted as the API is available. Taskworkers listen for those writes and execute them just as quickly as they can, alerting the client to their completion through push or some other server client protocol.

19.7   Conclusion

When you understand the building blocks of a distributed system, the possibilities become endless. You can piece these together in complex configurations to suit a multitude of needs. Computing on the fly, precaching, task scheduling, parallelization, and many other implementations are possible with the elements discussed in this chapter.

As you build out your architectural designs, diagramming and referring to those diagrams during discussions makes for well-informed, well-motivated conversations. There are many flavors of these diagrams, but the most important thing to remember is consistency.

Bibliography

[1] M. Herman, S. Rivera, S. Mills, J. Sullivan, P. Guerra, A. Cosmas, D. Farris, E. Kohlwey, P. Yacci, B. Keller, A. Kherlopian, and M. Kim, *The Field Guide to Data Science*. McLean, VA: Booz Allen, Nov. 2013.

[2] M. F. Smith, *Software Prototyping: Adoption, Practice and Management*. New York, NY: McGraw-Hill, Inc., 1991.

[3] Agile Alliance, "12 Principles Behind the Agile Manifesto," Nov. 2015. https://www.agilealliance.org/agile101/12-principles-behind-the-agile-manifesto/

[4] I. Goodfellow, Y. Bengio, and A. Courville, *Deep Learning*. Cambridge, MA: MIT Press, 2016.

[5] R. Kohavi, R. Longbotham, D. Sommerfield, and R. M. Henne, "Controlled Experiments on the Web: Survey and Practical Guide," *Data Min. Knowl. Discov.*, vol. 18, no. 1, pp. 140–181, Feb. 2009.

[6] R. Kohavi and R. Longbotham, "Online Controlled Experiments and A/B Testing," in *Encyclopedia of Machine Learning and Data Mining*, pp. 922–929, Boston, MA: Springer, 2017.

[7] T. Crook, B. Frasca, R. Kohavi, and R. Longbotham, "Seven Pitfalls to Avoid when Running Controlled Experiments on the Web," in *Proceedings of the 15th ACM SIGKDD International Conference on Knowledge Discovery and Data Mining*, KDD '09, (New York, NY), pp. 1105–1114, ACM, 2009.

[8] D. C. Montgomery, *Design and Analysis of Experiments*. New York: John Wiley & Sons, 2006.

[9] S. Newman, *Building Microservices*. Boston, MA: O'Reilly Media, Inc., 1st ed., 2015.

[10] "TimeComplexity," Python Wiki.

[11] L. Breiman, "Random Forests," *Mach. Learn.*, vol. 45, no. 1, pp. 5–32, Oct. 2001.

[12] T. Hastie, R. Tibshirani, and J. Friedman, *The Elements of Statistical Learning: Data Mining, Inference, and Prediction, Second Edition*. Springer Series in Statistics, New York: Springer-Verlag, 2 ed., 2009.

[13] T. P. Minka, "Algorithms for maximum-likelihood logistic regression," *Statistics Tech Report*, abstract, Sept. 19, 2003. http://www.stat.cmu.edu/tr/tr758/tr758.pdf

[14] D. Arthur and S. Vassilvitskii, "How Slow is the K-means Method?" in *Proceedings of the Twenty-second Annual Symposium on Computational Geometry*, SCG '06, (New York, NY), pp. 144–153, ACM, 2006.

[15] Y. Zhang, A. J. Friend, A. L. Traud, M. A. Porter, J. H. Fowler, and P. J. Mucha, "Community structure in Congressional cosponsorship networks," *Physica A: Statistical Mechanics and its Applications*, vol. 387, no. 7, pp. 1705–1712, Mar. 2008.

[16] M. E J Newman, "Analysis of Weighted Networks," *Physical review. E, Statistical, nonlinear, and soft matter physics*, vol. 70, p. 056131, Dec. 2004.

[17] S. Fortunato and M. Barthlemy, "Resolution limit in community detection," *Proceedings of the National Academy of Sciences*, vol. 104, no. 1, pp. 36–41, Jan. 2007.

[18] B. H. Good, Y.-A. de Montjoye, and A. Clauset, "Performance of modularity maximization in practical contexts," *Physical Review E*, vol. 81, no. 4, p. 046106, Apr. 2010.

[19] S. M. Omohundro, "Five Balltree Construction Algorithms," Tech. Rep., 1989.

[20] J. L. Bentley, "Multidimensional Binary Search Trees Used for Associative Searching," *Commun. ACM*, vol. 18, no. 9, pp. 509–517, Sept. 1975.

[21] "1.6. Nearest Neighbors," scikit-learn 0.19.1 documentation.

[22] J. Pearl, *Causality: Models, Reasoning and Inference*. New York, NY: Cambridge University Press, 2nd ed., 2009.

[23] D. J. C. MacKay, *Information Theory, Inference & Learning Algorithms*. New York, NY: Cambridge University Press, 2002.

[24] K. P. Murphy, *Machine Learning: A Probabilistic Perspective*. Cambridge, MA: MIT Press, 2012.

[25] E. J. Elton and M. J. Gruber, "A Practitioner's Guide to Factor Models," *Research Foundation Books*, vol. 1994, no. 4, pp. 1–85, Mar. 1994.

[26] D. Lay, *Linear Algebra and Its Applications*. Hoboken, NJ: Pearson, 3rd ed., 2016.

[27] I. M. Johnstone and A. Y. Lu, "Sparse Principal Components Analysis," *arXiv:0901.4392 [math, stat]*, Jan. 2009. arXiv: 0901.4392.

[28] "sklearn.decomposition.PCA," scikit-learn 0.19.1 documentation.

[29] M. E. Tipping and C. M. Bishop, "Probabilistic Principal Component Analysis," *Journal of the Royal Statistical Society: Series B (Statistical Methodology)*, vol. 61, no. 3, pp. 611–622, Jan. 2002.

[30] J. V. Stone, *Independent Component Analysis: A Tutorial Introduction*. Cambridge, MA: MIT Press, 2004.

[31] A. Hyvarinen, "Fast and Robust Fixed-point Algorithms for Independent Component Analysis," *Trans. Neur. Netw.*, vol. 10, no. 3, pp. 626–634, May 1999.

[32] S. Shwartz, M. Zibulevsky, and Y. Y. Schechner, "ICA Using Kernel Entropy Estimation with NlogN Complexity," in *Independent Component Analysis and Blind Signal Separation*, Lecture Notes in Computer Science, pp. 422–429, Berlin, Heidelberg: Springer, Sept. 2004.

[33] D. M. Blei, A. Y. Ng, and M. I. Jordan, "Latent Dirichlet Allocation," *Journal of Machine Learning Research*, vol. 3, no. Jan, pp. 993–1022, 2003.

[34] R. R. ehu and P. Sojka, "Software Framework for Topic Modelling with Large Corpora," abstract, p. 5. https://radimrehurek.com/gensim/lrec2010_final.pdf

Index

Numbers

12 principles of agile methodology, 11–14
"12-factor rules," 71
95 percent confidence interval, 20, 107

A

A/B replication, 229–230, 240–241
access, RAM (random access memory), 205–206
aggregation, 214
agile development, product focus and, 10–11
agile methodology, 12 principles, 11–14
algorithms
    Cannon's algorithm, 97
    classification algorithms, 117
        k-means, 125–127
        logistic regression, 118–122
        naive Bayes, 122–124
    clustering algorithms, 117
        greedy Louvain, 130–131
        k-means. *see* k-means
        leading eigenvalue, 128–130
        nearest neighbors, 131–133
    comparison algorithms. See comparison
        algorithms
Amazon, Route 53, 226–227
ANNoy, 133
API buffering, queues, 243
application-level caching, 236
architectures, 70–71
    batch computing, 72–73
    data sources, 72
    online computing, 72–73
    scaling, 73–74
    services, 71
    software architecture
        client-server architecture, 217–218
        microservices, 220
        mix-and-match architectures, 221

monolith, 220
n-tier/service-oriented architecture, 218–219
assumptions
greedy Louvain, 130
ICA (independent component analysis), 158
k-means, 127
linear least squares, 97
logistic regression, 121
MinHash, 83
naive Bayes, 124
nearest neighbors, 132
asynchronous process execution, queues, 242–243
ATE (average treatment effect), 168
auto-correlation, time-series plots, 60–61
availability, CAP theorem, 225
client-side load balancing, 228
data layers, 228–230
failover, 230–231
front ends and load balancers, 225–228
jobs and taskworkers, 230
redundancy, 225
average treatment effect (ATE), 168
avoiding locally caching sensitive information, 237

B

back-door conditioning, 178
bag of words, 27, 29
bar charts, 46–47
batch computing, 72–73
batch fitting, neural networks, 199–200
batched training algorithms, models, 74
Bayesian inference, 122
Bayesian networks, 135
casual graphs and conditional independence, 136–137
causal graphs, linear regression, 142–143
d-separation, 139–142
fitting models, 143–146
Markovity, factorization and, 138–139
stability and dependence, 137–138
Bernoulli distribution, 160
bias, 18
binary trees, 214
binary variables, 25
blocking, 142
blocking non-causal paths, 177–179
g-formula, 179–182
boosting, 113
bootstrap aggregating, 112–113
box plots, 55–57
branch prediction, processors, 210–212

C

cache invalidation, 72
cache services, 237
caches, 72, 235
application-level caching, 236
cache services, 237
write-through caches, 238
Cannon's algorithm, 97
CAP theorem, 223
availability, 225
client-side load balancing, 228
data layers, 228–230
failover, 230–231
front ends and load balancers, 225–228
jobs and taskworkers, 230
redundancy, 225
consistency/concurrency, 223–224
conflict-free data types, 224–225
partition tolerance, 231–232
capacity, neural networks, 193–196
career development, for data scientists, 5
CARP (Common Address Redundancy Protocol), 227–228
causal Bayesian networks, 136–137
causal graphs, Bayesian networks, 142–143
causal inference
controlling to block, g-formula, 179–182
controlling to block non-causal paths, 177–179
experiments, 168–171
machine-learning estimators, 182
examples, 182–187
g-formula, 182
observation, examples, 171–177
CCDF (complementary cumulative distribution function), 49–51
changing requirements, 11–12
choosing
models, regression, 90
objective functions, 90–91
classification algorithms, 117
k-means, 125–127
logistic regression, 118–122
naive Bayes, 122–124
clicks, 21
click-through rate (CTR), 21, 149–150
client-server architecture, 217–218
client-side load balancing, availability, 228
clock rate, processors, 209
clustering algorithms, 117
greedy Louvain, 130–131
k-means. *see* k-means

leading eigenvalue, 128–130
nearest neighbors, 131–133
clusters, 117
  k-means, 127
combined workflows, 10
Common Address Redundancy Protocol (CARP),
  227–228
communication, 13
company size, role of, data scientists, 3–4
comparison algorithms
  cosine similarity, 84–86
  Jaccard distance, 79–80
    algorithms, 80–81
    distributed approach, 81–82
    memory, 81
    time complexity, 81
  Mahalanobis distance, 86–87
  MinHash, 82–84
complementary cumulative distribution function
  (CCDF), 49–51
complexity
  cosine similarity, 85
  greedy Louvain, 130
  ICA (independent component analysis), 158
  k-means, 128
  leading eigenvalue, 129
  linear least squares, 97
  Mahalanobis distance, 86
  naive Bayes, 124
  nearest neighbors, 132–133
  PCA (principle components analysis), 154
concurrency, CAP theorem, 223–224
conditional independence, causal graphs and,
  136–137
confidence intervals, hypothesis testing, 40–41
conflict-free data types, 224–225
confounding, 174
consistency, CAP theorem, 223–224
context, hypothesis testing, 43–44
continuous variables, 46
convolutions, 191
cores, processors, 210
cosine similarity, 84–85
  complexity, 85
  distributed approach, 86
  memory, 85
critical value, 39
CTR (click-through rate), 21

D

daemon, 218
data, storing, 215

data analysts, 5
data layers, availability, 228–230
data preprocessing, 25
data scientists
  career development, 5
  importance of, 5–6
  role of
    company size, 3–4
    teams, 4–5
data sources, 72
data streams, 72
data teams, 7–8
  project workflows
    combined workflows, 10
    embedding versus pooling resources, 8
    prototyping, 9–10
    research, 8–9
data visualization, 45
  distributions and summary statistics, 45
    box plots and error bars, 55–57
    distributions and histograms, 46–51
    scatter plots and heat maps, 51–55
  graph visualization, 61
    layout algorithms, 62–64
    time complexity, 64
  time-series plots, 58
    auto-correlation, 60–61
    rolling statistics, 58–60
databases
  A/B replication, 240–241
  multimaster replication, 239–240
  primary and replica, 238–239
data-processing inequality, 33
debt, technical debt, 4, 13
decision boundaries, 118
decision trees, 109–112
  random forests, 112–115
deep feedforward networks, 186
  layers, 192
deliver value quickly, 12
dependence, stability and, Bayesian networks,
  137–138
dirichlet distributions, 160
discrete variables, 46
disks, 206–208
distributed approach
  cosine similarity, 86
  Jaccard distance, 81–82
  linear least squares, 98
  Mahalanobis distance, 87
  MinHash, 83–84
distributions and histograms, 46–51

distributions and summary statistics, 45
    box plots, 55–57
    distributions and histograms, 46–51
    error bars, 55–57
    heat maps, 51–55
    scatter plots, 51–55
do-operations, 180
d-separation, 139–142

E

ElastiCache, 231
Elasticsearch, 241
embedding versus pooling resources, 8
errors
    hypothesis testing, 39–40
    quantifying in measured values, 17–19
    random error, 18
    sampling error, 19–21
    systematic error, 18
    tracking impressions, 18
error bars, 55–57
error propagation, 21–23
ETL (extract, transfer/transform, load), 216
euclidean distance, 131
examples
    hypothesis testing, 42–43
    linear least squares, 98–105
    machine-learning estimators, 182–187
    observation, 171–177
execution-level locality, throughput, 208–209
experiments, causal inference, 168–171
extract, transfer/transform, load (ETL), 216

F

Facebook, Messenger app, 11
factor analysis, latent variable models, 151–152
factor loading matrix, 151
factorization, Markovity, 138–139
failover, availability, 230–231
FastICA, 159
feature selection, text preprocessing, 28–30
fitting models, 91–92, 143–146
front ends, availability, 225–228
functions
    objective functions, choosing, 90–91
    rand () function, 20

G

generate_signatures, 84
g-formula, 179–182

global minimum, 190
gradient descent, 190
granularity, 214–215
graph visualization, 61
    layout algorithms, 62–64
    time complexity, 64
graphical models, 135
    Bayesian networks, 135
    causal Bayesian networks, 136–137
greedy Louvain, 130–131
    assumptions, 130
    complexity, 130
    memory, 131
    tools, 131

H

hard disk drive (HDD), 206–208
hardware
    nonvolatile/persistent storage, 206–208
    processors, 209–212
    random access memory (RAM), 205–206
    throughput, 208–209
hash indexes, 214
HDD (hard disk drive), 206–208
heat maps, 51–55
histograms, 47–48
    distributions and, 46–51
horizontal sharding, 73
hyperparameters, 76
hypothesis, defined, 37–39
hypothesis testing, 37
    confidence intervals, 40–41
    context, 43–44
    errors, 39–40
    examples, 42–43
    multiple testing, 41–42
    p-hacking, 41–42
    planning, 43–44
    p-values, 40–41

I

ICA (independent component analysis), 154–159
igraph, 130
importance of, data scientists, 5–6
impressions, 21, 149
    tracking, 18
independent component analysis (ICA), 154–159
indexing, 214
information loss, 33–34
Internet, representations of, 234
Internet sockets, 217
interpretability, 111

intersection, 80
intervene, 179
interventions, g-formula, 179

J

Jaccard distance, 79–80
    algorithms, 80–81
    distributed approach, 81–82
    memory, 81
    time complexity, 81
Jarque-Bera test, 108
jobs, availability, 230
joint distributions, 139
junior scientists, 5
Jupyter Notebooks, 69–70

K

kernel density estimation, 49
k-fold cross-validation, 95
k-means, 125–127
    assumptions, 127
    complexity, 128
    memory, 128
    tools, 128
Kronecker delta, 128–129

L

ladders for data scientists, 5
lag, 60
lasso regression, 29
latency, 218–219
    nonvolatile/persistent storage, 207
latent dirichlet allocation, 159–165
latent variable models, 149
    factor analysis, 151–152
    ICA (independent component analysis), 154–159
    latent dirichlet allocation, 159–165
    PCA (principle components analysis), 152–154
layers, neural networks, 192–193
layout algorithms, 62–64
leading eigenvalue, 128–130
    complexity, 129
    memory, 130
    tools, 130
leaf nodes, 110
least recently used (LRU), 72
leave-one-out cross-validation, 95
ledger format, 214

LHS (locally sensitive hashing), 74, 82
life cycle of software prototypes, 9
linear least squares, 96–98
    examples, 98–105
linear regression, 29, 89, 96–97
    Bayesian networks, 142–143
    memory, 122
load balancers, 73
    availability, 225–228
load balancing, 234–235
local machines, 69
locality, throughput, 208
locally sensitive hashing (LHS), 74, 82
locking, 224–225
logistic regression, 25–26, 118–121
    assumptions, 121
    memory, 122
    time complexity, 121
    tools, 122
long-tailed distribution, 49
loss functions, neural networks, 200–201
LRU (least recently used), 72

M

machine learning
    neural networks, 191–192
        batch fitting, 199–200
        capacity, 193–196
        layers, 192–193
        loss functions, 200–201
        overfitting, 196–199
    optimization, 189–191
machine-learning estimators, 182
    examples, 182–187
    g-formula, 182
MAE (mean absolute error), 200
Mahalanobis distance, 86–87, 131
Markovity, factorization and, 138–139
master-slave configuration, 228
mean absolute error (MAE), 200
mean squared error (MSE), 91, 200
measured values, quantifying, error, 17–19
measurement noise, 18
memory
    cosine similarity, 85
    greedy Louvain, 131
    ICA (independent component analysis), 159
    Jaccard distance, 81
    k-means, 128
    leading eigenvalue, 130
    linear least squares, 97

linear regression, 122
logistic regression, 122
Mahalanobis distance, 87
naive Bayes, 124
nearest neighbors, 133
PCA (principle components analysis), 154
random access memory (RAM), 205–206
memory management unit (MMU), 206
Messenger app, Facebook, 11
microservices, 220
MinHash, 82–83
    assumptions, 83
    distributed approach, 83–84
    space complexity, 83
    time complexity, 83
    tools, 83
minimum viable product (MVP), 11
MINIPACK, 98
mix-and-match architectures, 221
MMU (memory management unit), 206
model fitting, 89, 91–92
model validation, 76–77
models, 74
    choosing, for regression, 90
    fitting, 91–92, 143–146
    graphical models, 135
    latent variable models, 149
        factor analysis, 151–152
        ICA (independent component analysis),
            154–159
        latent dirichlet allocation, 159–165
        PCA (principle components analysis), 152–154
    predictions, 75–76
    training, 74–75
    validating, 92–96
    validation, 76–77
modularity, 128–129
monolith, 220
MSE (mean squared error), 91, 200
multimaster replication, 230, 239–240
multiple testing, hypothesis testing, 41–42
MVP (minimum viable product), 11

N

naive Bayes, 122–124
    assumptions, 124
    complexity, 124
    memory, 124
    tools, 124
nearest neighbors, 131–133
network diagrams, 233–234
network locality, throughput, 209

networks
    Bayesian networks, 135
        casual graphs and conditional independence,
            136–137
        causal graphs, linear regression, 142–143
        d-separation, 139–142
        fitting models, 143–146
        Markovity, factorization and, 138–139
        stability and dependence, 137–138
    neural networks, 189, 191–192
        batch fitting, 199–200
        capacity, 193–196
        layers, 192–193
        loss functions, 200–201
        overfitting, 196–199
neural networks, 189, 191–192
    batch fitting, 199–200
    capacity, 193–196
    layers, 192–193
    loss functions, 200–201
    overfitting, 196–199
neurons, 192
nginx, 227
n-grams, text preprocessing, 27–28
non-causal paths, controlling to block, 177–179
    g-formula, 179–182
nonlinear regression with linear regression, 105–107
    uncertainty, 107–109
nonvolatile/persistent storage, 206–208
n-tier, 218–219
numpy, 98

O

objective functions, choosing, 90–91
observation, examples, 171–177
observational data, 6
online algorithms, 72–73
online computing, 72–73
online training algorithms, models, 74
OpenCV, 133
optimization, machine learning, 189–191
overfitting, 76
    neural networks, 196–199

P

paging, 213–214
    nonvolatile/persistent storage, 207–208
parallelization, queues, 241–242
parameters, 74
    hyperparameters, 76
partition tolerance, 231–232

paths, d-separation, 140
PCA (principle components analysis), 152–154
Pearl, Judea, 135
persistence, 216
p-hacking, hypothesis testing, 41–42
pie charts, 47–48
planning hypothesis testing, 43–44
pooling resources, versus embedding, 8
population, 19
potential outcomes, 169
power calculation, 39
practical cases, software architecture, 221
predictions, models, 75–76
preprocessing, text preprocessing, 26
    feature selection, 28–30
    n-grams, 27–28
    representation learning, 30–33
    sparsity, 28
    tokenization, 26–27
primary databases, 238–239
primary/replica, 228
principle components, 152
principle components analysis (PCA), 152–154
priorities, for teams, 4–5
priors, variables, 149–151
processors, 209
    branch prediction, 210–212
    clock rate, 209
    cores, 210
    threading, 210
product focus, agile development and, 10–11
production environments, 69
productionizing, 69
project workflows
    combined workflows, 10
    data teams, 7–8
        embedding versus pooling resources, 8
        prototyping, 9–10
        research, 8–9
prototyping, data teams, 9–10
p-value, 39
    hypothesis testing, 40–41
python-louvain, 131

Q

quantifying errors, in measured values, 17–19
queues, 241
    API buffering, 243
    asynchronous process execution, 242–243
    task scheduling and parallelization,
        241–242

R

RAM (random access memory), 205–206
rand () function, 20
random access memory (RAM), 205–206
random error, 18
random forests, 109, 112–115
randomized lasso, 30
receiver operator characteristic (ROC), 120
recurrent neural network (RNN), 31
Redis, 237
redundancy, availability, 225
regression, 89
    choosing
        models, 90
        objective functions, 90–91
    decision trees, 109–112
    fitting models, 91–92
    linear least squares, 96–98
        examples, 98–105
    logistic regression, 25–26, 118–121
        assumptions, 121
        memory, 122
        time complexity, 121
        tools, 122
    nonlinear regression with linear regression,
        105–107
        uncertainty, 107–109
    random forests, 109, 112–115
    validation, 92–96
regularization methods, 189, 198
replica databases, 238–239
replica lag, 239
replication, 229–230
    A/B replication, 229–230, 240–241
replication lag, 228
representation learning, text preprocessing, 30–33
representations, 30
research, data teams, workflows, 8–9
resources, embedding versus pooling resources, 8
RNN (recurrent neural network), 31
Robins G-Formula, 181
robustness, 216
ROC (receiver operator characteristic), 120
role of data scientists
    company size, 3–4
    teams, 4–5
rolling mean, 59
rolling statistics, 58–60
Route 53, 226–227

S

sampling error, 19–21
scaling, 73–74
scatter plots, 51–55
scikit learn, 122, 128
scipy.optimize.leastsq, 98
secondary, 228
SELECT FOR UPDATE, 224
self-organizing teams, 14
separation of concerns, 70–71
sequences, 79–80
service-oriented architectures (SOAs), 71, 218–219
services, 71
sets, 79–80
sharding, 229, 241
simplicity, 14
sklear.neighbors, 133
SOAs (service-oriented architectures), 71, 218–219
sockets, 217
software architecture
    client-server architecture, 217–218
    microservices, 220
    mix-and-match architectures, 221
    monolith, 220
    n-tier/service-oriented architecture, 218–219
solid-state drives (SSDs), nonvolatile/persistent storage, 207
space complexity, MinHash, 83
sparse vectors, 28
sparsity, text preprocessing, 28
spinning disks, 206–208
split brains, 231–232
SSDs (solid-state drives), 207
stability, dependence and (Bayesian networks), 137–138
static content, application-level caching, 236
stochastic gradient descent, 75, 200
stochasticity, 200
storage, nonvolatile/persistent storage, 206–208
storing data, 215
supervised learning, 125
survival plots, 51
swapping, 208
systematic error, 18

T

task scheduling, queues, 241–242
taskworkers, availability, 230
teams, 12
    role of, data scientists, 4–5
    self-organizing teams, 14

technical debt, 4, 13
terminal nodes, 110
test coverage, 34
testing
    hypothesis testing, 37
    multiple testing, 41–42
tests, Jarque-Bera test, 108
text preprocessing, 26
    feature selection, 28–30
    n-grams, 27–28
    representation learning, 30–33
    sparsity, 28
    tokenization, 26–27
thrashing, nonvolatile/persistent storage, 208
threading, processors, 210
threads, 208
threads of execution, 73
throughput, 208–209
time complexity, 64
    Jaccard distance, 81
    logistic regression, 121
    MinHash, 83
time to live (TTL), 72
time-series plots, 58
    auto-correlation, 60–61
    rolling statistics, 58–60
tokenization, text preprocessing, 26–27
tools
    greedy Louvain, 131
    ICA (independent component analysis), 159
    k-means, 128
    leading eigenvalue, 130
    linear least squares, 98
    logistic regression, 122
    MinHash, 83
    naive Bayes, 124
    nearest neighbors, 133
    PCA (principle components analysis), 154
topics, 159
topological ordering, 139
tracking impressions, 18
training models, 74–75
true value, 18
TTL (time to live), 72
Type I errors, 39
Type II errors, 39

U

uncertainty, nonlinear regression with linear regression, 107–109
underpowered, 39

union, 80
UNIX sockets, 217
unsupervised learning, 125
UPDATE statement, 224

V

validation, 92–96
    models, 76–77
value proposition, 10–11
variables
    binary variables, 25
    continuous variables, 46

discrete variables, 46
    priors, 149–151
vertical scaling, 73
vocabulary, 26
volatility, RAM (random access memory), 206

W

workstations, 69
write-through caches, 238

Z

Z statistic, 38–39

Credits

Cover: Digital technology web banner, big data machine learning algorithms, abstract banner analysis of information, isometric view, science dark blue background by Svetlana Avv/Shutterstock.

Chapter 2: "Build domain knowledge ... refine existing infrastructure". M. Herman, S. Rivera, S. Mills, J. Sullivan, P. Guerra, A. Cosmas, D. Farris, E. Kohlwey, P. Yacci, B. Keller, A. Kherlopian, and M. Kim, The Field Guide to Data Science. Nov. 2013.

Chapter 2, Figure 2.2: M. Herman, S. Rivera, S. Mills, J. Sullivan, P. Guerra, A. Cosmas, D. Farris, E. Kohlwey, P. Yacci, B. Keller, A. Kherlopian, and M. Kim, The Field Guide to Data Science. Nov. 2013.

Chapter 2: "Assess project requirements ... incorporating new information". M. F. Smith, Software Prototyping: Adoption, Practice and Management. New York, NY, USA: McGraw-Hill, Inc., 1991.

Chapter 2, Figure 2.3: M. F. Smith, Software Prototyping: Adoption, Practice and Management. New York, NY, USA: McGraw-Hill, Inc., 1991.

Chapter 2: "1. Our highest priority is to satisfy the customer ... and adjusts its behavior accordingly." Agile Manifesto.

Chapters 1, 2: "Individuals and interactions ... over following a plan". Agile Manifesto.

Chapter 3: "To kill an error ... truth or fact." Charles Darwin.

Chapter 7, Figure 7.1: Screenshot of Jupyter notebook © 2018 Project Jupyter.

Chapter 18, Figure 18.3: Screenshot of Amazon Route 53 console © 2018, Amazon Web Services, Inc.